Modern Social Work Theory

A critical introduction

Malcolm Payne

MACMILLAN

First published 1991

Published by
MACMILLAN EDUCATION LTD
Houndmills, Basingstoke, Hampshire RG21 2XS
and London
Companies and representatives
throughout the world

Typeset by Footnote Graphics
Warminster, Wilts

Printed in Hong Kong

British Library Cataloguing in Publication Data
Payne, Malcolm *1947–*
Modern social work theory: a critical introduction.
1. Welfare work. Theories
I. Title
361.3'01
ISBN 0—333—47477—5 (hardcover)
ISBN 0—333—47478-3 (paperback)

To Susan

Contents

List of Figures

List of Tables

Acknowledgements

I am grateful to the various people who have read all or part of this book and have saved me from many errors of judgement and fact; and also to the people who have provided personal support.

The publishers and the author wish to thank the following for permission to reproduce copyright material:

Colin Whittington and Ray Holland (1985) 'A Framework for Theory in Social Work', *Issues in Social Work Education*, 5 (1), published by the Association for Teachers in Social Work Education, and David Howe (1987) *An Introduction to Social Work Theory*, published by Wildwood House, for Figure 2.1; Peter Leonard (1975) 'Explanation and Education in Social Work', *British Journal of Social Work*, 5 (3) published by the British Association of Social Workers, for Table 2.1.

Every effort has been made to trace all the copyright-holders, but if any have been inadvertently overlooked the publishers will be pleased to make the necessary arrangement at the first opportunity.

Clearly, any writer of a review of social work theory relies on the ideas of other writers, and I commend any reader to progress from this introduction to the comprehensive accounts to be found in the books and articles referred to. I have found them stimulating and full of ideas for practice and understanding. I am sure you will do so, too.

Didsbury, Manchester   MALCOLM PAYNE

1

The Social Construction of Social Work Theory

Introduction: the starting point

This is the starting point: at this moment, somewhere in the world, 'clients' are struggling into an office to meet with a 'social worker'. Or perhaps the social worker is visiting the client's home, or is working with clients in groups, in residential or day-care settings, or in some form of community work. In some, but not all societies, this something called 'social work' goes on. It is widely enough spread for international associations of social workers and a shared language and literature of social work to exist.

This apparent shared understanding across many societies raises questions. Is social work a single entity? If so, presumably we should be able to say what it is and what it is not. But there is no agreed definition. It is hard to decide what might be included in social work, what its objectives might be, who its clients are, what its methods are, what a social worker is.

Perhaps these are insoluble problems, and no final decisions about them may be made. The answers may vary according to the time, social conditions and cultures within which the questions are raised. Nonetheless, to take part in social work you need a view about what you are doing – an interim view perhaps, but something which guides the actions you take. It will include values which are appropriate to doing social work, and theories about the nature of social work, for example sociological theories about its role in society, or its relationships with other occupational groups.

This book is concerned with *theories of social work* which try to explain, describe or justify what social workers do. Such theories

seem to be in a turmoil. There are a wide variety of them that may
be used; their proponents and other theoreticians compete and
have disputes about their value. Hartman (1971) argues that we
must each make our own definition of theory in order to practice,
and research by O'Connor and Dalgleish (1986) on beginning
social workers in Australia shows that they did create and retain
their personal models of social work during their early experience
of practice, but had difficulty in adjusting it to the agency setting.
Hugman (1987) in a similar British study did not find so many
difficulties, and argues that helping beginning workers to construct
personal models may avoid making therapeutic theories appropriate for their social and service context.

My personal reason for writing this book comes from a wish to
resolve theoretical turmoil for myself, and in doing so perhaps
to help others think about their own resolution. My career has
spanned the period of uncertainty, and I have learned, embraced
and used many apparently different and conflicting theories.
Although I have been involved in arguments with colleagues
holding different views, I have always seen these views as part of
social work. Throughout my theoretical travels, I have never seen
myself as moving away from social work as my fundamental base.
So, somehow I have managed to integrate different approaches to
social work into something that feels and is to me a whole. In
doing so, I must be saying something about social work: that it is,
or may contain, all these elements. Jordan (1989) contends that
social workers use 'a process of violent bodging' to adapt and mix
theories to 'render ideas more serviceable for their purposes.'
Accounts of social work theory often express their ideas in a
coherent form, using evidence and ideas drawn from the social
sciences. Yet social workers often take into their practice lives
only a hazy set of concepts which, while they may be recognised
(Curnock and Hardiker, 1979), do not form a co-ordinated theory.
Loewenberg (1984) argues that this is because less wide-ranging
'middle-range' theories, fitted into an overall professional ideology,
are needed. I am interested in how ideas come to be made practical within social work and form a coherent (if theoretically
messy) basis for practice.

Another reason for writing this book is that I am concerned by
students and practitioners who either reject or simply parrot the
different kinds of theory that they have been taught about, or

repudiate the rich heritage of ideas which is theirs. They do not see the need to understand where their theory comes from, how one theory differs from another, how they connect. Clarity about theoretical ideas is, to me, necessary to being part of the occupation of social work since these ideas are an important pillar of mutual understanding and identity among social workers. It also helps in practice, because being able to specifiy what we should do, and why, is an important purpose of theory and a vital necessity to anyone working with and trying to help human beings. It is particularly crucial if, as I have suggested, we tend to use practical amalgamations of ideas from different sources, instead of one set theory for all our practice. Doing this without understanding is likely to risk confusion, and possibly damage, to our clients. Understanding connections and disparities among the ideas we use can help avoid such problems.

The *aim* of this book, then, is to review a range of theories about social work practice, to offer an assessment of those theories, and to arrive at an understanding of them and their value in modern social work practice. I contend that social work theories may be understood in relationship to each other as a whole body of knowledge.

This first Chapter sets out how social work theory may be understood as part of the social construction of the activity of social work and how this activity itself helps to construct theory. I say that, contrary to some views, the body of theoretical knowledge is useful in practice. Chapter 2 considers and rejects the pragmatic argument that social work theory is no use in practice, discusses the positivist and eclectic approaches to using social work theory, and examines some ways of analysing social work theories and their relationships with one another.

I find it useful to think about these theories in relation to one another and compare and assess them against each other. Chapters 3–11 look at nine groupings of social work theories, their history, relationships with other theories and their prescriptions for practice. Reasons why these theories have been selected and why certain material has been included or excluded are given towards the end of this Chapter and in Chapter 2. Chapter 12 seeks to assess the value of these theories in relation to one another and arrive at a view of their value in modern social work practice. I say modern, because understanding a social phenomenon such as social work can only be for this time. Also, it is only possible to consider social work theory within a limited cultural frame. Rein and White make this point in an important paper on the development of new understandings of how we seek and use knowledge:

> ...the basic movement of knowledge gathering is to provide for contexts in transition. The knowledge that is gathered – the perceived utility or relevance of the knowledge – is bounded in time, place, and person. (Rein and White, 1981, p.37)

Cultural differences in social work theories

Differences in cultural frame are important. Much writing about social work and its histories derives from Western cultures, and may not apply to non-Western cultures. Moreover, the significance of American (and to a lesser extent European) social work theory, and of colonial influences from Europe on Third World countries has led to an impression that techniques appropriate in these countries can be transferred to completely different cultures. This is increasingly disputed, and some points should be made about the applicability of Western social work theory in non-Western countries.

First, not all such influences are identical. Heisler (1970) makes the point, for instance, that the British colonial tradition tended to lead to a reliance on local, decentralised and informal initiatives for social welfare, while French colonies reflected a more centralising and co-ordinated tendency. In turn, the reaction to these trends by governments and people after decolonisation also varied.

Second, while English language theories tend to be pervasive, the different forms of service organisation and professional education in different countries lead to different sets of ideas which are not widely available in the USA and Britain. For example, in France, a range of welfare workers exists, all of whom have roles which are related to but different from social work as it is known in Britain and the USA (Birks, 1987). Similarly, Western European ideas about social pedagogy (e.g. Hamalainen, 1989), in which education rather than therapeutic approaches are taken to social assistance, are not widely used in Britain and the USA.

Third, while Christian influences were important in European and North American developments (e.g. Philpot, 1986), their impact in colonial countries was entirely different, since they were part of a missionary effort to convert a subject population to the dominant culture of the colonists. In some places, this was kept astutely apart from conflicting local pressures (as Haile Selassie achieved in Ethiopia in the 1930s; Schenk and Schenk, 1987). In others, there was an uneasy co-existence of cultures, as in India where legislative attempts were made in the 19th century to change conflicting cultural practices such as widow sacrifice and thuggery, but few social reforms were attempted (Chakrabarti, 1987). Other countries, including many in Africa (Dixon, 1987), found that what social provision there was largely comprised Christian missionary and voluntary services, with little attempt at organised public provision until the late 1940s.

So, even major non-Christian religions have had unreasonably little influence on conceptualisations of social work. Danisoglu (1987), for example, in discussing Turkish services, maintains the importance in predominantly Muslim countries of the Islamic tradition of equity and justice and their history of charitable provision. Often, the implementation of such philosophies in public services is distant from Western political assumptions particularly because of authoritarian regimes. However, Chow (1987), considering Chinese and Western philosophies of care, makes the point that social assumptions may be different. Western social work is based on the importance of the individual, with an associated concept of individual rights, and services have developed from a residual policy where they are provided only to those who cannot be helped otherwise, to an institutional model, in which the aim of social services is to varying extents social equity and redistribution of wealth (although it is doubtful that social work contributes much to such objectives). In Chinese social assumptions, the rights of individuals are not emphasised, rather the duties and responsibilities of being part of a network of family relationships are central.

There is considerable discussion of these issues in India. Wadia (1961) proposes the Hindu concepts of *Dharma* (concern for society as a whole and help for others) and *Karma* (actions which lead to consequences in life) as actual and potential influences on Indian social reform and social work values. There are also attempts to locate a different philosophy of social work in India in the ideas of leaders like Gandhi and Nehru on the welfare of untouchables, women and rural areas (Muzumdar, 1964; J. Howard, 1971). Gangrade (1970) argues that India requires more concentration on the responsibilities of the family network for maintaining contacts throughout life than the individualistic Western social work model, in which the role of the family is to prepare people for separation and independence from it. Similarly, Western social work tends to encourage plurality and diversity through competition, whereas Hindu philosophy is to try to build connections and avoid conflict. Although casework services exist in urban areas, and adapt Western non-directive techniques to a more culturally acceptable authoritarian approach (Kassim Ejaz, 1989), there has been much criticism of the failure of Western social work to offer viable models and appropriate training particularly in the areas of rural development and social change (Nagpaul, 1972; Nanavatty, 1981; Ghosh, 1984; Ilango, 1988). Even here, Bryant (1985) argues that the theoretical and practice needs of different countries are not necessarily the same, since African and Asian rural development work varies due to different economies and approaches to farming. For a completely different cultural response to the inadequacies of Western models of social work, which has had some reciprocal influence in Western social work, see Chapter 10 on the reconceptualisation movement in Latin American social work.

Fourth, colonial powers were little concerned with welfare matters, since they tended, according to Asamoah and Beverly (1988), to split up different aspects of human and social problems rather than seek comprehensive social provision. They gave great importance to political and economic issues rather than social needs, were concerned to reduce for such reasons the importance of traditional (e.g. tribal) structures which provided a base for welfare, and tended to make decisions for short-term expediency rather than long-term benefit for the colonies. This tended to mean that services and ideas associated with them were underdeveloped, and made the assumption that Western theories would be transferable. Provision by international agencies can be poorly integrated with local services (Schenk and Schenk, 1987; Whang, 1988) and often focused on children rather than other client groups (Dixon, 1987; Dixon and Schuerall, 1989; Onokerkoraye, 1984).

Fifth, the post-colonial experience has shown that such ideas were not transferable. This is partly because the individualistic bias of social work in the 1950s and 1960s when most colonies became independent was particularly inappropriate where major social and economic problems existed. Yelaja (1970) noted around this period that a much broader concept of social work, taking in social change and social policy development was required. In some cases, the economic problems have been so severe (e.g. in many African countries; Dixon, 1987) and ideological considerations and other priorities have been so important (as in mainland China; Starak, 1988) that it might be argued that any form of social work recognisable to developed Western countries is inappropriate. Elsewhere, there seems to have been the slow development of a locally appropriate form of social work. Walton and Nasr (1988) propose, using the example of Egypt, that this is a parallel process of indigenisation, in which important ideas are altered to make them appropriate to local conditions, and authentisation, where local ideas are developed in association with imported theories to form a new structure of ideas. It may be that similar processes occur even among Western countries as, for example, American theories generated in an elitist, voluntary social service system, become adapted to use in Britain and other European countries with a more bureaucratic and governmental system of social work.

As indigenisation and authentisation take place, it can be useful to study the original theories and the way they fit together to help in the process of analysing their use in another culture. But this book concentrates primarily on Western theories of social work until other ideas can have the influence necessary to conceive of their international influence as part of this pattern of ideas, or until a completely different form of practice emerges from non-Western countries.

The argument of the book: social work is socially constructed

The major principle of this book is that *social work is a socially constructed activity*. We have seen that social work is complex and varies in different cultures. It is part of a complex theoretical, occupational and service network. Therefore, it can only be understood in the social and cultural context of the participants.

Theories about it are products of the context in which they arise, and they also influence that context, because theories affect what people do and say within social work, and that affects social attitudes towards the people within social work and their ideas and values. To understand what social work is, therefore, we have to look at its participants, its organisation and its theories about itself, and we can only understand these things if we also see how they are constructed by the society which surrounds them and of which they are a part. Rein and White make this point forcefully:

> ... the knowledge that social work seeks cannot be made in universities by individuals who presumptively seek timeless, contextless truths about human nature, societies, institutions, and policy. The knowledge *must* be developed in the living situations that are confronted by the contemporary episodes in the field ... it is necessary to enlarge the notion of context to include not only the client's situation but the agency itself and more broadly the institutional setting of practice. This involves the intersecting network of offices, agencies, professionals, government structures and political pressure groups that all act together on the agency. (Rein and White, 1981, p. 37)

The idea of social construction is an application of the ideas of Berger and Luckmann (1971). They maintain that 'reality' is knowledge which guides our behaviour, but we all have different views of it. We arrive at shared views of reality by sharing our knowledge through various social processes which organise and make it objective. Social activity tends to become habitual, so that we share assumptions about how things are and behave in accordance with social conventions based on that shared knowledge. This leads to the institutionalisation of these conventions as large numbers of people come to share similar understandings of that aspect of society. Then, these understandings become legitimised by a process which attaches 'meanings' which integrate these ideas about reality into an organised and plausible system. Social understanding is, in this way, the product of human understandings. As far as those humans are concerned, it is also objective, because the knowledge of what is reality is widely shared, and since people are brought up within those social understandings to accept their reality, they are in a sense the product of society.

Applying these ideas to social work, I have argued that it has a reality, in that it is seen to exist; theories about it express that reality, are created by the human beings in their interactions which define social realities. The human beings are themselves created by the social realities of the common understandings of what social work is.

The three elements of social work from which I started out in this Chapter were the social worker, the client and the setting in which they meet. The next three sections of this Chapter look at how each of these is socially constructed by expectations, cultural norms and patterns of behaviour. The argument is as follows. Social work theory is created within social work, out of an interaction with social work practice, which in turn interacts with wider social contacts. Three sets of forces construct social work: those which create and control social work as an occupation; those which create clienthood among people who seek or are sent for social work help; and those which create the social context in which social work is practised. Social work is a special activity where people interact in special social roles as 'social worker' and 'client'; its nature is thus partly defined by those roles. Understanding social work involves examining the factors which establish the social positions of these actors in a complex of social relationships. In the next section, the worker is the subject.

Defining a social worker

Social workers in encounters with clients are constructed by occupational expectations, that is, the organised statements and understandings which say what a social worker is, and the social processes which define someone as a social worker. The various histories of social work, together with its relationships with other occupational groups and social institutions will form its nature as an occupation. That nature changes, grows, perhaps declines in response to social changes. So, the knowledge and ideas that social workers use also respond to social changes.

There are as many histories of social work as countries where it is acknowledged to exist; there is no one set of developments to explore. Its written history is about Western European countries and North America. Much of the literature about its institutional

Table 1.1   *Factors in the development of social work as an occupation*

Factors	Examples
Moves to organise personal help systematically	charity organisation movements in Britain and the USA in the 19th century; the importance of social work services as the base for co-ordinating other activities
Moves to control, limit or manage the use made by members of the public of other social and welfare services	development of Poor Law workhouses in the 19th century; growth of education welfare in Britain to control absence from compulsory schooling
Development or change in new social institutions	workhouses, hospitals, schools, and housing services stimulating services to provide help to make use of them; development of settlements and community services in the 19th century; the role of trades unions in providing social services for their members in countries like Ghana (Asamoah and Nortey, 1987), and Canada (food banks for poor people; Bellamy and Irving, 1989); changes in family and community services in the UK in the 1960s
Economic and political ideologies and trends	paternalism in the 19th century intended to limit the harmful effects of uncontrolled market forces; the influence of the German middle-class women's movement in the early 20th century in developing services for families and young people (Muller, 1989); the development of socialist principles among reformers, particularly in the early 20th century (especially the influential Fabians), which also had effects in some colonial and European countries, e.g. Mauritius (Joynathsing, 1987), and Sweden (Olsson, 1989); the mid-20th century growth of social work services as part of the welfare state in European countries (Dixon and Scheurall, 1989); new methods of education in Third World countries gaining commitment from oppressed groups leading to techniques such as conscientisation;

Factors	Examples
	the privatisation of welfare services in response to conservative ideology and social legislation in the 1980s (e.g. residential care for elderly people in Britain); reduction in finance for social services in development economies due to international economic problems in the 1970s and 1980s (Dixon and Scheurall, 1989)
Changing needs or changing perceptions of need in public debate or among influential groups	the influence of the temperance movement in Victorian society; 'moral panics' about vandalism or hooliganism among young people in the 1950s and 1960s; concern about drug abuse in the 1960s and 1980s; concern about child abuse and sexual abuse in the 1970s and 1980s; the 'rediscovery of poverty' and civil rights movements of the 1960s and 1970s leading to the use of individual cases in advocacy for social causes, and stimulating advocacy in social work practice; anxiety about services needed to combat AIDS in the 1980s
Changes or perceived changes in the need for or methods of social control	the acceptance of probation as an appropriate way of dealing with some offenders in the late 19th and early 20th centuries; changes in British mental health legislation in 1890, 1959 and 1983 altering the system for compulsory admissions to mental hospitals changed the balance of legal, medical and social influence, making social workers more powerful in decision-making
Implementation of values and beliefs which are influencing society	the efforts of evangelical Christians to 'rescue' orphan or abandoned children in the 19th century stimulating nationwide and local services; the importance of family, tribal and mutual aid, and availability of rural work in countries like Nigeria, retarding formal

Table 1.1   (*contd.*)

Factors	Examples
	social services until economic changes led to more need for collective responses to social need (Sanda, 1987); opposition to welfare activities in Ethiopia in the 19th century due to the philosophy of the Coptic church that 'poverty and pain were the gifts of God' (Schenk and Schenk, 1987); the influence of the Christian churches in moral welfare work with prostitutes, unmarried mothers and illegitimate children, and in broad caring services such as child care and family agencies (Young and Ashton, 1956); the influence of liberal and Fabian ideas of equality, provision of services according to need, territorial justice, altruism and services free at the point of delivery, implicit in the British welfare state reforms of the 1940s and 1950s; the influence of the women's movement on ideologies of care in the 1970s and 1980s
Changing legislation	the British Children Act, 1948, which established an independent local authority service for children enhancing the standing of social work; the Local Authority Social Service Act, 1970, built on that development to establish a powerful, generic social work department in local authorities; the importance of central government provision of social services in New Zealand (Uttley, 1989); the 1978 law resulting in the deinstitutionalisation of mental health services in Italy and the consequent growth of social work-related community services (Ferrera, 1989); the Chronically Sick and Disabled Persons Act, 1970, which established improved services in Britain for disabled people
Academic and intellectual developments	the introduction of social work education into universities and other institutions of higher education in Britain and the USA,

Factors	Examples
	giving it a higher status than, say, nursing, in the early part of the 20th century; the impact of psychoanalytic ideas in the 1920s; the impact of professional moves towards seeing social work as generic in the 1950s in the USA and the 1960s in the UK; the growth of academic social research and the impact of academic development in the social sciences in the 1950s, and 1960s; the importance of ideas of positivism, consumer research, and critical evaluation of services; the influence of sociological and Marxist ideas in the 1960s
Agencies employing or organising social workers	the influence of the large number of small voluntary agencies supported by charitable donations in the USA; the influence of trade unions organising social workers in European countries (where often professional associations are also trade unions) on the organisation of work and professional practice
Related occupations	medicine, the law, the churches, counsellors, psychologists and professional sociologists affect the way in which social work is organised, so that it fits in with related services, with the result that various methods, theories and techniques are borrowed from related professions

NOTE: many of these historical developments are covered in later parts of this book; references are given where examples (mainly covering countries other than Britain and the USA) are not dealt with more extensively elsewhere.

relationships comes also from these cultures. This material offers clues about the sort of factors which are important in its establishment and may well be relevant elsewhere; these are summarised with some examples in Table 1.1.

It is not possible to identify a complete list of every factor influencing the development of social work, but this brief exploration and the examples given draw attention to a number of features:

- social work practice and theory is influenced by many social forces which are nothing to do with the academic and practice development of the occupation. Changing social needs, the influence and needs of related occupations, political and legislative changes are just some of the examples noted above.

- those social forces are conditioned by political and public perceptions of social and personal need and the way in which services should be organised to meet such need. Thus, political debate and media coverage of social work and its activities influence the climate of perceptions which create social work's tasks and interests. This is because public perceptions influence services and because social workers are themselves part of the public and are influenced by media and political change.

- the organisation of services and agencies, and the legislation, economic capacity and managerial techniques which underpin that organisation affect how social work is able to do its job. If social work is part of a powerful independent agency, there is likely to be freedom to develop social work techniques independently. This is less likely where social work is performed in agencies dominated by other occupations (e.g. hospitals and medicine) but the status and influence of the dominant profession may offer other benefits as well as disadvantages. Industrial organisation may be particularly important. Where trade unions control to some degree the negotiations for conditions of employment (as they do in many European countries), they are also bound to affect the nature of the work in ways which will be different from the situation where employers or members of an occupational group themselves define the task and methods of work.

- many of these social groups and institutions are in conflict either actually or potentially. The academic development of social work theories and techniques may well be in conflict with the wishes of other occupational groups (e.g. medical resistance to the independent establishment of social work), or with employers' definitions of the social work task (e.g.

complaints from employers in several European countries that the theoretical approach of training courses for social workers is not practically applicable), or with political objectives for the services. There may well be a struggle for control of the theory and practice of social work among these and other groups, each attempting to apply various forms of influence in public perception, organisational structure or political systems and legislative change.

From this point of view, social work is part of a network of related occupations, and we need to see how it has been established and controlled, and how it relates to the network around it. Part of such an understanding requires us to see how its theories have grown up and exerted influence on it, and how they relate to the network of theories around social work in related occupations.

Such theories are themselves social influences which help to position social work among the network of other services, occupations, professions and agencies. I also argue that the theories are constructed in part by those social factors which create the social worker. This must be so as social work theory is created by people within the socially-constructed occupation. The socially defined purposes and origins of that occupation shed light upon the theory, and the theory as it is created affects the occupation and thence the social influences which form the context of practice.

Defining a client

Clients' influences on social work are ignored in much professional writing; they are merely the object of an activity which is defined by theory. In fact, I argue that they partly construct the activity through the process by which they become the special people called 'clients'. The client-making process is itself socially constructed, because it relies on general social understandings of the nature of social work. As they bring the outside world into social work activity with them, clients change the nature of social work. In this sense, social work is an interactive process in which client changes worker *and* the nature of social work *and* therefore changes also the theory of social work. The aim of this argument is to dispute the conception that social work is a catalytic process in which the client is changed by an unchanging worker and agency, and to propose instead that the worker and agency are changed by their clients.

Clienthood is not an invariable or absolute *state*. Generally, people are socially defined as clients if they are interacting with workers using techniques where social work is considered appropriate, but this is not always an accurate representation of their position, as they, the worker, or as some others involved might see the situation. For example, a social worker acting as an advocate on behalf of a client is more a colleague of the client than a helper. A foster parent may have an ambivalent relationship with a worker, being treated as someone who is a colleague and as someone who needs help. The parent of a mentally-handicapped child may be a colleague of the worker in helping the child, the object of the social worker's help in coping with the child or part of a family being helped as a whole.

Clienthood is partly a matter of perception, so that if a person is seen by others as a client, they may be treated as such. People's own definition of their status affects, but does not determine, whether they are seen as clients. Formal designation is also relevant, so that official categorisation as a client may set off or reinforce perceptions that someone is a client. Such perceptions may be held by clients, by workers, by officials in the worker's agency, by people in other agencies, by the client's family or by others in the client's social environment. Once clienthood is ascribed to someone, it often persists even if social work activity is intermittent or has stopped.

Clienthood tends to be associated with certain sorts of people, for example, those of a particular social class, or those living on a particular housing estate. People in such groups may be more easily defined by agencies or observers as a client than they would if they came from another group. Stigma often comes with being a client because people who need help in managing their everyday lives tend to be disapproved of; if they are in some way held to blame for their dependence, disapproval will be stronger.

All these factors may interact or conflict. So, for example, an agency and its worker may see Albert as a client, and to outsiders that might be reasonable, but he may see himself as a friend of the worker. If so, is what the worker does with Albert social work? It is intended to be, but if the client sees it as something else, has it failed and become something else? This example shows how people's definitions of clienthood may affect how we understand the nature of social work.

Since different people's perceptions of clienthood vary, we must see where those perceptions come from. It is likely that the social institutions and their history that we examined as originators of the definition of a social worker are also influential in defining clienthood. This brings us to defining clienthood as a process.

Since clienthood is hard to understand as a state, it is more appropriate to understand it as a *process*; people are becoming, acting as and moving away from being clients of social work. That process occurs around coming into contact with a social work agency providing them with services from people who are defined as social workers. Since, as we saw in the previous section, the nature of social work and therefore its agencies is socially defined so also is the process of attaining clienthood. Attitudes to particular human conditions such as alcoholism will define whether they are seen as relevant to social work, and so whether people suffering from that condition will see themselves or be seen by others as appropriate candidates for clienthood. They might, for example, be seen as candidates for prison, or medical intervention, or for help from a priest.

The *route to clienthood* only begins when someone becomes aware of some issues in their lives which need resolution; often this arises from coming to see these issues as a problem. Awareness, together with various social pressures may create an *impulsion* towards receiving help. At some point consciousness of the availability of the agency arises, and leads the client to arrive at the agency, where interaction with the social worker begins.

Up to this point, the decisions made may not have been subjected to any professional influence. The definition of problem, the social pressures, the route to the agency and options which were closed off on that route which led to the selection of this particular agency; all these may arise from general social perceptions about a problem and the agencies available. Wikler's research (1986) into the pathways to help followed by Jewish clients in New York confirms that self-referral and referral from nonprofessionals was by far the most significant route.

Then begins the process of *intake*. The aim is to explore clients' circumstances and establish a definition of them as relevant to the agency, including, often, an assessment of their motivation. Specht and Specht (1986a) see the point at which assessment begins as the beginning of the route to clienthood, although I think they pitch this at too late a stage in the process I have outlined here. Certainly at this stage clienthood is not final. People are often described as 'applicants' being investigated to see whether they may fall within the definition of a client suitable to the agency according to the agency's policies, the training and social institutions which form the social worker's view of appropriateness, and professional, personal, public and political trends. Some services such as welfare rights advice may be offered without a caller being defined as a client.

All this assumes that visiting the agency is a matter of choice, but in fact many clients are *involuntary*, and are forced to visit the agency by court order, or by being investigated through one of the agency's policing functions such as an investigation for child abuse or neglect. Cingolani (1984) argues that workers should see themselves as in a process of continual negotiation of an acceptable relationship with clients. She proposes that a social conflict model in which roles are taken by the social worker to mediate and negotiate between an unwilling client and the social environment may be most appropriate.

Specht and Specht argue (1986b) that making a contract with the client for providing service is the final stage in establishing the definition of clienthood. Contracts are not necessarily formal written documents but may be no more than loose agreements between worker and client. Even after intake and designation as a client, the status of clients may change, as they are passed to different parts of a large agency for different forms of help, or as their own, community, family and other agencies' perceptions change as it becomes known that they are receiving services.

Becoming and being a client leads also to the process of ceasing to be one. This, again, involves recognising circumstances which lead to an impulsion – this time away from the agency. Understanding when it is appropriate to stop involvement with an agency is also an important factor. In any of these moves, clients are again affected by their own social understanding, information gained from the worker, legal pressures, and knowledge and attitudes deriving from the client's social circle.

Defining the context of social work

So far, we have seen that the clients and social workers who arrive to work together in the process called 'social work' are brought by a route that is socially and historically formed. This view presents the relationship between workers and clients as *interactive*; they each affect the other.

Much social work theory recognises this fact inadequately because it is also based on a catalytic model in which the competent social worker helps to resolve or cure the problems of an inexpert client. This *medical model* is a traditional feature of social work, criticised as leading to fragmented help being offered according to specialisations which treat clients as problems rather than as whole beings, and as being characterised by poor communication with and involvement of clients in the helping process, which consequently reduces the independence and personal power of clients (Katz, 1983). Weick (1983, 1986) argues that the medical model should be replaced by a health model, where everyone is seen as responsible for healthy living, and the worker's task is to facilitate healing processes in which the interaction of a variety of personal and environmental factors are recognised and rebalanced to provide a more healthy environment for everyone.

In a catalytic model of social work, the worker's expertise comes from understanding of theory, which may be supported by empirical research. Agencies and workers are relatively unchanging, and interpret information according to their professional assumptions. Clients cannot present themselves in a radically different way, because their presentation will be reinterpreted in accordance with the workers' conventional assumptions; in any case, the route to clienthood reinforces those assumptions, so that the clients learn what to expect and how to behave. New knowledge and theory are brought into social work through social pressures on the political and community leaders who form the highest echelon of management, and through social science and other research which affects the literature and training of workers. So new knowledge and theory is applied to social work by collective academic and social processes rather than by response to actual social situations presented by clients. Some social trends are likely to be absent from or under-represented in agencies because of the process by which clients come to it.

I call such a view of social work *catalytic* because catalysis is a chemical reaction in which substances are put together with a catalyst. A reaction takes place between the substances that would not occur if the catalyst were not present. By a series of combinations with the other substances, it helps the reaction to work, but it emerges from the process having reformed into its original state.

Is the picture presented by this model accurate? Some evidence for it is contained in the unresponsiveness of social work agencies to radically different social trends. For example, social agencies were slow to recognise failures in providing services to ethnic minorities in western countries, because of endemic racism in training, management and practice (Lum, 1982; Dominelli, 1988) and in social policies (Granger and Portner, 1985). There was distrust of agencies and white people by black people, and a failure to communicate across racial and social boundaries because of different life styles and cultures. A general social movement recognising these issues applied political and intellectual influence to social work. Personal responses to the world that workers saw around them did not seem to reflect the changes. Similar points might be made about the failure to recognise serious inequities in the response to women's roles in caring within welfare and conventional social systems.

Such an inadequacy in response, however, probably derives more from the inflexibility of agency structures and socially-formed attitudes among workers, rather than theory and knowledge not taking account of social changes. J. Ellis (1977), for example, showed that European conceptions of children's needs differed from those held by West Africans, leading to inappropriate interventions in West African families. Further examples may illustrate the point. There are many grass-roots agencies which are acceptable to ethnic minorities and respond appropriately to women's roles and wishes. These seem to show that with workers and managements who have appropriate attitudes, and outside large institutionalised agencies, ideas and theories which are basically similar to conventional social work theories are helpful to groups which otherwise seem to be rejected by social work agencies. Some agencies are able to incorporate ethnic elements as a positive attribute of their work (Jenkins, 1980). This also happens in sympathetic enclaves within institutionalised agencies. Such a view cannot be taken too far, however. Midgley (1981) shows that Third World countries have often found the Western model of social work inappropriate to their needs and have created more pragmatic and radical practices.

There is also evidence that social workers do respond to social trends which appear in their work, but cannot always affect their agencies or attitudes within them to take this further. One particularly important example is increasing violence towards workers. Brown *et al.* (1986) argue that there is more violence because people who would have stayed in institutions are being discharged to the community. Small (1987) similarly claims that violence to social workers reflects changing social patterns, and is incorrectly ascribed to breakdowns in relationships. Violence towards social workers and the fact that they suffer from stress and possibly burnout (Gibson *et al.*, 1989; Davis-Sacks *et al.*, 1985; Jayaratne *et al.*, 1983; Fineman, 1985; Cherniss, 1980) draws attention to the fact they are affected and changed by their relationships with clients. So, the potential exists for social work and its agencies to be affected by their clients directly.

The catalytic model, then, does not adequately describe some aspects of social work. An *interactive* or transactional model sees social workers and agencies, not as catalysts, but as capable of change by their interaction with clients. Gitterman (1983) argues that many difficulties in getting clients to accept help can usefully be seen as part of a struggle for dominance between the worker and professional prerogatives, the client's wish for control and the agency's attempts to manage what goes on within it. Since theory describes and explains what workers do, it must also respond to the realities of its social constructions. Otherwise, it would be rejected or amended. A major feature of any acceptable model of social work theory, therefore, is the extent to which it can offer explanations of and guidance in dealing with the pressures clients put on social workers and how this affects their perceptions of the clients' social circumstances. A theory which is inadequate at any time in representing the real needs of clients as presented to agencies is likely only to be partially accepted, or to become supplanted.

So far, I have argued that social work *itself* is interactive because it responds to clients' demands on a service affecting workers, and that theoretical development reflects this, because theories are rejected or amended as they fail to deal with the demands actually made.

To take this further, *theory* must also develop in response to demands made by clients on agencies and workers affecting the interpretation or acceptance of theoretical ideas. Since theory is a statement of what social work is and prescribes what social workers should do in various situations, it follows that the nature of social work and its theory are defined, not by some independent process of academic development and experimental testing but by what social workers actually do. And that is created by their reality, the demands made by clients in the context of the basic values and social structures established within the occupation of social work. A modern social work theory must therefore respond to the modern social construction of reality both by clients and by social workers and their social environments; if it fails to do so, it will be unsuccessful. The recognition of the need for theory to be interactive or *reflexive* in this way is a feature of more modern social work theories such as ecological systems approaches, where the interaction with the environment is strongly recognised (Germain, 1981), and Marxist and radical approaches (see Chapters 10–11).

According to this view of social work, its theory must be constantly changing in response to practice constructions by its participants. Therefore, accounts of its nature cannot arise from a theory or model of what social work is in general. Instead, it is a variety of activities which have common features in most social constructions of it. The balance of those features, the degree to which they are present, and their significance to the participants in a social work activity offer a structure against which social work theories may be tested. If a theory explains or describes helpfully a particular combination of circumstances it provides an adequate account of that form of social work. If it cannot offer such guidance it is inadequate as a theory for that purpose, although it might be useful in some other context.

The features which offer a useful set of categories for assessing theories are those aspects of social work activity which affect the social construction of participants. They specify areas which it is helpful for theory to deal with. It is then possible to compare their adequacy in different circumstances. The fact that these elements are always present in social work, although in different combinations, gives its nature a stability so that it is recognisably social work even though its implementation varies. These features relate

Table 1.2 *Common features in the social context of social work*

Feature	Implications
Individualisation	people are treated as *individuals* not categories
Use of knowledge	clients and actions are understood through *psychological and social knowledge* evidence and argument
Relationship	social work operates through *relationships*
Organisational context	social work uses the *organisational context* of its relationships to carry out its activities
Need	social work defines *need*
Maintenance of social institutions	social work is concerned with *maintaining important social structures*
Advocacy	social work *advocates* for clients

closely to values which some writers would see as basic to social work. They are set out in Table 1.2. Many of them are what Rojek *et al.* (1989) call 'received ideas' in social work; they argue that such ideas, whether traditional, radical or feminist, constitute powerful influences on what workers actually do.

The remainder of this section explores each of these points, and considers the social work literature about them, to argue in each case that they are an essential part of social work. Their existence in an activity defines it as social work, but the nature of the description of social work which emerges from using these features to define an activity as social work varies, because how they are balanced and interact with each other affects how the activity looks. This is apparent in Chapter 12, which shows how different groups of theories reflect different balances of these features, and respond to different perceptions and analyses of the worlds within which social workers work.

Individualisation means that social work deals with people as individuals and avoids, for example, operating simply through bureaucratic procedures. Such procedures in agencies are often misused in dealing with clients but are more properly used in providing services which are adjuncts to social work, or in the administration of the agency. Clients' needs may be common ones, or reflect social trends, but social work activities are always designed to respond individually. Other agencies use set criteria, such as housing points systems, or social security eligibility rules, for assessment.

As a result, social work is often used within other services, easing problems of access to bureaucratic or complex services. Social workers also sort out the problems caused for clients by the management requirements of other services. The role of social workers in social security agencies in countries where social security and social work services are combined, and the role of medical social workers in hospitals are examples.

Individualisation is closely allied to 'advocacy' as a feature of social work. Writing a report for court, or a mental health worker providing a social history for a psychiatric team aims to individualise and personalise the client who might otherwise be just another offender or a psychiatric category.

Individualisation is a feature of social work even when groups or communities are the clients. Group or residential work aims to provide settings enabling individuals to use the group or environment to gain personal competences and perhaps insight to function more effectively in groups and in ordinary life. Even where the aim is to help a family, group or community function better as a whole, it includes how the individuals concerned take part, and how others use their contribution.

Part of the individualisation of people is individualising the circumstances which clients face. Individual or group clients are respected as human beings, and so the circumstances about which they seek help are differentiated from others' similar circumstances. Each individual point of their problems is considered as well as being seen as part of a whole. This is the purpose of much social work diagnosis or assessment, and their connection with individualisation is why such aspects or phases of social work are so important in the accounts given by many writers from many different theoretical perspectives.

Individualisation is not only an important value, it is significant for technical reasons. Social workers often deal with the exceptional or unusual which cannot be dealt with by more cost-effective bureaucratic means. They avoid generalities and categories and concentrate on the special features of the circumstances they are dealing with in order to fulfil this role. Doing so also enhances clients' feelings that their problems are being attended to. Relationship, another important feature of social work, is connected with individualisation, since the quality of the relationship partly depends on individualisation. Social workers tend to be criticised when they fail to act individualistically. In Cleveland, in the UK, for instance, a large number of referrals of child sexual abuse were made to the social services department, which was criticised for automatically taking legal proceedings, rather than considering each case on its merits (DHSS, 1988).

The classic statement of individualisation is by Biestek (1965) in his account of the main features of the social work relationship. The underlying philosophical idea is about respect for persons. These propose that social workers should always *accept* each individual client as a valuable human being, even though the client's behaviour is unacceptable; this distinguishes people from their actions. One aspect of respect for the client as an individual is commitment to that idea of *self-determination* by the client. Originally, this had a technical purpose in enabling the worker to influence the client more successfully by getting them to take an active part in the work and so engage their motivation more strongly. This has developed to an ethic that clients should have a degree of, or complete control of the process in which both worker and client share (Payne, 1989).

Use of knowledge is a corollary of individualisation since if people are dealt with as individuals, there must be some basis for understanding them as such. Social work uses social and psychological evidence and argument for this purpose. In this, it differs from, say, the law, religion, or politics where the basis of understanding is respect for authority, faith, belief, or interest. Although other occupations use similar material to that used by social work, the balance is different. Medicine has a greater emphasis on biological and chemical science; psychology rather neglects the sociological; counselling leans away from political, organisational and social understanding; public administration concentrates on the political and social rather than the psychological.

The history of rational assessment in social work goes back at least to the work of the charity organisation societies whose purpose was to plan personal help so that it was focused effectively. This involved assessing individual clients on the basis of organised record-making and investigation of the client's life circumstances. An early text from the USA 'Social Diagnosis' (Richmond, 1917) set out systematic schemas for investigating clients' affairs. These developments were sometimes in conflict with the Fabian or socialist view of social action, particularly in the UK (C. Jones 1979), and with Evangelical Christian workers such as Barnardo who was in conflict with the London COS (Wagner, 1979). Their view was that services should be non-selective as far as possible and everyone who came forward and met the criteria for services should receive them.

Social work took from its medical connections the value of systematic observation and assessment to form the basis of a diagnosis. The medical model is also an important aspect of the influence of psychoanalytic theory. Sociological origins of the importance of understanding through evidence lie in the tradition of empirical social investigation pioneered by people like Booth (1892–1903) in the 19th century, and by empirical sociologists such as Durkheim (1938) and American sociologists. This approach to understanding social problems has been extended into the work of social policy analysts such as Titmuss and his followers (e.g. Titmuss, 1963, 1968) who promoted the use of detailed investigations of social problems. Subsequently, there has grown up an approach to political pressure-group activity which relies on detailed empirical analysis of case material.

The range of theories and knowledge used in social work, reviewed by Barker and Hardiker (1981) among others includes sociological, psychological, social policy and organisational theories. These are generally used to understand and explain:

- behaviour of clients
- social origins of clients' behaviour and problems
- social environment of clients' lives
- interactions between clients and workers
- organisational environment of the work
- effectiveness or otherwise of the work.

Relationship between client and worker is the vehicle of the continuity of the social work process, because a broad involvement in clients' lives is needed which cannot be achieved in distinct episodes or limited interactions, and because of the effectiveness of relationship as a medium for achieving change in people's lives.

Using a relationship is closely connected with the idea that social work is a process, rather than a series of discrete events. Clients are involved in a sequence of activities which connect with and influence one another. The whole is designed to do more than a series of separate activities could do. The relationship carries the sequences along and makes the connection. It is the practical implementation of individualisation and respect for persons.

Relationship implies a two-way influence so that social workers are changed interactively by clients as well as vice-versa. Their emotions and mutual interests are involved with each other. Perlman (1979) stresses the emotional and individualising aspect of relationship in social work and in general. This creates a connection between people which continues even when they are not together. Clients and workers understand social work as something which continues between them. A sales assistant and a shopper, by contrast, may well communicate in much the same way, but each has a distinct role in which the seller services the requests which the customer defines, after which contact ceases. In a service organisation such as a hotel, contacts may persist longer and involve closer personal interactions, but the exchange between the parties is still a customer-servant one.

In some other caring occupations, the contact may be similarly highly personal, sustained and may rely on an element of trust generated by an appropriate manner or approach to clients or patients. Such relationships, unlike social work, are based on activities around a particular form of services (as in clinical psychology, physiotherapy or speech therapy) or episodes of care (as in nursing) or on particular sets of symptoms or conditions (as in medicine). Only in social work is the establishment and maintenance of the relationship the main instrument of service with the client.

Social work and related activities such as counselling are concerned with a much broader range of the client's circumstances. The openness required of the client for this sort of process demands of the worker a responsive involvement which only the relationship can offer. As other nearby occupations such as psychiatry move away from their own centres of speciality towards using similar techniques, they also make greater use of this sort of relationship. Similarly, as social workers move towards service provision in their role, their approach may take on more aspects of the customer-servant style.

Relationship became important in social work principally because of its importance in psychoanalytic theory, but other therapeutic theories also give importance to relationship, including behaviour modification and humanist therapies. Research has shown that the nature of the relationship between a client and worker is important in many different kinds of counselling and psychotherapeutic activities (Patterson, 1986). The effective features of a relationship are empathic understanding by the worker of the client, respect and warmth for the client and genuineness in the worker's behaviour; these are considered further in Chapter 8.

Cultural assumptions and expectations are also carried by relationships, so that sociologists and anthropologists are also interested in how they create social institutions. An example of this relevant to social work is how the value base of social work is reflected in the sort of relationships which workers establish with their clients (Biestek, 1965).

Organisational context, as we have seen, forms and controls social work as an occupation and the establishment of clienthood for a particular person. Organisations are social institutions with certain social goals. They have to achieve the commitment of their members to meeting those goals. Clients and social workers are within and surrounded by many organisations as well as the agency which is the base of their work. Working in an organisation raises, therefore, issues about the goals of the institution and whether they are consistent with the goals and activities of those working within it, and how compliance with organisational goals is achieved or not (Etzioni, 1975).

Since they are social institutions, organisations are also media for managing various kinds of social relationships. Such relationships include interactions between organisations and other social institutions and power and influence within the organisation and between it and others. How this is done often reflects existing social and cultural patterns within society, such as geographical, class, sexual, racial, political and family divisions. Therefore, not only the social work agency but its relationships with others and the general social context are relevant to an understanding of social work. The organisational goals and forms of social relationships set by social agencies are transmitted to and affect the social work activities which are carried out to meet both the formal and informal goals. The agency is also a conduit transmitting the effects of clients' demands and responses into the organisational and social networks around it. That transmission, of course, is equally affected by the social factors affecting the nature of the agency.

Importance was first attributed to the role of the agency in social work by functional social work theory (see Chapter 3). This proposes that the agency's role gives focus and purpose to social work activity undertaken within it. While this is so, the agency is also affected by clients and workers in complex ways, as we have seen in earlier parts of this Chapter.

Need is a complex concept; individual and social needs are hard to unravel, and one of social work's roles is to assess needs. Two important areas are relevant. First, 'need' is often used to refer to something within us which drives us to achieve some purpose. So, if we are hungry we 'need' food. Second, 'need' can be socially defined to be things which it is to some degree essential that we have. For example, it may be said that everybody needs good health care. Sometimes the two ideas are related. Most people, for example, have an emotional commitment to feeling healthy and would accept that it is socially beneficial to be provided with health services.

The origins of the importance of need in social work are:

- psychoanalytic theory, which is based on a theory of motivation so that people who lack emotional or physical necessities are driven to attain them, so that 'need' gained associations with emotions, often strong and irrational ones.
- early Poor Law welfare work and charity organisation work, which made distinctions between people deserving and undeserving of assistance; in modern times, government social provision is often related to entitlement or assessment of the extent to which a service is needed according to set criteria; therefore the assessment of need comes to be seen as a prerequisite of receiving services and of fair allocation of services.
- medical services, where doctors provide an authoritative diagnosis, and prescribe treatment; so it comes to be said that a diagnosis and prescription define need for medical care, and social work, using a medical model of study, diagnosis and treatment as the basis for its service, has developed a similar concept.

The complexities of need have given rise to a considerable literature, which has influenced social work thinking. Different types of need exist, according to Maslow (1970), and some types are more important than others, giving rise to a hierarchy in which there will not be emotional pressure to meet needs lower in the hierarchy until the more important levels of need are met.

The social definition of need is equally complex. With the importance of defining need as an entitlement to service, need has acquired a political importance. To say that something is a need makes it more necessary to take action to deal with it than with something which is not. Assessing need thus becomes associated with rationing services. As social workers define something as a need, they are making it more likely or, in an ideal world, necessary that it should be provided for.

Bradshaw (1972) has produced a taxonomy of need which sets out different sorts of need which would have different consequences for services. These are:

- *normative need*, defined by an expert or professional
- *felt need*, which is the same as wants
- *expressed need*, where felt need is turned by some action (e.g. applying for services) into demand
- *comparative need*, where people are in need if they suffer the same conditions as others who do receive a service.

Defining need is also part of the assessment stage of the route to clienthood. Reviewing this process, G. Smith (1980) argues that need is an administrative construct which describes decisions made by officials. Kemshall (1986) in a study of intake in a social services office shows that such decisions are constructed by workers' everyday reactions to the problems that they faced, reinterpreting by social consensus the official definition of need. As well as these formal determinations of need, clients and others around them, other agencies and other workers and officials also define clients' need in relation to the services of a social worker. Social workers may also define need on behalf of other agencies. Their reports, social histories or referrals may lead to the provision of services or to reactions to the client by other agencies.

Assessment of needs by social workers is related to the role of advocacy for clients, since often the worker's credibility as a spokesman relies on their assumed expertise in assessing needs.

Maintenance of social institutions is another important role of social workers and their agencies. Davies (1985) argues that in doing so, social work helps to maintain social norms and values; it does so in the process of helping people maintain a satisfactory life in society. The two most important institutions upheld by social work are the family and the community, as we saw in examining important factors in the development of social work as an occupation. Social work's role in maintaining the family and the community is paradoxical, since some social work is concerned with supporting and developing such institutions so that they work well, while in some cases the institution is maintained because social work makes substitute arrangements when it does not work well. So, where an elderly person is living with children and this is causing relationship difficulties, the social worker would help resolve these so that the family could continue to be together. Where there is no family, the social services often provide services which substitute for the care and support that the family would provide.

This is support for the institution because:

- making alternative or supportive services available encourages families to continue with helping their members thus maintaining their family involvement in such activities.
- it expresses a public policy demonstrating commitment to maintaining family and community if possible.
- providing alternatives when family and community are not present demonstrates their value.

Giving importance to family and community in social work is a long-standing ideal but it is not without its critics. Hamilton (1957) argues that early social workers worked with the problem, rather than social structures. The importance of the family in social work theory arose because of the importance of early life in psychodynamic theory, and the role of social workers, particularly in child guidance, in investigating the early social history of clients. Much writing on casework sees it as work with individuals and families. The importance given to families in psychosocial theory and crisis intervention (see several chapters in Parad, 1965) are examples of this in traditional social work. Concern for the risks to family life during the Second World War (and also in other wars) were an important aspect of the development of supportive social services, particularly in Europe. During the latter part of the

Second World War and the period afterwards in England, for example, family problems were an important focus (Rustin, 1979), leading to concern about multi-problem families. Families were seen as the focus of work with offenders and as the basis of a new organisation of the social services in the UK following the Seebohm report (1968). A number of techniques for working with families in a distinctive way, grew up to form family therapy (Walrond-Skinner, 1976) which has generated considerable interest among social workers, even being adapted from its psychiatric and therapeutic base for use in the bureaucratic climate of official agencies (Dimmock and Dungworth, 1983; Nuttall, 1985).

Two major criticisms of social work's emphasis on the family come from radical perspectives. Marxist theorists see the family as the place where the labour force is 'reproduced' (in the sense of both being born and socialised into acceptance of the ideological oppression of capitalist societies). Maintaining the family in this instance may be detrimental to the interests of working class people, but, according to Corrigan and Leonard (1978) it may also be the only place where people may experience sharing and collaborative relationships. Feminists argue that 'the emphasis on appropriate mother-centred child-rearing practices in social work has . . . more to do with the regulation of women's lives than the successful negotiation of childhood' (Sullivan, 1987, p. 164). Thus, the emphasis on family work may stress the role of women as carers rather than respecting their capacity for broader roles. Women receive most of the attention from social workers dealing with families, and suffer more of the practical consequences of social problems than men (Wilson, 1980).

The community as a social institution is also an important focus for social work activity. Many early social work agencies had an educational and leisure bias, rather than or as well as being concerned with personal help and therapeutic activity. One important strand of the history of social work derives from settlement work in Britain and the USA. Parts of this activity have been divided into community work and group work and in the UK (but not in other parts of Europe and the USA) a fairly clear division has grown up between youth work and social work.

One of the characteristics of social work is that it is either carried out in the community (i.e. with clients who live in their own homes) or with the aim of helping people in residential or hospital care to deal with their problems outside the setting and often as part of the process of discharge from the setting. Social policy in many countries is emphasising deinstitutionalisation, resulting in the social services becoming increasingly important, and, as we saw earlier, more pressurised. In the UK, for example, a policy of 'community care' outside residential settings has been developed for most client groups since the Second World War, and has origins in policies and developments going back to the early part of the century (Walker, 1982). Such policies for deinstitutionalisation are apparent in services associated with social work in the USA, Italy and other countries (P. Brown, 1985; Ramon and Giannichedda, 1988).

Related to these ideas that living in the community as opposed to residential settings is preferable, is a romanticism about 'the community' as an important factor in our lives. This has led to the development of ideas about promoting and strengthening informal care and networks of people offering support in 'the community'. There has been a movement for the decentralisation of bureaucratic social services (Hadley and Hatch, 1981) which has led in the UK to the development of ideas of community social work (Barclay report, 1982; Hadley and McGrath, 1984). This term is sometimes misunderstood since it is used in the USA to refer to what in Britain would be called community work.

While they have their supporters, ideas of the community as the essential base of social work and personal support for individuals with problems have been questioned, as has the emphasis on family in social work. Support offered in working-class communities came from shared adversity, rather than commitment to some community ideal, and demographic and social changes mean that it is harder for families and local social networks to provide care for people with problems than at one time it was. As with families, 'community care' seems likely to place a particular burden on women who are usually seen as the people who should provide caring in most situations.

Social work, then, is intimately bound up in social policies and ideologies concerned with the support of several social institutions of which family and community have been selected as the most important. How a social work theory deals with these institutional and ideological demands is a crucial part of assessing its relevance to social work.

Advocacy is another important aspect of social work, both in the sense of arguing clients' cases for the provision of resources within the worker's agency or elsewhere, and more generally in seeking to establish or re-establish clients' acceptability and participation in society. Advocacy is a crucial element of all social work for two reasons. First, it is an important and rather neglected skill which, although recognised (Jordan, 1987), has not received its place in most general accounts of social work practice (Payne, 1986). Second, and more importantly, it is an essential element in social work's knowledge structure which defines the characteristics of social work (Philp, 1979).

Social work includes advocacy because, as we have seen, social work's role is to define needs and individualise clients on the basis of evidence so that, within organisational structures, clients' demands can be appropriately represented. In some countries, advocacy forms a determining part of the social worker's role, e.g. in Italy social workers administer the social security system, and having assessed their client and worked out their needs for financial resources, must put the client's needs to a lay committee (Cigno, 1985).

However, agencies do not necessarily respond well to clients' demands because they are often outside the expectations and rules of the agency, and because social work clients often possess characteristics which make them stigmatised such as mental illness, disability and a history of offending behaviour or drug addiction.

Advocacy from social workers, therefore, goes beyond arguing the client's case. Philp (1979) contends that the essential role of social work is to create a picture of the client as an individual which is both subjective in that it presents an individualised view and social in that it shows how that person is created and affected by their social surroundings. This creates the client as a 'subject'. Objective knowledge is integrated into this picture of the client (hence the importance to social work of the use of evidence in spite of the fact that much of what is done is concerned with subjective feeling and personal interaction) to give credibility to the *humanisation* of the client which the social worker tries to achieve. This presents the client as a candidate for acceptability for the services required or for admission to normal life after a period of unacceptability, and in doing this the social worker is creating a realistic case for the client. This process can be seen in the functions of social workers in producing social histories and reports for court which use objective evidence to explain and present the client appropriately for medical or judicial decision-making. It is also present when social workers try to demonstrate their clients' needs for services. Philp (1979) would argue that the whole process of casework and other therapeutic activities is directed towards showing, either by the fact that activity has gone on or by the changes wrought, that clients have been humanised to the point where they can be accorded full human and citizen status.

Philp's vision of social work accords a central place to its role in humanising and advocating for the client in the eyes of society. One important consequence of this view is to play down the role of therapy and personal change as an objective of social work in favour of achieving social changes in the position both of clients, as individuals, and of the social groupings of which they are part.

Seeing social work as fundamentally concerned with this broadly defined advocacy shows why relationships and an organisational role are important as part of social work. The closeness of social workers to their clients, allied with their official position and the credibility of their agency, demonstrates that they have the involvement which enables them to make a fuller and more detailed evaluation of their clients than most other officials, and gives organisational backing to their advocacy.

Social work and its theory: the organisation of the book

I have argued that social work is socially constructed through its interactions with clients, because they themselves become defined as clients by social processes, through its formation as an occupation among a network of related occupations, and through the social forces which define it through its context. I have characterised social work as an activity in which workers humanise through individualisation and advocate the needs of their clients in and from an organisational setting among whose aims is the maintenance of important social institutions, a factor which gives credibility to their efforts. Social workers achieve a close and credible understanding and assessment of clients' needs through their relationship with the clients and the use of objective evidence from the psychological and social sciences.

Going on from these points, the social construction of social work suggests that its theory at any one time is constructed by the same social forces that construct the activity. This makes it possible to see among the turmoil of conflicting and debated theory a way of organising theory for practice at any particular time.

Theory for practice will inevitably respond to current social pressures, so that present interests and concerns colour it. And yet it also reflects the histories of theoretical, occupational and service context. The strength of influence of those histories in the construction of present theory varies from time to place to person, but they are always there, alongside present social forces. In trying to make some sense from the turmoil of debated theory in this book, I am trying to reflect the histories of theory as they seem important as a contribution now, and to see what theory may be available and how it may be used. Examining how it fits together with other theories offers the opportunity of seeing what present and immediate future developments hold.

Inevitably, I have made decisions about what to include and exclude from the accounts of social work theory given in this book. I have, first, selected theories which have historical importance, or are subject to contemporary debate. These are grouped with related theories into individual Chapters (3–11) covering similar sets of concepts which form a theoretical *perspective*. In each case one or two of the theories is selected for more detailed treatment as an example of how that group of theories describes and accounts for social work activities. The aim of selecting a few writers in this way is to give enough detail to show how the writers actually apply their theoretical concepts to social work. Not enough detail can be given to allow a worker to practice from the accounts contained in this book, but there is enough to show the practical utility of each theory, and how its prescriptions differ from other theories.

Around the main account of the use of a theoretical perspective, is material about *connections*. Each chapter gives some account of the origins of that perspective and how it came to have influence in social work, identifies and makes connections with other ideas and writers whose work is related to the main concept. This is so that the reader can position the theory among other theories and ideas, and can appreciate connections among writers and ideas as he or she comes across them.

In Chapters 2 and 12, I consider the problems of relating theory to practice, of selecting from and understanding the relationships between theories, and finally the problems of assessing the utility of the various theories and their future. In these three Chapters I am trying to arrive at a view about how social work theory may be used in practice as a whole.

The naturalisation of social work theory

My fundamental position is that social work theories share common features, which are far more important than the differences between them. These features derive, as we have seen, from the social contexts in which social work is practised. New ideas within social work theory arise in various ways and go through a process of *naturalisation* by which they become adjusted to the conventional framework of social work. Some theories have not fully naturalised, because they do not deal well with some of the important features of social work within the period in which they become important. Theories which do naturalise affect the common features of social work. Cheers (1978), in a rather humanist approach, argues that particular theories only deal with parts of a client's problems and need to be co-ordinated to form one holistic view of them and the help they need. In his view, as part of the process of naturalisation:

- ideas must be studied and grasped intellectually
- they must be analysed and criticised intellectually
- individual workers must 'make sense' of them as part of their own experience
- workers must interpret the theory and link it into the total pattern of their thinking
- they must try it out and experience how it works in practice.

At this point, it is appropriate to introduce the idea of *paradigm*. In general terms, this concept means a pattern or template, something which is commonly reproduced in an activity. Kuhn

(1970) uses paradigm to describe a general view of the nature of physical or natural phenomena in science. His influential book on the history of science suggests that such paradigms arise, and scientific activity (theory-making, experimentation, methods of research, debate etc.) builds on them, until, in a scientific revolution, a completely new world view of phenomena is constructed which totally changes the conception of those phenomena. Using 'paradigm' as Kuhn uses it, I am arguing that there is a paradigm of social work, which is socially constructed and into which all current theory and practice may be fitted. This is in practice agreed, even though there are theoretical disputes and minor variations, since most social workers recognisably do similar sorts of things in interactions with their clients. Kuhn questions (1970, p. 15) whether parts of the social sciences are well enough developed to have acquired a paradigm, let alone experienced one of these revolutions. Yet some writers (e.g. Fischer, 1981) argue that such shifts in the conception of social work have taken place. Kuhn (1970, p. 49) accepts that many minor paradigms will grow up in what he calls the ramshackle structure of specialities, and gives these paradigmatic status before they have acquired wide agreement. This seems to me to be the status of many of the competing theories in social work; the fact that they exist does not alter my view that one fundamental approach in daily practice exists. My argument that all theories are in practice collected together in the basic paradigm of social work may therefore be considered to be controversial.

The basic paradigm of social work derives from psychoanalytic theory carried out within a humanist ethic, but it is a derivation which is now at some distance both from psychoanalysis and humanism. Nonetheless, in discussing the basic contexts of social work, we saw that several of these had their original roots in psychoanalytic theory, and this is true also of several approaches to practice. Psychoanalytic ideas, then, form the groundwork which other ideas in social work either naturalise to or respond and reject, while often still assuming deeply-rooted approaches to clients whose origins lie in distant psychoanalysis.

Having given this outline of some important points in the argument of the book, it is time to move on to the first step of examining relationships between theory and practice.

2

Using Social Work Theory in Practice

Many people have difficulty in applying social work theory in practice. The first part of this chapter considers three debates about this issue. The *pragmatic* argument proposes that there is a confusing array of theories, mainly imported from outside social work practice by academic theory-builders, and that these are not practically useful. It relates to a pragmatic tradition of social work practice particularly associated with official agencies rather than with social reform or therapy, which offer alternative traditions of social work theory. In response to these arguments I propose a social constructionist view suggesting that this debate is basically a struggle for control of social work theory and practice between different interests within social work.

The *positivist* argument is that many social work theories are insufficiently rigorous, and are not genuine theories at all because they only describe and hypothesise rather than explain which actions by a social worker will achieve precise results. The positivist would limit the theories which can be used to those which can be supported by empirical testing, so excluding many of the perspectives which might be available to social workers. I argue that this would be an extreme and unjustified position to take.

The next section of this chapter considers the *eclecticism* debate. Eclecticism is the idea that it is possible to use all or many of the theories available together, or in sequence, or to select parts of them to use in combination. I show that there are problems with eclecticism, which must be used with caution.

The fourth section considers a number of ways in which social work theory might be related to practice, and argues that problems and advantages arise with each of them, suggesting again that the pragmatic argument is misleading in suggesting that only one relationship is desirable, and that only an unhelpful model of the relationship between practice and theory is being used. I argue, instead, that a variety of alternative approaches to relating theory and practice is possible, and use of a number of them is desirable.

What theories, then, are available within social work to be used in practice? The final section reviews various analyses of social work theory, and theory in related areas, and explains how particular theories have been presented in this book.

The pragmatic argument

All practical occupations face the problem of relating theory about their activities to the practice of them. People who take a pragmatic view of practice argue that present social work theory (and perhaps all possible social work theory) cannot be applied to practice. Pragmatists would say:

- there are a wide range of competing theories making it impossible to use them; so many are available that to select only one may discredit the user
- theories are too highly generalised to prescribe specific actions in practice
- theories either conflict with the legal and procedural responsibilities of many workers, particularly in official agencies, or do not make provision for those responsibilities, which are seen as outside social work and part of agency roles, or are allocated a lower status than therapeutic interventions
- theories emphasise voluntary and therapeutic or reform aspects of social work and are thus hostile to the social control, legal and procedural responsibilities of workers in many agencies.

If theory is, as I have suggested in Chapter 1, socially constructed, these arguments have some inadequacies. First, theory is constructed to respond to demands which are made upon it in various settings. So its many varieties may be useful in responding to different needs in different agencies. There is adequate coverage of the needs of compulsory clients and social control work in social work theories; indeed many theories are criticised for being excessively authoritarian and controlling. The fact that such criticisms are made does not exclude the usefulness of these theories to some social workers.

Second, if the problem is one of prescription, it is important to acknowledge that everything we do is always theoretical (Howe, 1987) and the problem is one of seeing how action relates to the theory formulated in books. It is a misunderstanding of theory, in the social construction perspective, to say that it must spring fully-formed with explanatory power from academic development. Instead, it must, according to this perspective, always be adapted by and responsive to action in daily practice. How it is adapted and how it responds are the crucial questions. Much of this criticism and debate reflects a struggle for control of theory and how social work may be seen.

Third, I have argued that social work theory actually demonstrates considerable stability. This is for two reasons. The first is that, as I have said in Chapter 1, social work always comprises a balance of the seven characteristics which interact to create it in any particular social context. Those features are always present, and give social work a distinguishable form and nature to which the theory always relates.

The second reason that I argue for the essential stability of social work, is that I have asserted that there is a basic approach and model of social work practice which reflects both an implicit and explicit theory.

Pragmatists often mistake the basic paradigm as common sense or ordinary social work. Critics and supporters of paradigmatic status for alternative theories often characterise it as traditional social work. This too is a mistaken view, since this fundamental social work perspective does develop and grow. The following account of the history of theory development in social work is, therefore, a further argument against the pragmatic view.

There are three separate traditions of theory in social work. The *pragmatic* tradition is associated with work in official agencies, particularly deriving from the Poor Law, and latterly social security agencies in the USA, Canada and European countries other than the UK where social workers are employed in helping roles associated with financial aid. I have suggested above that this tradition is associated with the pragmatic view of theory. In this view, practical developments, and such things as legal and administrative constraints, rather than theoretical perspectives, are the crucial elements in the development of practice. The second is the *socialist* tradition which concentrates on reform, social criticism and intervention at a collective level with communities and large groupings of disadvantaged or oppressed people. The *therapeutic* tradition is concerned with working with individuals or groups who present personal or social difficulties.

Many histories of social work identify the origins of social work as a separate occupation within the charity-organisation societies as also being the origins of its theoretical development. This is true primarily of the therapeutic tradition. Early theoretical developments were generally concerned with effective influence on the competence of individuals, particularly in families, to manage their financial and social affairs. There was a degree of moral judgement aligning competence in provision for family responsibilities with social acceptability. Theory was concerned with methods of investigation and assessment, so that judgements made were justifiable, and influence based on rationally obtained evidence. The apotheosis of this approach lies in the 'scientific social work' particularly of Mary Richmond (1917). She proposes an extensive set of schemas for assessment, and accurate diagnosis of problems.

Strean (1971a; 1979, p. 5) argues that psychodynamic casework, based on Freud's work (see Chapter 3), grew out of recognition that the moral element brought a relatively unscientific element to social work, that explanations were required for circumstances in which clients resisted logical and practical advice and that 'scientific' social work offered little assistance where problems arose from behaviour difficulties. Germain (1970) characterises the enthusiasm for using psychodynamic theory in the 1920s and 1930s as a quest for scientific respectability and association with high-status medical activity in hospitals rather than lower-status nursing or caring tasks; this is a professionalisation explanation. The growth of criminological work using psychology and social research influenced the perception that more practical intervention with offenders was possible, desirable and an appropriate role for social work. It also led to association with and a role within the criminal-justice system alongside another high-status profession – the law.

During the 1950s and 1960s, ego psychology displaced older

forms of psychodynamic theory as the most influential approach, and applications in groupwork and residential work through the development of therapeutic communities and planned environment therapy became important (see Chapter 3). Two aspects of theoretical growth then became significant. Their impact became evident towards the end of the 1960s. The first was the growth of interest in an alternative system of psychological explanation: behavioural approaches based on learning theory. Much of this interest came from perceived inadequacies in the practice of psychodynamic theory, particularly in the light of psychological research which clarified the importance of learning, cognition motivation (other than through internal drives) and social psychological factors in behaviour.

The second development was the growth of interest in the application of sociological theories in social work. These developments also were a reaction to perceived inadequacies in psychodynamic theory, but they were responsive too. Significant theoretical growth in sociology and an expansion of academic departments led to greater influence for this area of social science. Marxist theory strengthened its influence, particularly in Europe. At the same time, after a period in the 1950s when relatively conservative administrations dominated governments in the West, democrat (in the USA) and socialist governments (in Europe) gained power more widely, and this led to a flowering of interest in various social reforms. The poverty programme in the USA and various community developments elsewhere aroused greater interest in the social tradition of social work and in community work and development.

The decolonisation of many Third World countries led to broadly left-wing governments, and also to the separation of social welfare systems from the dominance of Western thought, and a greater emphasis on indigenous ideas, concerned more with social and community development rather than the more individualised social work of the Western world. Some of the ideas arising from these also began to have influence in Western society. Particularly noticeable is the work of Freire (see Chapter 10). In the UK and some other European countries, the end of colonial power led to the return of colonial administrators who brought some experiences of community development techniques used to prepare Third World countries for independence.

The social response led to two different sorts of theoretical change. One was a synthetic or integrating approach giving greater importance to social factors in casework practice. The most important ideas relied on systems theory, and a number of formulations are considered in Chapter 6. The alternative approach was politically radical in nature, proposing that substantial social change was necessary, and emphasising community and collective interventions. This was particularly important in the development of empowerment and advocacy approaches to social work. From this point, it is impossible to outline any particular path of theory development. A number of alternative perspectives and therapeutic approaches became available, taking up the reform, radical and therapeutic traditions.

I have tried to show in this account of the development of social work theory that generally changes took place because of perceived inadequacies in available theory in practice, which stimulated new developments. Many of these changes came from academic and professional sources and sometimes responded to academic assessments of the inadequacies of existing theories, but generally this was an inadequacy perceived in practice rather than being simply a matter, as the pragmatists would argue, of effete academic development. Similarly, some developments were conditioned by a perception of the inadequacy of theories which needed development for the benefit of a more effective profession. The growth of theory is thus often associated with occupational development. Many theoretical changes responded directly to theoretical and practice gaps identified in practice and academic environments at the time.

If we must reject the pragmatic argument, then, is the confusing turmoil of theory capable of being organised in other ways? There are fundamentally two approaches to doing so. One, the positivist view, argues that only a restricted range of theories is practically useful, because only a few can be supported by empirical evidence. To the positivist, it is these theories which should be used; others should be rejected. The second approach is the eclectic approach, which maintains that theories can be used in combination.

The positivist debate

Positivism is the view that understanding about human activity should be based on the methods of natural science. This would mean that a theory would not be considered true or worthwhile unless it made clear predictions of outcomes from actions taken, and the outcomes could be shown to have occurred as predicted. Positivist or logical empirical approaches to theory imply a strict attention to experimental and statistical design of the tests of prediction and carefully tested logic in deriving and expounding the theory.

Leonard (1975b), in an important paper, distinguished two different systems of explanation in the social sciences and applied them to social work: a physical-sciences and human-sciences paradigm. In each, he identified two positions about types of explanation. These are set out in Table 2.1.

Table 2.1 *Types of explanation in social work*

Physical-sciences paradigm	
Position A	*Position B*
aim at status of physical science	aims and methods in physical and social sciences similar
importance given to measurement and objectivity	physical sciences are inexact
only data capable of exploration by the senses counts as scientific knowledge	probability important in both physical and social sciences

Human-sciences paradigm	
Position C	*Position D*
social sciences rely on subjective understanding	social sciences are socially-determined
questions are value-laden: answers can be value-free	ideological influences important socio-economic context of theories important

Source: Leonard (1975b).

Leonard argues that position A reflects the view of supporters of behavioural approaches, that only a 'hard science' form of explanation is credible, whereas position B in the physical-sciences paradigm emphasises that many areas of both physical and social sciences are inexact, and reflects a less extreme view. The human-sciences paradigm implies a different sort of explanatory model, with position D emphasising that not only are values and subjective understanding important in the social sciences but, typical of a radical view, the social and economic context in which theories are formed must also be considered. Different views about explanation reflect, in Leonard's view, different philosophies about the social and economic system, with people taking position A not acknowledging the importance of social contexts in the formation and use of their theories.

As we have seen, social work has a scientific ideology, and has constantly sought status and respectability through having a scientific approach to understanding human problems. This came under attack in the 1960s for two reasons. First, the experimental validity of behavioural psychology led to increasing criticism of the scientific status of psychodynamic theory, and had great impact on social work because of its intense reliance at that time on psychodynamic theory. Second, empirical testing of the effectiveness of social work intervention, both in the USA and Britain, did not show that it was effective.

Criticism from a positivist perspective came from two important writers, Fischer (1973, 1976, 1981) in the USA and Sheldon (1978, 1982a, 1984, 1986) in Britain. Their argument was that since traditional social work practice could not be shown to be effective, it should be abandoned and replaced with empirically tested practice, which would be based on behavioural approaches. Fischer produced a book (1978) outlining such an approach.

The positivist critique as presented by Fischer and Sheldon led to a considerable reaction, paralleling that in the field of psychoanalysis, and some intemperate debate. It can also be claimed that positivism is part of the struggle for control of theory and practice rather than a debate about evidence for theories. Such a view is taken by Karger (1983), who suggests that arguments for scientific method as the basis for knowledge in social work are designed to enhance the academic and professional status of the profession in general and particular groupings within it, without having much interest or value for many practitioners.

The answers to the positivist critique fall into three groups:

● validation of social work effectiveness has been achieved with studies which have concentrated on more closely-defined services and outcome in recent years, as compared with the broader studies of earlier years. Also, some earlier research which has been seen as evidence of ineffectiveness does not have to be read so pessimistically (D. Smith, 1987). This would be generally accepted, and is treated as evidence that more focused techniques similar to or derived from behavioural approaches are having their effect. Fischer (1981) has gone so far as to claim that this change constitutes a change in the basic 'paradigm' (in the Kuhnian sense – see Chapter 1) of social work. Gordon (1983) argues, correctly in my view, that Kuhn's model is not intended to apply to professional knowledge areas or to debate about appropriate methods for research in any given area, that Kuhn himself is opposed to 'rank empiricism', and that Fischer wrongly equates 'quantifiable' with 'empirical' which has a broader meaning and should include qualitative research and tested accumulation of experience.

- to follow on from the previous point, the positivist critique ignores, according to D. Smith (1987) and Heineman (1981), a variety of other philosophical and research traditions which are equally acceptable and useful in related fields. Smith argues that the positivist view has an unreasonable hold among lay people and within social work. Jordan (1978) and England (1986) argue for an artistic and imaginative approach to understanding social work, although Smith rejects this because it does not provide clear enough practice guidance.

- there are always problems with the positivist view when dealing with human activities because human behaviour is hard to define clearly, and outcomes which are tested may not connect with the inputs which are examined. It is very hard to identify incontrovertible facts about human activity – nearly everything is in fact subject to interpretation and differences of perception and is affected by the context in which it occurs (D. Smith, 1987; Ruckdeschel and Farris, 1982; Rein and White, 1981).

Putting theories together: eclecticism

Can the confusion of theories be dealt with in practice by putting all or several together in some way to provide an overall theory? This approach to theory is called *eclecticism*.

Dryden (1984) identifies a number of forms of eclecticism in the literature on therapy. Among them are:

- *theoretical*, using one school of thought but adding particular techniques from other schools according to the aims of the major theory used
- *structural*, assessing clients' circumstances according to various categories of information and selecting techniques from a variety of theories accordingly
- *combination*, trying to combine two or more approaches at theoretical and other levels
- *existential*, following a general set of existential principles, such as the idea that encountering and coping with the problems of life exposes clients' basic dilemmas in life, and using any available techniques to tackle these problems, so that what workers do is conditioned both by belief in the principles and the dilemmas revealed
- *technical*, using techniques from a variety of theories without any commitment to the theories or disciplines which underlie them
- *integrationism*, identifying the shared features of many theories and defining and using these
- *developmental*, treating therapy as a series of stages to which theory is secondary
- *haphazard*, choosing a theory according to its appeal to the worker.

Is there evidence that social workers are eclectic, or that eclectic theories exist? Three forms of evidence are relevant. First, there are research studies of social workers' attitudes. Second, there are texts which explicitly attempt an eclectic approach. Third, there are texts which approach social work in a fundamentally eclectic way.

The evidence for a degree of eclecticism exists in research studies of social workers. Jayaratne (1978) surveyed 267 American social workers in the mid-1970s and found that there was a primary allegiance to psychodynamic approaches but that '. . . eclecticism is the predominant mode of intervention . . .' (p. 626). 29.6 per cent of eclectics were (according to Dryden's much later categorisation, described above) combinationists, 22.5 per cent were structuralists,

17.2 per cent were technical eclectics and 5.6 per cent simply thought that no one theory was adequate. Research by Kolevson and Maykranz (1982), covering nearly 700 American practitioners and teachers, shows that they have very weak allegiances to specific theories; they speculate that this may be because of poor theoretical grounding in their training. British studies (e.g. DHSS, 1978, pp. 134–6) comment on the pronounced lack of theory in the approach of many workers surveyed, although there is also evidence (e.g. Curnock and Hardiker, 1979) that some inexplicit use of theory takes place.

Fischer (1978) has produced a text on social work which is specifically eclectic. He argues that we should select techniques appropriate to the needs of the client. He is quite committed to the behavioural approach, and selects techniques according to their effectiveness as demonstrated by research evidence, so he could be seen as a theoretical eclectic, enhancing a basic theoretical approach with insights from other related ideas.

Many other social work texts are eclectic in other ways. Some are theoretically eclectic in that they specifically include aspects of other theories (e.g. Hollis and Woods, 1981, on psychosocial theory include family therapy, role and communication theory). Most humanist writers (e.g. Krill, Brandon, Goldstein) are existential eclectics, since their theories do not propose techniques of practice specific to their approach, but concentrate on how we should understand and work with the human condition using a variety of techniques.

Many basic social work texts are integrationist, structural or developmental, since they concentrate on presenting the processes, skills or techniques of social work rather than offering any particular theory to help understand personal or social behaviour. It might be claimed that these, or developments in service delivery such as community social work (in Britain) or case management, are more relevant to practice prescription than the sort of theories which seek to provide an explanation of why particular behaviours from social workers result in worthwhile change in clients – this latter being the approach of most social work theories which are viewed as such in this book and elsewhere. Against this, it may be argued that ideas such as case management do not seek to explain how social work works, but merely to establish an administrative system within which social work may be more effectively provided.

Systems theories explicitly seek to be combination-eclectic, since they try to offer an overarching theory which includes many or all other social work theories.

Moore (1976) argues that being eclectic relies on the skill, knowledge and value base of a worker, which offers a secure base for moving among theoretical ideas. Since there is evidence that eclecticism is widely apparent in social work, is it a satisfactory way of dealing with the problem that there is a multiplicity of theories to choose from in practice? To go further, should we take up an eclectic or inclusive theory in preference to others, because it allows us to use a variety of approaches within it? Further still, are the sorts of theories that we have been examining basically irrelevant to practice, and is a technical or developmental theory which simply presents a range of techniques or offers descriptions of stages of work all that is necessary? To answer these questions, we need to look at the arguments for and criticism of eclecticism and these are set out in Table 2.2.

As an overall judgement, it is clear that there are strong arguments in favour of eclecticism in using theory, but that there are difficulties, which mean that doing so should be a cautious act.

Theory and practice

Theory offers:

- *models* describing what happens during practice in a general way, applying to a wide range of situations, in a structured way, so that they extract certain principles and patterns of activity which give the practice consistency
- *approaches* to or *perspectives* on a complex human activity which allow participants to order their minds sufficiently to be able to manage themselves while participating
- *explanations* which account for why an action results in particular consequences and the circumstances in which it does so
- *prescriptions* for action so that workers know what to do when faced with particular circumstances
- *accountability* to managers, politicians, clients and public by describing acceptable practice sufficiently to enable social work activities to be checked to see that they are appropriate

Table 2.2 *Arguments for and against eclecticism*

For	Against
Clients should be able to benefit from all available knowledge, so theoretical perspectives should not be limited	Clients may not benefit, since workers acquire work styles early in their career and may miss theories which are devised later
Empirical knowledge about skills or communication are valid irrespective of theory, and should be used as part of applying any theories	Eclecticism avoids the professional responsibility to accumulate and integrate knowledge of social work
There are many links between different ways of helping	
Theories work at different levels (e.g. task-centred theory gives specific guidance about particular situations while psychodynamic theory offers very wide-ranging ideas about interpreting behaviour); theories at different levels can be used together	There is no clear basis for deciding how to use one theory rather than another, or selecting one from a range; therefore, the decision to use one theory rather than another is purely arbitrary or based on personal feeling rather than rational decision
Some theories do not pretend to cover all areas of work (e.g. Marxist theory does not provide psychological knowledge or skills guidance) and so must be used in conjunction with others, provided care is taken about how they match	Workers would need to understand many theoretical approaches, some very complex and needing supervision and study; this is not possible for most workers much of the time; if something went wrong with a highly technical theory, they might not notice or be able to put it right
Many aspects of social work are the same whatever theory is used (e.g. the sequence of beginning, middle and end phases; assessment, diagnosis and planning; use of tasks and contracts) so a broad approach to social work can be constructed from these without worrying about theory	Practising so as to join many different theories together may cause a worker to lose a common core of practice
Many of the distinctions drawn between theories are not relevant to practice which concerns itself with general and practical ideas like assessment, rather than ideas about human behaviour, social environment or the human condition which are secondary to helping people	Many theories use similar techniques but with different justifications, or within a completely different understanding of society or human beings; theories might inherently conflict without the worker being aware of or understanding the contradictions; this may be confusing for clients and workers
Social work involves personal commitment and use of personality in a close relationship with clients, and sticking to one theory may be uncongenial for the worker or client in a particular case; human variety requires us to choose from the widest possible range of theories to make the personal element of social work possible	

- *justifications* for the use of the models and explanations of practice

Positivists would distinguish models from theories, since they would say that theory must explain in a provable way *why* something happens, not simply describe it in an organised way.

The use of theory for justification may also be questioned. Some theories in social work, however, seem to be concerned with relating social work activities to broader categories of activity in society, rather than seeking to explain, describe or prescribe social work activities systematically. A particular system of social work activities is then justified because they meet some wider social aims. Many social work theories do this to some extent, especially where they claim to rely on particular human values: existential or humanist therapies are examples. Some theories seem to be primarily intended for this purpose: Marxist and feminist therapies are examples. Other theories tend to justify or explain social work theories by showing how they relate to general models or theories about human behaviour or society. The social work branch is then justified to some extent because it can be shown to fit into an accepted model of explanation or description. Systems or psycho-analytic theory are examples of this use of theory in social work.

Different types of theories in social work have different purposes:

- theories *about* social work explain the nature and role of social work in society
- theories *of* social work describe which activities constitute social work, set aims for social work activities and explain why those activities are relevant and effective in meeting the aims
- theories *contributing to* social work are the psychological, sociological and other theories which explain or describe personal and social behaviour and are used to make theories of social work systematic, related to general social science explanations and to give supporting evidence for the social work theory's prescriptions
- theories of social work *practice and method* prescribe in detail how the other theories so far outlined may be applied in the interaction between workers and clients.

Theories of social work are strategic in nature, theories of practice and method specific. They often apply to a wide range of settings within social work and to work in related occupations. Practice and method theories frequently form the links in the network of occupations, while theories of social work create the boundaries of an occupational grouping.

There has been a long-lived debate in social work (and in other occupations) about how theory may be linked with practice. Carew (1979) identifies a number of different issues of concern in the theory/practice link.

First, there is the concern that social work should be empirical or scientific; this issue is sometimes really about the use of research rather than theory. Thus, Sheldon (1978) describes the link as 'tenuous' primarily because social workers are not clear that their enterprise should be based on a positivistic regard for the evidence of social science, and do not use the available means of rational evaluation of their work. This meaning of the problem of relating theory to practice is a particular presentation of the positivism debate, considered above. The relevance of this point to social work knowledge is, however, that it may be argued that the sorts of knowledge available to social workers are not concrete enough ever to be useful. For example, a doctor may have precise information about the effects of a drug on the patient, and this degree of certainty can never be available to the social worker. Either social work as an activity can never aspire to the same professional standing because of the inadequacy of its knowledge base or it is fundamentally a different kind of activity, or, again, efforts must be made to improve its scientific standing and to use only the most credible knowledge available. If this latter aim can be achieved, some writers would claim that researched knowledge and practice can inform each other. In an American study, Siegel (1984) experimented with teaching on a social work course so that a researcher and practitioner taught together, and found that there were five ways in which research and practice could be effectively linked:

- working with clients can include research activities
- research findings can be used to decide on practice actions and on personal models of practice
- both research and practice share their nature as problem-solving processes
- research concepts can also be used as practice concepts
- both forms of activity involve the use of 'applied logic'.

Second, there is a concern for the effective implementation of theory from specific sources, so that various authors wish to see more (or less) use of ideas and knowledge from the social sciences in general, psychology, psychoanalysis or Marxist theory. This is a concern that practice may be partial, or not take account of the range of available information. Another difficulty may be that social workers find it hard to integrate these many ideas into one system of thought which may be practically applied; the problem here is that there is so much to know that it is hard to use it in an organised way.

Third, there is a concern that social workers find it hard to operationalise knowledge and theories that they may possess and understand. The problem here is that the ideas cannot be turned into practical action.

Many reasons have been put forward for the existence of these difficulties. One issue may be that social work knowledge is largely borrowed from other disciplines, and so therefore it has been created for other purposes, and may be hard to convert to practical use. This reason is about the knowledge contributing to social work rather than theories of practice.

Another issue which often arises is the inadequacy of social work's education and training in helping social workers to transfer knowledge effectively. On the other side, there is a view that agencies do not provide appropriate environments for the effective practice of good social work which is taught within courses, perhaps because agencies are too bureaucratic, or have too many conflicting objectives. This is, in essence, a replaying of the pragmatic debate in terms, not of the nature of theory and knowledge being inappropriate, but of the incorrect way they are transferred. As Smid and van Krieken (1984) point out, these arguments are, like the pragmatic debate, reasonably seen as a struggle between academic and practice for influence over the nature of practice.

A further issue is about whether the theories available in social work are actually suitable for practice; they may, for example, be too generalised to enable workers to apply them to specific circumstances or too limited so that, while apparently useful, they never apply to the complex situations which social workers have to deal with

There is some evidence about how social workers see the

relationship between practice and theory. Carew (1979) found in a study of 20 social workers in the north of England that few used theory explicitly in their work; most thought it was important, but that its use was unconscious or as a framework rather than as an explicit guide to action. Mostly, they had acquired through practice a series of skills which allowed them to follow procedures for dealing with problems that clients raised. These were unrelated to specific knowledge, but were generally gained from casework literature. Barbour (1984) studied 20 English social work students and distinguished two approaches to using theory. Students who took a 'helping perspective' sought sets of directly applicable principles. Others took a 'healing perspective' and had a more generalised view of what a good social worker brought to inter-action with clients. Sometimes respect for the dignity and worth of clients was seen as incompatible with the use of theory, which was seen as treating clients like guinea-pigs. This approach is consist-ent with Pithouse's (1987) study of teams in Wales, where he found an informal consensus about and ways of assessing what characterised a good social worker, which were unrelated to theoretical or agency expectations. Barbour found that there were three models by which the students understood the integration of theory with practice:

- *'seeping-in'* where students had acquired general ideas and methods but were unable to say where these had come from
- *amalgam* where particular theories were used where they seemed relevant, and each student built up a stock of 'professional lore' to be used as required
- *personal style* where knowledge was said to be integrated with the student's personality to form a seamless whole.

In an important series of studies, Curnock and Hardiker (1979) and Hardiker (1981) showed that in several English settings workers used theoretical knowledge inexplicitly, although this may be subject to the criticism that such knowledge may have been gained from general rather than professional sources, and Carew (1979) argues that inexplicit knowledge cannot be described as organised theoretical understanding. Cocozzelli and Constable (1985) in an American study also confirmed the impression of the British work that general approaches to clients rather than explicit use of theory is the most common relationship between theory and practice. They found that a theoretical preference for technique (active vs reflective), emotional attitude to the client (task-oriented vs person-oriented) and for defining problems (as stemming from the individual or from society) correlated with practice actions.

J. Hearn (1982) notes that one of the difficulties with these debates is the problem of defining what 'theory' and 'practice' actually mean. Often, in the pragmatic debate for example, they are caricatured so that theory means what is learned on courses and practice is what is done in agencies, and Sibeon (1982) suggests that one model of the relationship is that of an academic division of labour between colleges and the field. This problem is confirmed by Barbour (1984) who has three different meanings of theory:

● grand theory providing a comprehensive conceptual scheme
● middle-range theory about specific aspects of society (e.g. labelling theory) or of undertaking practice (e.g. task-centred casework)
● anything learned in college rather than in placement.

Another difficulty identified by Hearn (1982) is that there is confusion about the nature of the relationship between theory and practice. A variety of such relationships are possible, and often complaints about the relationships between theory and practice come from a failure to recognise, or a rejection of, some of the possibilities. In arguing for practitioners to take an active role in testing and developing theory, for example, Brennan (1973) shows that the conventional conception is that such activity is outside normal practice. Six different models (derived partly from Carr, 1986) of the relationship between theory and practice are identified and these are set out in Table 2.3, together with some of the objections to each of their approaches to dealing with theory-practice relationships.

It is evident then that none of the models described offers a full and indisputable analysis of how theory and practice in social work are related. Table 2.3 draws attention to the fact that various models of this relationship exist, and are disputed. It is entirely possible to conceive of a set of theories for social work which derive from academic, practitioner or managerial sources, and which recognise the primacy or balance of one or several of those sources. This suggests that we should be looking for a number of ways of joining theory and practice from different positions, and avoiding struggle between different elements of occupational control for influence concealed as a debate about the 'true' nature of social work theory. Hearn (1982) contends that we should avoid seeing theory and practice as two ends of a dumb-bell, but rather as always intertwined and relating to each other in a variety of ways.

It seems useful therefore to move from these debates about how social work theory may be used in practice to see how the panoply of theories may be understood as part of an integrated area of knowledge, instead of as competing perspectives. This involves looking at attempts to classify and understand the relationships between different types of social work theory.

Analysis of social work theories

Practitioners selecting theories are faced with a wide choice among apparently comparable and useful theories. The purpose of the remainder of this book is to offer information about some of those theories, to enable comparisons of their value and to see how they may be selected and combined. Some would ask whether this is a useful enterprise. Solomon (1976), for example, considers that theories and models of social work are not comparable because they often deal with different things (e.g. the functions of practice, the process of change, the sequence of helping processes, the nature of problems to be dealt with). Some, she argues, are based on particular methods of change, while others extend into fields of therapeutic change beyond social work. This sort of criticism shows why it is so important to consider carefully the basis on which selection and grouping of theories is carried out.

Various attempts have been made in the past to select and group theories in useful ways, and we now turn to discussion of how this might be done. A number of books exist whose writers and editors try to review and compare a range of social work theories. Table 2.4 summarises the coverage of some of these. This is not a complete analysis, since many of these works specifically deal only

Table 2.3 *Different types of relationship between theory and practice*

Types	Objections	Arguments against the objections
General theories of behaviour or social life contributing to social work are used to originate practice theories, and existing practice is tested to see if it accords with the theory; if not, it is adapted; if the theory still fails, practice experience discredits it or forces a change in the practice theory or the contributing social and psychological theories	theories persist because of academic support when practitioners find them hard to use (e.g. many social science concepts – Hardiker, 1981)	theories can be used to stimulate debate and for teaching clarity, and do not need to be applicable; they may helpfully give ways of looking at things, rather than guidance in action; theories may not be universally useful, but may help some practitioners – the objectors may be non-users who are not justified in rejecting a theory
General theories are designed to produce practice prescriptions which are testable according to scientific method; theories which will not produce testable prescriptions are rejected; those which fail in testing are rejected	many social workers (according to positivists) accept theories without empirical validity	empirical testing may be difficult with human beings, and action may be needed in which an untested theory gives useful guidance; people disagree about what kinds of evidence are acceptable – positivists may be too strict

Theory is a process of enquiry and debate in which proposals for action are tested against accumulations of experience and ideas	leads to cycles of disagreement on ideological grounds rather than clarity; leads to acceptance of ideas in debate without any empirical validity	theory about practice is always unfinished, there is no final certainty, so a cycle of debate may be realistic; at least this approach allows practitioners to take part in theory development, rather than simply being given theory to use
Theory is a series of generalisations based on the accumulation of practice experience which it articulates and conceptualises	unlikely to have public credibility because it is not 'scientifically' tested	public may prefer theory tested by experience rather than by experiment
Theory comes from a variety of sources to offer models of practice, but action according to such models is altered or limited by organisational and political constraints	leads to a too-ready acceptance of constraints which may be unjust impositions on clients; difficulty of deciding when constraints should apply and when they should be opposed	constraints are real and need to be included in theory if it is to be practically useful
Theory develops from practice experience but is tested and altered by empirical research and intellectual debate	practice-derived theories may be hard to test; they may also be used without testing	this approach allows practitioner involvement – even primacy – in theory development; ensures that academic work is developed on firm practice base

Table 2.4 *Alternative reviews of social work theories*

Categories of theory	Roberts and Nee (1970)	Strean (1971)	Hopkins (1986)	Turner (1986)	Howe (1987)
Psycho-dynamic	psychosocial functional problem-solving	psychoanalysis ego psychology	psychosocial functional egocentred diagnostic individual overdeveloped superego separation-individuation transactional analysis	psychosocial psychoanalytic functional problem-solving ego psychology transactional analysis	psychoanalytic
Behaviourist	behavioural modification	behaviour modification	behaviour modification	behaviour therapy	behavioural social work

60

Family treatment	family therapy		family therapy: *psychoanalytic crisis strategic structural experiential family-focused marital (couple) casework*	family treatment	
Crisis theories	crisis intervention		crisis	crisis	
Social learning theories	socialisation		imitative learning		
Systems theories		systems	systems	systems / life model	not seen as a major category
Role theories		role theory	role model	role theory	
Organisation theories		organisation theory			
Communication theories		communication theory		communication theory / neuro-linguistic programming	
Group theories	(separate volume in series)	small groups	(casework only)	(casework only)	(casework only)

Table 2.4 (*continued*)

Categories of theory	Roberts and Nee (1970)	Strean (1971)	Hopkins (1986)	Turner (1986)	Howe (1987)
Task-centred theories			task-centred	task-centred	(allies with behavioural approaches)
Cognitive theories			cognitive	cognitive	
Humanist theories			client-centred existential fantasy-reality gestalt encounter life space presentation of self	client-centred existential gestalt meditation	client-centred (groups a number of existential ideas under the heading of 'seekers after the self')
Radical theories				Marxist feminist	Marxist radical consciousness raising (includes feminist social work)

with casework (e.g. Hopkins, Roberts and Nee). There are two companion books of Roberts and Nee (Roberts and Northen, 1976, Taylor and Roberts, 1985) which review and compare group and community-work theories; these are considered later. I include some discussion of group, residential and community work in chapters with related casework or general theories. Some of these works of review, while not defining their coverage as casework, concentrate on this field (e.g. Howe, 1987).

There are some analyses of social work theories which are empirical and so presumably reflect actual distinctions used in the field. Cocozzelli and Constable's (1985), study of clinical social work in the USA for example, distinguishes between psychodynamic, behavioural, existential, family, gestalt and problem-solving therapies.

Some writers have attempted more than just a description of social work theories. They have tried to group them to show connections, or underlying principles which different theories share. One possible way of doing this is to demonstrate the content of each theory according to a standard set of categories. An alternative and more sophisticated method is to have a conceptual scheme which places theories in relation to one another.

Table 2.5 gives three examples (one based on Meyer (1983), another on Kettner (1975), and the last on the instructions by Roberts and Nee to the contributors in their 1970 publication) of this approach of evaluating or describing theories according to a common set of categories. Meyer is primarily concerned with examining the internal consistency of theories, and their fitness for modern practice – hence her analysis requires less description and includes capacity for use with self-help groups and non-professional staff. Roberts and Nee's categories seek a largely descriptive analysis, whereas Kettner includes some measure of both elements. The categories used vary, therefore, but there is a degree of overlap.

An alternative approach is to look at theories which underlie models of social work practice. Whittaker (1974) argues that there are only four: psychodynamic, behavioural and systems theories, and the existential and humanist approach (he distinguishes here between theories and approaches). This seems to exclude radical approaches, probably because he was writing before they reached prominence – and in the USA where less importance is attached to them.

Table 2.5 *Frameworks for comparing social work theories*

Meyer (1983)	Kettner (1975)	Roberts and Nee (1970)
ideological base	writer's philosophy of social work	general characteristics of approach
values	basic values	
underlying social and psychological theories	knowledge base from psychology and sociology	behavioural science foundations
unit of attention	level of intervention	
◄——— (i.e. individual, group or community) ———►		
problem definition (i.e. how sorts of issues dealt with are decided)	how specifically are aims, procedures and outcomes stated?	target group (includes definition of problems)
are prescribed actions relevant to above and explicit?	roles and responsibilities of client and worker:	
use of professional relationship	*fully stated?*	
	active or passive	
	importance of relationship	

desired outcomes
use of time (long- or short-term)
differential use of staff (i.e. is it possible?)
work with self-help groups (i.e. is it possible?)
effectiveness research (i.e. is it possible?)

research validation (i.e. has it been done?)

target groups of clients
input of worker and client to decisions
description of process:
 beginning phase
 assessment
 strategies and techniques of interaction
 how effectiveness is evaluated
 ending phase

target group

initial phase

assessment of client in situation
treatment principles and methods

The second method of grouping theories is by categorising them according to an organising concept. A particularly important classification of social work theories is attempted by Whittington and Holland (1985) which is taken up by Howe (1987) in his review of social work theory. This classification is based on the work of Burrell and Morgan (1979) in sociology. They propose that philosophical positions about the nature of society range from the subjective to the objective. The subjective position includes views which say that the world cannot be understood except through the perception and interpretation of human beings (a broadly pheno-menological, humanist view), whereas objective views propose that knowledge about the world is possible outside human percep-tion, so that there can be facts about society, human behaviour and natural phenomena which are generally true and can be tested experimentally (a broadly positivistic, empirical view). This way of organising views of the world is related to Leonard's (1975b) paper, considered in Table 2.1, since it is concerned with showing how different sorts of explanation may be validly held in different theoretical positions; there is no one agreed form of explanation.

There is an alternative dimension along which philosophical positions about the nature of society are ranged, that of whether they try to understand society as fundamentally changing in a radical way or as a regulated set of social interactions. Social work theories can be assessed according to where they fit into these two continua. Figure 2.1 gives some examples of how this works. This approach to categorisation and others like it can be criticised because they set arbitrary continua for analysis and because the placing of theories within the axes may always be questioned (Stenson and Gould, 1986). For example, theories tend to be regarded as mutually exclusive and neatly set in a particular position, whereas often they overlap and share things in common. Equally, conflicts of ideology which do not relate to these axes may not be represented. D. Howe (1987) treats both psycho-dynamic theory and behavioural approaches to social work as representative of functional ideas, whereas there are considerable differences between them.

A number of attempts have been made to classify *groupwork* theories, and some of these are set out in Table 2.6. Roberts and Northen (1976) present an analysis which includes several forms of groupwork allied to casework theories, such as functional and

Figure 2.1 *Analysis of social work theories*

Theories of radical change

Subjective	radical social work ('raisers of consciousness')	Marxist social work ('revolutionaries')
	interactionist ('seekers after meaning')	traditional social work ('fixers')

Objective

Theories of regulation

(note: Howe's labels for each grouping are given in brackets)

Sources: Whittington and Holland (1985), D. Howe (1987).

problem-solving groupwork, and their book attempts to parallel the models of practice covered in their book on casework theories. More recent classifications rely on the seminal article by Papell and Rothman (1966), and there is broad agreement from a perspective which is strongly based in current groupwork ideology.

This offers three fundamental approaches. The social goals model assumes that participation in the group assists people to achieve desired social changes outside it. The aim is empowerment and social skill development. The remedial model, particularly associated with the work of Vinter, presents the group as a place in which individuals who have problems, very often of how they function in social roles, are brought together in a group to help them change their deviant patterns of behaviour. Any model of groupwork which is fundamentally therapeutic might be regarded as remedial in approach. The reciprocal or mediating model, associated with the work of Schwartz, is humanistic in philosophy, using a terminology associated with systems theory. In this approach the group is a place for helping people examine and establish their social roles in a safe, supportive but challenging environment. Although normally regarded as a separate humanist and gestalt form of groupwork concerned with personal growth, encounter groups, associated with Perls (see Chapter 8) might also be regarded as mediating in philosophy. Developmental approaches, developed after these three approaches, are associated with Bernstein, and are concerned with group dynamics. It is assumed that groups have a life of their own independently of the actions and thoughts of members, and the purpose of the group is understanding of self- and group-dynamics. Developmental approaches are broadly psychodynamic, based particularly on the work of Erikson and ego psychology, theories of group dynamics and social psychological ideas about conflict and group membership (Balgopal and Vassil, 1983). Although this is a typology from the USA, British group dynamics theory, associated with the work of Bion (1961) could also broadly be described as developmental.

Feldman and Wodarski (1975) carried out an empirical study of groupwork methods in the USA, and found traditional (broadly developmental) styles of work, remedial approaches and some behavioural approaches in which the group was used as a supporter and place of management of behavioural changes (see Chapter 5). They also designated a group-centred or non-treatment method, in which, while clients met as a group, the worker made no apparent efforts to achieve change in any organised way, but assumed that the presence of people possibly with shared circumstances or problems would be beneficial and that clients could help each other. This may be typical of many pragmatic uses of groups in everyday practice, and with self-help groups which do not seek to promote therapeutic change.

There are some tentative approaches to analyse *community work* theory relevant to social work. Taylor and Roberts (1985) for example, recognise the distance of community work theory from casework, and offer few connections. They regard community work theory as fluid, but identify five major approaches:

- *community development* which enables deprived groups to come together and promote services in the interests of their community
- *political action* which encourages disadvantaged groups to find ways of representing their views to more powerful groups in society
- *programme development and co-ordination* which is concerned with promoting new services and more effective co-operation in services working with deprived communities
- *planning* which is concerned with more effective planning of

Table 2.6 Classifications of groupwork theory

Roberts and Northen (1976)	Feldman and Wodarski (1975)	Papell and Rothman (1966)	Douglas (1979)	Balgopal and Vassil (1983)
generic			eclectic	
organisational				
psychosocial	traditional	remedial	remedial	remedial
functional				
mediating		reciprocal	reciprocal/ mediating	mediating
developmental/ humanist	group-centred		group-centred/process/ developmental/maturational stage/ personal growth	developmental
task-centred			task-centred	
socialisation				
crisis intervention				
problem-solving	behaviour modification	social goals	behavioural social goals	behavioural

services in the community and processes which involve members of the community in such planning
• *community liaison* which is about promoting better links between agencies with similar interests in the community.

York (1984) suggests that a number of conceptualisations of community work divide it into three types. Table 2.7 sets out several of these '3-model' conceptualisations of community work.

Tahble 2.7 *'3-model' conceptualisations of community work*

Ross (1968)	Rothman (1968)	Gulbenkian (1968)	Phases of development in community work; York (1984)
reform (action towards)	locality development	direct work with people to help community development	organising community agencies
planning (community organising)	social planning	facilitating agency plus interagency co-operation and promoting community groups	developing local competences
community development	social action	community planning and policy formation	political action for change

Source: York (1984).

York rejects these '3-model' arrangements in favour of a number of dichotomies which apply to all community work:

• directive vs non-directive (Batten, 1967)
• task or problem vs process approaches
• initiating vs enabling roles for the worker
• treatment vs reform.

Community work is not treated in this book, although many social workers practice it and a community orientation is an important aspect of the organisation of many agencies. Community work, however, must be regarded as a distinct form of practice, which calls upon a theoretical and knowledge base which is more sociological and less psychological than casework and groupwork. There are some views of social work which give more importance to using community approaches as part of social work, particularly radical, Marxist and empowerment approaches, and this is considered in the relevant chapters.

A number of writers include *family therapy* within social work theory (e.g. Hopkins, see Table 2.4). This is a form of practice in which all or several members of the family are treated together on the assumption that their problems arise from interactions among them all. These therapies are excluded from this volume, although their use in social work and connections with social work theories are considered in relevant places. One reason for this exclusion is that there are a considerable number of schools of thought in family therapy, and exploring them would extend the length of the book (and the competence of the author). Also, family therapy is more a multi-disciplinary area of practice in which several occupational groups operate and to which several, including social work, have made contributions. It is reasonable to regard it as a form of practice which some social workers borrow from as part of social work, or an occupational grouping into which they move, rather than as an activity which has been adapted to social work.

Residental care can be viewed as a setting in which other treatment theories are used (e.g. Jones, 1979, Ward, 1980) in which case no separate theoretical perspectives are relevant, or as a distinct form of social work activity justifying theories of its own. Writers such as Ainsworth and Fulcher (1981; Fulcher and Ainsworth, 1985) regard residential care as a form of groupwork carried out in residence and call it *group care*, a term which they extend to day care, and to settings in health care, education and criminal justice systems outside the social services. They see group care as an occupational focus, a field of study and a domain of practice in each of these settings. Lennox (1982) also sees residential care as a setting for groupwork, but identifies different forms of groupwork:

- behavioural approaches
- encounter groups
- transactional analysis.

A number of ideological approaches to residential care may be identified. A. Davis (1981, pp. 9–21) proposes three:

- *optimists* who claim that although many institutions are damaging to their inmates, this is not necessarily the case, and beneficial residential care is possible
- *pessimists* who claim that institutionalising features of residential care will always be damaging to inmates, so it should be abandoned
- *radicals* who argue that residential care as presently offered may be damaging, but that communal living should in principal offer opportunities for unselfish self-actualisation which are not present in ordinary capitalist society or in other therapies.

Sinclair (1988, pp. 162–3) reviewed the evidence presented to the British Wagner committee on residential care and detected three ideologies within it:

- *Christian love* proposing that care should be guided by a recognition of the importance of every individual, is similar to the social work philosophy of respect for persons
- *therapeutic value of communal living* espoused by therapeutic communities who argue that 'living together' must be used as part of therapy for removal from normal environments to be valuable; this is similar to the radical view outlined above, except that supporters of therapeutic communities would not necessarily agree that the purpose of communal living should be to enhance people's experience of co-operative living in order to combat the alienating effects of isolation in capitalist societies
- *individual rights* the normalisation approach, which suggests that the aim of residential care should be to return people to life styles which are valued by ordinary people in that culture.

Such ideologies have a bearing on possible theoretical perspectives in residential care. Much of the literature is pragmatic and draws on skills without a theoretical base (e.g. Clough, 1982), but a number of perspectives are identified by some writers. They are connected to other theoretical approaches, and are dealt with in the relevant chapters below. *Behavioural* approaches rely on behaviour modification techniques often using token economies (see Chapter 5), and *radical* approaches implement the ideology identified above (see Chapter 10). *Reality therapy* is a form of cognitive therapy having residential care origins (see Chapter 9). *Therapeutic environment* theory is psychodynamic in origin and is dealt with in Chapter 3.

Conclusion

This Chapter completes the first part of the book, which examines the place of social work theory in social work, and argues that it is practically useful, and the variety and confusion about theory can be organised and understood. The relationships and oppositions between theories provide a context in which their value can be assessed against one another, and against the modern social context in which they must be used. We can now move on to examining the selected groups of theories in Chapters 3–11 and assessing their value to social workers in the modern context in Chapter 12.

3

Psychodynamic Models

Connections

Psychodynamic models are based on the work of Freud (e.g. Freud, 1974) and his followers (Roazen, 1979), and on developments of their work. They are called psychodynamic because the theory underlying them assumes that behaviour comes from movements and interactions in people's minds and also because it emphasises the way in which the mind stimulates behaviour and both mind and behaviour influence and are influenced by the person's social environment.

Understanding psychodynamic theory is a prerequisite to examining other social work theories, since its influence is pervasive, as we shall see. A variety of schools of thought and applications or developments have grown up. Although most use psychodynamic concepts in general, there is, mainly in the USA, interest in applying ideas from psychodynamic theorists who are a long way from Freud and the mainstream development of psychoanalysis (e.g. Borensweig on Jung, 1980). Modern psychoanalytic theory has moved away from the idea of drives as the basic influence on behaviour (Lowenstein, 1985), and is more concerned with how individuals interact with their social world; it has become more social than biological. This has come about through the influence of ego psychology (E. Goldstein, 1984).

A recent appraisal of the role of psychoanalysis in social work (Pearson *et al.*, 1988) shows that there is a wide range of developments, and in different countries various streams of thought. Ego psychology, for example, has been much more strongly influential in the USA than elsewhere, whereas object relations theory has two differing streams of thought; one British, based around the work of psychoanalysts such as Fairbairn (1954) and Guntrip (1968), and a rather different approach in the USA (E. Goldstein, 1984). Lacan (1979) has developed a line of psychoanalytic thought which has enabled some writers to make links with Marxism (see Bocock, 1988, p. 76) since he reinterprets the unconscious as a structure of symbols like language which are pointed to by our conscious behaviour; these symbols are imposed upon us by our society and culture (Dowrick, 1983); if this is so, ideas from Marxist historical materialism can be made to fit with some interpretations of psychoanalysis. Another radical ideology, feminism, has also attempted an interpretation of psychoanalysis as an explanation of patriarchy (that is, male domination of social relations and oppression of women). Leonard (1984) in his attempt to construct a Marxist approach to individual psychology is doubtful of the intellectual viability of these attempts to inter-pret psychoanalysis in a radical way.

Some general account is given here of major psychodynamic ideas, and then a summary of the work of Hollis and Woods as an example of how these ideas are translated into social work. Their psychosocial theory is a modern formulation of a long tradition in social work. Various other applications of psychodynamic theory in social work are then discussed in briefer form as variations on the general theme.

Some basic psychoanalytic ideas

Psychoanalytic theory has three parts: it is a theory of human development, of personality and abnormal psychology and of treatment. Two important basic ideas underpin the theory (Yelloly, 1980; Wood, 1971):

- *psychic determinism*, the principle that actions or behaviour arise from people's thought processes rather than just happen
- *the unconscious*, the idea that some thinking and mental activity is hidden from our knowledge.

These ideas are widely accepted. For example, the assumption that slips of the tongue (colloquially, Freudian slips) and jokes

reflect hidden or unknown confusions in people's thought processes includes both ideas. Commonsense meanings do not always
fully represent the complexity of psychodynamic ideas. Yelloly
(1980, pp. 8–9) gives the example of the meaning of 'unconscious'
to show how full psychodynamic ideas are. *Resistance* arises when
some thoughts and feelings are not compatible with other beliefs
that we hold strongly. In this case, the mind does not allow the
contested ideas into the conscious by a process called *repression*.
Many repressed thoughts are dynamic in the sense that they cause
us to act, even if we are unaware of them. The psychodynamic
unconscious consists of these forcibly hidden ideas. They are not
just available if we think about it; in many cases they are deeply
concealed. Great importance is given to *aggression*, where people
turn destructive impulses against others.

In the *developmental theory* of psychoanalysis children are
thought to go through a series of developmental stages. These occur
as *drives* (originally translated as 'instincts') which are mental
pressures to relieve physical needs such as hunger or thirst. Having
such a need creates tension or *libido* which gives us the energy to
act to meet the need. Among physical needs, sexual tension, even
among young children, is very important in creating drives.

At each stage, particular behaviours are important, but as we
progress through the stages we use the behaviours associated with
previous stages. So, in an early stage, satisfaction is gained from
sucking (for example at a mother's breast to satisfy the need for
food). Later on, sucking can also be satisfying (for example in the
use of cigarettes, sweets or in sexual activities) although the adult
has a wider range of satisfying activities to choose from. Some
people become unconsciously attached to behaviour associated
with particular stages (*fixation*) and are driven to seek that
particular form of satisfaction to an unreasonable degree so that
they cannot use the full repertoire of behaviour available to them.

The child starts off in a stage of *primary narcissism* seeking only
gratification of its own needs and learns through social interaction,
at first with parents, that these must be compromised. In each
stage the focus of attention is on a different need; oral (hunger),
anal (excretion), phallic (identification with same-sex parent),
oedipal (attraction to opposite-sex parent), latency (drives are
managed through resolution of oedipal conflicts) and puberty
(social learning). Erikson (1965) has expanded on the stages of

development by suggesting that at each stage the rational mind deals with a maturational crisis presented by the social circumstances of our life. His work, which has been influential in social work and especially in crisis intervention, emphasises cultural and social pressures rather than inner drives (Yelloly, 1980, p. 12). Associated with stages of development is the idea of *regression*. This occurs when people who have progressed through the later stages fall back to behaviour associated with earlier stages under some present stress. Regression should be contrasted with fixation, when the individual is stuck in the behaviour of the early stage.

Psychoanalytic *personality theory* assumes that people are a complex of drives forming the *id* (literally 'it', a sort of undifferentiated pressure from an unknown source; Wood, 1971). The id pushes us to act to resolve our needs but our actions do not always bring the desired results. Development of the *ego* follows from this. It is a set of pragmatic ideas about how the environment can be understood and manipulated. The ego controls the id. For example, children control the excretion of faeces as the ego learns that disapproval and discomfort follow inappropriate excretion. The ego manages relationships with people and things outside ourselves; *object relations*. The *superego* develops general moral principles which guide the ego.

One of the important features of the personality is how the ego manages conflict, and how the need of the ego and superego to exert control over the id in the cause of social responsibility creates further conflicts. *Anxiety* results from such conflicts. The ego deals with anxiety by bringing into play various *defence mechanisms*, of which repression, already mentioned, is one. Other important ones are:

- *projection*, where unwanted ideas associated with something the ego wants to protect become attached in our minds to another person or thing
- *sublimation*, where energy which is directed towards unwanted activities (often sexual) is redirected towards more acceptable activities
- *rationalisation*, where acceptable reasons for particular activities are devised, when the real ones are unacceptable and repressed.

Freud's later work concentrated on ego and object relations. This was picked up after his death (in classic works by Anna Freud and

Hartman) and has been influential as the basis of much psycho-analytic thought today. In social work, it is the most modern form of psychoanalytic theory to be used, and has strongly influenced crisis intervention and systems theories.

Ego psychology and object relations theories consider that children have the capacity to deal with the outside world (object relations) from an early age. Development of the ego is the growth of our capacity to learn from experience, and especially using the rational parts of our minds through using rational thinking (cognition), perception and memory.

Widespread and sometimes criticised influence on social work has been achieved by the work of psychodynamic theorists and practitioners, pre-eminently Bowlby (1951), who in the 1940s and 1950s directed the psychoanalytic interest in early mother-child relationships, in research and theory about maternal deprivation. This is the idea that if a child is deprived of contact with its mother, its personal development is impeded. In recent years, this has developed into a more extensive theory about the importance of attachment (Bowlby, 1969, 1973, 1980), particularly to the mother but also in other ways, and the significance of the effects of loss of attachment. There is extensive evidence that deprivation and disadvantage have major damaging effects on children's development and later life, but in the relationships between children and parents, a wide variety of factors, including the social environment, are relevant, not just maternal deprivation, and there are many social and psychological factors which help protect against the damaging effects of deprivation (Rutter, 1981).

Loss is more widely an important idea in psychoanalysis; mourning is regarded as a response to all kinds of loss, not just the death of someone close (Salzberger-Wittenberg, 1970). Parkes (1972) interprets bereavement in a number of situations as a regression to childhood experiences of stress due to loss. L. Pincus (1976) argues that in typical family reactions to death, signs of hidden feelings about past relationships may be disclosed. The intensity of feeling when grief takes hold is particularly susceptible to psychoanalysis, although C. Smith (1982) argues that much behaviour in bereavement and loss comes from social expectations of behaviour in such situations, and proposes that a phenomenological or existential interpretation of bereavement is more appropriate (see Chapters 7 and 8).

One of the important aspects of these more modern psychoanalytic developments is that they provide a link with sociological ideas, in particular the idea that people are part of social systems and play a social role. Recent work in the object relations tradition particularly by Kohut (1978; see also Eisenhuth, 1981, Lane, 1984, Lowenstein, 1985) has emphasised that children develop a perception of their 'self' and their difference from the surrounding world at a very young age.

Treatment theory in classic psychoanalysis required therapists to be 'blank screens', making themselves as anonymous as possible so that patients projected their fantasies onto the therapists. *Transference* occurred when the patient transferred unconscious feelings about their parents onto the therapists, and treated the therapist as though they were that parent. This was a way of revealing unconscious ideas. By stimulating transference, the conflicts arising from early relationship difficulties with parents and causing present behaviour difficulties would be revealed. This idea has been adapted in social work to refer rather more generally to the idea that our present behaviour, particularly in relationships, is affected by the emotional remains of past relationships and experiences (Irvine, 1956). Counter-transference occurred when analysts reacted to patients irrationally bringing in past experiences to the relationship. An example is given later in this chapter.

Most psychoanalytic techniques are concerned with revealing hidden thoughts and feelings. It is assumed that undesirable behaviour caused by repressed conflicts leaking out in various ways required more than ordinary attempts to disclose its origins. Once revealed and properly understood, the conflicts would no longer cause difficulties in behaviour. Thus, traditional psychoanalytic therapy is concerned with giving people *insight* into their repressed feelings. This is another emphasis which has been altered in ego psychology, where there is often a concentration on how people manage their relationships with the outside world through extending their rational control of their lives.

Psychoanalysis and social work

Social work theory has been greatly influenced by psychoanalytic theory; its approach underlies virtually all social work practice.

But its theories of development, personality and therapy are not explicitly practised in a widespread way. Its influence is more complex and indirect in the following ways:

- Freud's influence on Western culture, so that many of his ideas are common currency, and may appear in social work because of this rather than because the theory has been directly applied to social work
- there are different aspects to his work, developed at different times so that ideas came into social work at intervals: ego psychology, which is now important, arrived later than basic psychodynamic ideas
- Freud inspired both followers and dissidents, so some related theories share ideas with Freud but sometimes disagree with his approach
- psychodynamic ideas were the first strong explanatory theory in social work and so have created the environment to which later theories have naturalised: they thus tend to influence a range of theoretically distinct ideas in practice
- the influence of its therapy in producing a permissive, open, listening (Wallen, 1982) style of relationship (indeed the emphasis on relationship at all; see Perlman, 1957b) rather than a directive and controlling style, and one which seeks explanation and understanding of personality rather than action
- the importance attached to feelings and unconscious factors in particular (Yelloly, 1980) rather than to events and thought and to many ideas such as the unconscious, insight, aggression, conflict, anxiety, maternal relationships, transference; these are terms which are often used in watered down strength as a common language in social work and in everyday life, and they gain in importance by their continued availability to practitioners
- the theoretical sophistication and complexity of its ideas, which make it attractive and interesting to explore, as compared with newer and less developed theories (Fraiberg, 1978; Lowenstein, 1985)
- the continued influence of the specialised settings and groups of social workers who practise psychodynamic work explicitly (in Britain, for example, the Group for the Advancement of

Psychodynamics and Psychotherapy in Social Work – GAPS – and its journal)
- the important focus in social work on childhood and early relationships and maternal deprivation
- the emphasis on mental illness and disturbed behaviour as a focus of much social work
- insight as an important part of social work understanding and treatment
- less emphasis is given to social factors in social work than to psychological and emotional ones (Weick, 1981).

Features of psychodynamic social work which arouse critical comment are:

- its *scientific*, and originally biological, approach to explanation, in a theory which cannot be easily tested in conventional scientific ways, and many people would argue does not reflect respect for human self-determination (Strean, 1979).
- it is weak in its account of female development and personality to the extent that it is seen as reinforcing *stereotypes of women* as domestic, childbearing, and socially, intellectually and perhaps morally inferior, although some use has been made of it in developing feminist perspectives on psychology. Mitchell (1975), for example, argues that psychoanalysis is a useful means of understanding how men achieve and maintain supremacy in a patriarchal society. Sayers (1986, 1988) contends that not enough attention has been given to explaining women's resistance to subordination in a patriarchal society and that psychoanalytic theory can also be helpful here.
- related to its scientific approach, psychoanalysis operates on a *medical model* which assumes the patient's sickness, which is cured by an expert therapist, rather than a more equal model of relationships between client and worker.
- originating in middle-class Jewish Vienna, it is very limited in its *cultural assumptions*, so that it assumes that deviations from a limited, white, middle-class norm are abnormal behaviour to be cured; in recent years this has been controversial in that variations due to ethnic difference may be seen by psychoanalysts as abnormalities needing treatment, and

their attitude to homosexuality as requiring treatment and as being associated with maternal relationships has been regarded as objectionable (Strean, 1979, p. 56).

- the use of *insight* as a major therapeutic technique tends to lead psychodynamic workers to stop at the point that clients have understood what is happening to them emotionally, but does not help them to take practical action to do something about it; this, associated with the non-directiveness of psychoanalytic techniques, tends to make social workers' help insubstantial.
- the use of concepts in ways which enable workers to *blame the victim* for social problems or agency inadequacies, by interpreting the client's behaviour as maladjusted if it conflicts with the assumptions of the worker or agency; Gitterman's (1983) example is the use of psychological 'resistance' to avoid responsibility when clients are unhappy with aspects of the agency's service.
- a preference for verbally able clients with psychological problems, who can take part in discussion and self-examination, thus playing down the importance of less articulate, working-class clients with more practical problems (Strean, 1979).
- environmental factors are given less prominence than internal psychological ones, which limits the possible range of interventions, and narrows the assumptions from which social workers start their work (Strean, 1979).
- a limited concern for social reform, which excludes a major element of social work (Strean, 1979).

Some accounts of the history of social work have emphasised the importance of the *psychiatric deluge* (Woodroofe, 1962), the period in which psychoanalysis was the dominant force in social work and gained its ascendency in social work theory. While this is important it should not be exaggerated.

First, Woodroofe refers to a psychiatric rather than psycho-analytic deluge. As Pearson (1975) shows, two important issues were the association of community services with the medical model of treatment, and social work's close association with psychiatrists from the 1930s to the 1960s. This emphasised a tendency to regard mental abnormality rather than social problems as the focus of social work. In spite of the fact that the literature was often predominantly psychodynamic (e.g. in a survey of American journals from 1957–72 by Howe and Schuerman, 1974), research both in Britain (Lees, 1971) and in the USA (Alexander, 1972) has shown that in daily practice, psychodynamic ideas may have been limited to a few trained workers and high-status agencies rather than being widely spread. Even by the early 1960s, N. Timms (1964) shows that in the UK the diffusion of trained psychiatric social workers was very limited. In many ordinary social work settings the pragmatic and commonsense provision of service must have been the primary activity. The dominance of relatively unsophisticated services through the Poor Law in the UK until the 1940s is also significant. Both psychiatry and psychoanalysis made relatively little headway in these environments.

Concentration on internal mental processes also did not have it all its own way. There has always been a tradition of social reform and socialism in social work. Attlee's 1920 British text on social work, for example contains sections on the social worker as agitator. In the USA a concern for reform is reflected in the career of Bertha Reynolds (Germain and Hartman, 1980; Hartman, 1986; Freedberg, 1986), the literature of the 1920s (Alexander, 1972) and in Lurie's unavailing criticism of trends in the 1930s (Schriver, 1987).

Hollis and Woods: psychosocial therapy

Hollis and Woods (1981) offer the benchmark account of psychodynamic casework. The 1981 edition is the third, the first two were by Hollis alone. It is in the tradition of diagnostic theory, whose most important exponent was Hamilton (1950). The crucial elements are the idea of the *person-in-situation* and the *classification of casework treatment*.

Casework is about people, their environments and the relationships between them – the person-in-situation. People are affected by *press* from the environment and by *stress* from conflicts within themselves. Press and stress interact with each other in a complex way. The second and third editions of the book use systems theory to analyse action in the 'situation', and psychoanalytic theory for 'stress', which is given more attention. Defence mechanisms are

important for understanding how people interact with the environment. This sort of emphasis gives the book a psychoanalytic and
psychological bias, despite claimed concern for social issues. The
most significant sociological concept used is role theory; communication problems are also relevant.

Sources of distress come from:

- strong childhood needs and drives retained into adulthood
  causing unreasonable demands on the situation (for example,
  Christine, who felt rejected by a rather cold mother and
  father who were busy with their careers, and continued to
  seek love and affection, making her husband feel unable to
  respond enough).
- press from the environment (for example, Sandra, a young
  mother, was worried because she was getting angry and
  hitting her children; her stress came from the necessity to
  manage an old damp house in a street where there was a
  great deal of stealing from houses).
- damaged ego or superego (for example, George, a mentally
  handicapped man who had been over-protected by his
  mother, so that he had not learned socially acceptable
  methods of relating to women, and tended in a day centre to
  be aggressive or over-affectionate – he had not learned to
  manage relationships very well with people and things outside himself).

Sometimes all are present and adding to each other. Press may be
modified directly, or clients can be helped to make changes
themselves, which also produces beneficial personality changes in
the client. Problems in the client's mind are dealt with by altering
the balance of forces assumed to be operating within the client, by
working on current behaviour or memories. This is done by:

ventilation	the client expresses feelings such as hostility or aggression which while suppressed are misdirecting their thinking and action, a treatment approach related to catharsis and abreaction in traditional psychoanalytic theory

corrective	the client experiences with the worker a
relationship	relationship like that of mother and child
	which compensates for a previous
	unsatisfactory relationship
examining	helping the client understand how these are
current personal	affected by past relationships and experience.
interactions	

The treatment model emphasises clients' thinking about and trying to understand their person-in-situation in a helpful relationship with the worker. So in the cases of Christine, Sandra and George (above), the worker would establish a relationship with each. In Christine's case, she could discuss how she had experienced her parents' attitudes. The worker could join with her in discussing her own experience; they could see together how their experiences were leading them to act now in relation to others. Advising clients or using the worker's authority to change behaviour or attempting changes in the environment is only used to augment (Hollis and Woods, 1981; p. 50) the main approach which is *reflective*. Reflection here means thinking about and trying to understand. In Sandra's case, alongside an understanding relationship concerned with exploring her feelings, the worker would help Sandra to say to herself that she would not hit her children, to identify times when and situations in which this happened and find ways of avoiding them. The authority of the agency would be used to try to get Sandra rehoused. With George, authority would allow a worker in the day centre to work out with George a simple set of rules of appropriate behaviour, and as he made mistakes in applying them to stop him at the time and show him what sorts of behaviour might be more appropriate.

Hollis' *classification of casework methods* covers communications with interviews with clients and communications during environmental changes. It is summarised in Table 3.1.

From this brief summary table, it is obvious that the environmental work is much less fully realised than the individual work, and is largely seen in terms of the worker's relationships with individuals surrounding the client rather than intervention in agencies and communities or at a political level. Responsibilities for changing inappropriate agency services are acknowledged.

Moving on to other aspects of psychosocial casework, Hollis and

Table 3.1 *Hollis' classification of casework methods*

| Procedure | Procedures in client-worker communications | |
	Purpose	*Worker's actions*
Sustainment	reduce anxiety, poor self-image, and low self-confidence; set up relationship with worker	express interest and shared concern with clients; reassure clients of worker's understanding of strong and irrational feelings; express confidence; encourage clients in the relationship and planned activities; reach out by showing a wish to help; non-verbal behaviour such as eye-contact and touch may be sustaining
Direct influence	promote particular behaviours by force of worker's opinion	advice given by trusted worker is appreciated (Hollis and Woods, 1981, pp. 116–17; Rees and Wallace, 1982); emphasise approved behaviours; urge; insist
Exploration, description, ventilation	understand clients' view of situation and selves; bring out feelings	psychosocial study; anger, hatred, grief, anxiety, guilt are all feelings to be brought out and so reduce in strength by being expressed; avoid ventilation if it becomes habitual; ventilation comes from psychoanalytic technique of abreaction
Person-situation reflection	improve clients' understanding	extraflection about knowledge and understanding of situation (e.g. housing, money); effects of clients' behaviour on others and selves; intraflection about clients' own responses to situation; rarely explained directly, technique is to lead clients to look at issues and achieve self-revelation; clients examine how external stimuli affect internal responses and produce behaviour; self-evaluation about values and self-image; clients should examine agency limitations, requirements, the worker and feelings about coming for help
Developmental reflection	clients' understanding of the effects of the past	unlike psychoanalysis, not a major feature, should only be used when relevant; avoid intellectualising as a defence; transference sometimes explains unexpected bahaviour towards worker

| Procedure | Procedures in environmental work | |
	Purpose	*Worker's actions*
Types of communication	relationships with collaterals	same procedures used as in worker-client communications with other people who are relevant to the clients (see first four procedures above)
Types of resources	services for clients	use other agency services efficiently, seek to improve them; use resources of secondary setting (e.g. hospital, school, court) where worker works; use workers in other agencies;

Procedure	Purpose	*Procedures in environmental work* Worker's actions
Types of roles	acting on behalf of clients	use non-social work agencies; use 'instrumental collaterals' (e.g. employers, landlord) in relationship with clients; use 'expressive collaterals' in relationship involving feelings with clients; worker should identify with clients act as provider, locator or creator of resources; act as interpreter of the clients to others; act as mediators between clients and others; act as aggressive intervenor between clients and others (e.g. child protection)

Source: Hollis and Woods (1981).

Woods attach importance to integrating family therapy into social work, which has always focused on individuals within families. This is an example of the strong concern in social work for the family as a social institution.

Psychosocial study reflects the origins of psychosocial casework in diagnostic theory, one of whose principal tenets was the importance of distinguishing between the different categories of problems presented by clients so that casework could be directed appropriately. Giving importance to *differential diagnosis* is a mark of psychodynamic theory (see Turner, 1986). In Christine's case, for example, it is important to distinguish between the effects of her past relationships with her parents and other factors which might be possibilities in such a case. For example, women often become depressed because of lack of support from their husbands in their life; the demand for love and affection from the husband might easily have been a product of such feelings.

Psychosocial study at the beginning of contact with clients gives an interim view of the problem and direction of work on it. After this, psychosocial study (gathering and ordering information), diagnostic understanding (thinking about the information) and treatment proceed together. *Study* involves observation, examination and deduction about existing and recent relationships, environment and events in the client's life. Early history would be explored if particularly relevant. *Diagnostic understanding* involves both worker and client deciding what is the trouble, and what can be changed. Then, *dynamic understanding* is an attempt to explain why the problems exist. They are then classified into categories which help identify social consequences. *Health* problems show where social consequences need to be prepared for; for example, a cancer patient may need preparing for death. *Problem* categories, for example, parent-child, old age, unemployment, show where others may be involved and need to share in the work. *Clinical* diagnosis identifies major personality characteristics which will be relevant.

The next stage is to choose *treatment objectives*. Long-range aims will be an improvement in the client's personal and social life. Motivation and the client's and others' social values are relevant in deciding on a particular target. Intermediate aims come from the problems and dynamic understanding. Workers must consider whether change is realistically possible and select aims accordingly. The needs, wishes and policies of other family members, agencies and important individuals will be factors in the decision.

Treatment procedures must be chosen to accord with the aims. When clients are anxious in the early stages, care must be taken to choose acceptable procedures, without sacrificing the need for movement. The client's personality and situational factors should affect the choice of procedures. For example, if the client is overwhelmed with practical problems such as poverty these should be the focus. Ethnic factors, where present, may well predominate.

Commentary

This account of Hollis and Woods' analysis of psychosocial casework shows how its roots lie in psychoanalytic theory, but it is an adapted theory, relying particularly on later ideas, and focusing on functioning in the present rather than exploration of the past. There is a concentration on feelings, personal reactions to social situations rather than the situations themselves, exploratory reflection rather than action. Personality structure, defences and anxiety make significant appearances.

It is a caricature to say that there is no concern for social change. This is considered and approved (p. 162); social control as an aim of casework is rejected (p. 413); social workers have responsibility for policy change (p. 173), priority for ethnic and practical problems is acknowledged (*passim*). Even so, the focus of this quite modern account of casework is on internal feelings about the outside world and on person and family rather than social factors. The reliance on psychoanalytic, systems and role theories is evidence of a theory which fundamentally accepts social order: it is social and personal disorder which must be understood and dealt with. Although there may be things wrong with the present environment for clients, the burden of this perspective is to help them accept it and the worker seeks social reform as a separate activity. The view is medical – health is a frequently mentioned issue; diagnosis and treatment are uncritically accepted as the model. Controversial interpretations of internal dynamics are accepted as accurate representations to guide treatment. Study is about finding facts, when many sociologists and humanists would quarrel with the assumption that there is one understanding of any social situation to be identified. While Hollis and Woods would accept a conflict perspective and it is true that feelings are facts to be worked with, they do not press the possibility that the nature of the phenomena worked with may be fundamentally ambivalent, unreconcilable with clients' interests or unresolvable.

The existential critique of psychoanalysis would go further. These personality structures are illusions, and the adjustment achieved always inadequate or provisional since the only true understanding of humanity is an appreciation of the wholeness of internal and external experience and the paradoxes of existing but being unable to understand the meaning of existence (Krill, 1978, p. 40). Insight techniques may encourage self-preoccupation rather than change.

The behaviourist and cognitive critique also doubts the value of inferring personality structures. However, the main thrust of criticism from this perspective is that the approach is not easily testable empirically, since it relies on such inferences. Behaviourists argue that it is better to depend on careful observation and description of definable behaviour. The emphasis on feelings and emotions rather than rational thought is also a failing according to this view; it leads to lack of clarity and means that people may be disabled from acting if it is believed that unchangeable things in the past are causing their present behaviour. A cognitive theorist would argue that people can manage their behaviour from their own rational minds and need training to do so. It is important not to caricature psychodynamic theory from this perspective. Modern psychoanalysis too largely concentrates on how people can manage their world rationally through the ego and object relations.

Alternative psychodynamic formulations of social work

Functional theory arose in the USA during the 1930s, contesting pre-eminence with diagnostic theory, which became the forerunner of psychosocial casework. The latest extensive book expressing the view is Smalley's, published in 1967. It can only be regarded as a significantly distinct form of practice in the USA, although some ideas have been incorporated into social work more widely. Functional theory is distinct from structural-functionalism (see Chapter 7). The term 'functional' is applied because it emphasises that the *function of social work agencies* gives form and direction to practice in each setting.

Another distinctive feature of functional social work is that its psychological base derives from the work of Rank, a disciple of Freud. Rather than work from diagnosing illnesses and treating problems, functional social workers emphasise helping their clients in personal *growth*. Capacity for growth is released by the casework relationship. Greater emphasis than in psychosocial casework is given to social and cultural issues in human development. Functional social work stresses that social work is a *process* of interaction between clients and workers rather than a series of acts or procedures as psychosocial casework has it. Hofstein (1964, p. 15) defines process as '. . . recurrent patterning of a sequence of changes over time and in a particular direction.'

Smalley also applies functional theory specifically to group and community work. Ryder (1976) elaborates on the approach to groupwork, and Phillips (1957) offers the classic account of functional groupwork.

Five basic principles of functional social work (Smalley, 1970) are:

- involving clients in diagnosis and understanding of the issues being worked on, which are constantly changing
- conscious understanding, and use of *time phases* (beginning,

middle and end); this is a classic feature of functional social work

- use of *agency function* gives form to the work, offers accountability and a concrete role for clients to understand
- clear understanding of the structure or form of the *social work process*; again a classic feature of functional social work
- social work uses relationships to engage clients in helping themselves.

Functional theory avoids taking a medical and problem-based model, and emphasises positive forward-looking change instead. Social causation and issues are more important than in psychosocial casework. It is also rather less concerned with internal feelings and more with interactions with the outside world.

Problem-solving casework is another analysis of casework practice made by Perlman (1957a). Her book was an important text for many years, and is psychodynamic in its approach because that was the accepted psychological base of social work at the time it was written (Perlman, 1986). Her work was distinct from the conventions of diagnostic social work because it emphasised dealing with the presenting problems of the client and current difficulties in the environment (Abrams, 1983). There is less emphasis on irrational and internal motivation.

Perlman emphasises the importance of looking at four aspects of the situation: the *person* with whom the work is done, the *problem* presented, the *place* in which the work was done, and the *process* of the work. The model thus takes in these two latter aspects which are associated with functional social work; Perlman was influenced by several ideas from functional theory (Perlman, 1986). Clients are assumed to have failings in their capacity to solve problems, and need help in overcoming obstacles to improving their coping capacity. This approach is rooted in ego psychology (Perlman, 1970, p. 169; 1986, p. 261) with its emphasis on how the ego manages outside relationships. The book concentrates especially on study and diagnosis of the problems; treatment is rather ill-defined. Perlman (1986, p. 261) claims this is intentional since 'the essential elements of the total helping process ... are to be found ... within the first few hours.'

Perlman's model is an important forerunner of task-centred

casework, which has developed the idea of problem analysis (see Chapter 4). The idea of 'problem' as a concrete definition of the issues being looked at by a social worker and client is such that it is widely used as a pragmatic basis for planning work, outside a formal problem-solving perspective (e.g. Bunston, 1985; Sucato, 1978). Such uses of 'problem' should not necessarily be seen as allied to Perlman's model.

Ego psychology and ego-oriented casework offers a more explicit formulation of modern psychoanalytic theory to casework activities. Early influential works promoting this perspective (Parad, 1958; Parad and Miller, 1963) laid the foundations for it as a separate and identifiable stream of social work thought. E. Goldstein's recent (1984) comprehensive formulation provides a clear and practical introduction. She identifies two sets of contributing ideas:

- classic Freudian theory with its emphasis on the unconscious and the ego's role in defending the mind and mediating between different parts of the mind
- modern ego psychology with its emphasis on the ego as the rational problem-solving part of the mind, dealing with the outside world and minimising the aspect of managing unconscious drives.

She deals with ego-oriented practice in three aspects: assessment, intervention and the worker-client relationship.

Assessment involves looking at clients' present and past ways of *coping* (an important concept in ego psychology) both emotionally and practically with things that happen to them and things that they have to do; their inner capacity and external circumstances. The starting point is to share the problem, discuss the ways clients have already tried, and look for other possible ways of dealing with it. The plan of action will then involve choosing between three major strategies:

- improving clients' internal capacities
- changing outside circumstances affecting them
- improving how their internal and external worlds fit together.

Intervention may be either ego-supporting or ego-modifying, and applied either directly through psychological means or indirectly on clients' environments. Goldstein's distinction of these two approaches makes useful differences in practice clear. *Ego-supporting* interventions tend to focus on present behaviour, conscious thought and environmental change, involve learning or mastering new skills, through experiencing a worthwhile relationship with the worker using directive and educational techniques, and are more likely to be short- rather than long-term.

Ego-modifying interventions, by contrast, tend to concentrate on past and present unconscious feelings and drives, and avoid environmental changes. Efforts concentrate on giving insight into feelings and resolving emotional conflicts, understanding transference in the worker-client relationship; they use non-directive and reflective techniques and are generally long-term.

Client-worker relationships are like but different from ordinary human relationships. Their special features are:

- client needs form the basic aim of the interactions, instead of both parties' needs being involved, as in most relationships
- the workers involve themselves in the relationship in a disciplined and controlled way, rather than simply by inclination and emotional response
- important social work professional values are always involved, so whatever the client's personal characteristics or behaviour, the worker is always prepared to take part; this is not typical of ordinary relationships where inclination, liking and the sort of responses made affect relationships.

Client-worker relationships have rational and irrational aspects. The former are about the tasks to be undertaken and work towards the agreed objectives. The latter come from the feelings involved in past relationships. So, for example, Howard was a social worker who in his teens had been homosexually assaulted, and was working with Joe, who had come for help because of his feelings of isolation and lack of self-worth arising from concealing his homosexual life-style, which he had not been able to reveal to his parents, his brother and sisters. A plan for talking to his brother and then disclosing this important part of his person to his family was agreed, but this relied on Howard's personal support and involvement through these proceedings. However, Joe came to experience Howard as rather cold and rejecting and felt that he could not go on. In exploration with his supervisor, Howard identified his anger towards the person who had assaulted him as the past event which had caused present feelings which were getting in the way of his relationship with Joe. Howard's feelings about this event were unresolved; that is, he had hidden his anger at this exploitation of his person, rather than expressing it fully and coming to a rational view that he had not been badly hurt. He could not avoid fearing that others, like Joe, might cause similar hurt elsewhere. He was entitled to his anger and fear, but hid it because he accepted that applying it to others like Joe was unreasonable. Nonetheless, his rational understanding of that did not overcome the expression of his hidden feelings, and this is why Joe was able to sense his rejection. This case is an example of counter-transference; how irrational aspects of a past relationship brought forward to a present one can get in the way of using the special helping features of worker-client relationships. It also illustrates the importance and role of supervision.

Transactional analysis (TA) derives from the work of Eric Berne (1961, 1964), and is included here because he started as a psychoanalyst and his theories have some obvious links with psychoanalytic personality structures, and some aspects of psychoanalytic terminology. It could equally validly be regarded as a form of humanistic therapy (see Chapter 8) since its basic principles rely, unlike the more deterministic psychoanalytic theory, on the assumption that people are responsible, autonomous agents who have the energy and capacity to control their own lives and solve their own problems – they are prevented from doing so only by leftover failings of early childhood behaviour patterns (Pitman 1982a). TA has now developed completely independently of psychoanalysis, with its own literature and training schemes. Pitman (1982b) provides an extensive introduction to its application to social work, Coburn (1986) a briefer account, but it has not been widely integrated into social work with other techniques. It is, rather, a system of therapy which specially and separately trained people sometimes undertake within social work agencies. Some of the jargon, especially 'games' and 'strokes', is used without calling on the full system of thought.

There are four elements of TA: structural, transactional, games and script analyses. *Structural* analysis proposes that our personality has three 'ego states'; ways of thinking about the world which have typical behaviour patterns associated with them. The parent state is a collection of attitudes typical of the sort of injunctions that a parent figure might give to a child, and the sort of perceptions that a child might have of such a figure. The child state contains feelings and attitudes left over from childhood, typically rather self-centred, but also uncontrolled and potentially creative. The adult state manages, mostly rationally, the relationships between the ego states and with the outside world. These concepts are like the psychoanalytic structures of superego, id and ego, but TA is less concerned with internal interactions among parts of the mind and with drives and irrational responses.

An example of the interaction of ego states is in a residential setting for mentally-ill people. One of the residents, Colette, takes offence at a minor transgression of the rules by Mike, shouts at him and runs to her room and locks the door. The worker has an internal debate. His 'child' says: 'That stupid woman. I'll go and tell her off.' His 'parent' says: 'There are always two sides to a story, and Mike can be very irritating.' His 'adult' works out a compromise and executes an appropriate action: 'I'll go and say she must not get angry like that, but I'll also find out what happened and then bring them together to talk over how they can live better together in future.' This sort of debate goes on continuously within all of us.

In social work practice, we need to work out the internal interactions, strengthen the adult's ability to deal appropriately with the world (rather like ego-oriented work) and redirect energy from one state to another. For example, where people are driven too much by the demands of their parent, the worker can help let their child have a greater influence; this may lead them to be more creative in how their adult reacts. Colette, for instance, has a parent which says 'gentlemen should always be courteous and respectful towards women' and 'ladies always behave with decorum.' A lot of energy is used in applying these ideas, which could be partly transferred to her child which says 'it's fun to get really involved in a lively argument.' If this happened, she would be able to deal more flexibly and creatively with Mike's occasional aggressive responses, instead of closing down her own emotions, and criticising his response to her.

Transactional analysis is about how ego states in one person interact with those in another. Transactions are exchanges between

Table 3.2 *Examples of transactional analysis*

Colette: Please, Mike, would you not use my kettle without asking me, because I worry in case it gets damaged. *Mike*: I'm sorry, but the fuse has blown on mine and I couldn't find a replacement.	*Complementary*: Colette's adult to Mike's adult; Mike's adult to Colette's adult
Colette: You've really upset me, please don't do it again. *Mike*: I've explained the problem; shall we go and see if we can find a fuse in the toolbox? *Colette*: You really shouldn't upset me like this.	*Crossed*: Colette's child to Mike's adult; Mike's adult to Colette's adult; Colette's parent to Mike's child
Mike (deliberately): We can try to find a way out of this together. *Colette* (coldly): I'm sure you are better at mending fuses than me.	*Ulterior*: Mike's adult to Colette's adult hides an angry parent to her child; Colette's adult to his adult hides her child to his parent.

people's ego states, which may be open or hidden. When open and hidden messages involve different ego states or transactions, problems arise. There are three kinds of transaction: 'complementary' where only two ego states are in play; 'crossed,' where several are involved but verbal and non-verbal messages are consistent; and 'ulterior' where again several ego states are involved, but the open messages are different from the hidden ones. The examples in Table 3.2 come from Colette and Mike's interactions. In practice, the worker uses transactional analysis to find out which ego states are involved in transactions, and helps clients to use communication more constructively.

Games analysis is concerned with patterns of interaction and behaviour. People have three groups of emotional needs:

- stimulation, which they fulfil by artistic, leisure and work activities
- recognition, which is met by receiving 'strokes' either non-verbal or verbal, positive or negative, from others (e.g. respectively a smile and a thank you; or a scowl and a criticism)
- structure in life, particularly of time.

Table 3.3 *The four life positions in transactional analysis*

Life position	Meaning
I'm OK – you're OK	you feel good about yourself and others
I'm OK – you're not OK	you feel good about yourself but not about others, so you tend to blame others for your own problems, and criticise them (rather like projection in psychoanalysis)
I'm not OK – you're OK	you feel bad about yourself and see others as more powerful and capable than yourself, so you tend to feel inferior and incompetent all the time
I'm not OK – you're not OK	you are critical of both yourself and others

Source: T. Harris (1973).

The pattern of strokes and life experiences that we get used to in childhood sets up our life position, which is about how we feel about ourselves and others, and our general attitude to the world. There are four life positions (T. Harris, 1973), set out in Table 3.3.

Games are a typical pattern of ulterior transactions which recurs and reflects and promotes damaging life positions. So, if Mike is at 'I'm OK, you're not OK' and Colette is at 'I'm not OK, you're OK,' their game of 'kettle' in Table 3.2 encourages him to continue to feel he is being reasonable, her to feel inferior. In practice, workers can analyse games with clients, so that they can understand and avoid them in favour of more satisfying interactions.

Script analysis is concerned with seeing how transactions in the past have led to present life positions and games.

From this brief account, it will be seen that TA is an attractive formulation of behaviour, with an emphasis particularly on communication patterns, which relates closely to more conventional communication theory (see Chapter 7). Its evident links with psychoanalysis should not be overemphasised, since it has travelled a long way from instinctual drives and determinism. There are clear relationships with ego psychology and psychodynamic structures of the personality. As a method, it may be criticised in the same way as psychodynamic theory for relying on insight. Other criticisms are that the technique is largely psychotherapeutic and

Figure 3.1 *Diagrammatic representation of ego states in transactional analysis*

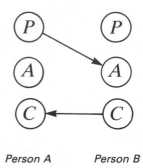

Person A   Person B

Explanatory note: In this case, person *A*'s parent is communicating with person *B*'s adult, while person *B*'s child is communicating with person *A*'s child.

does not have much to say about clients' practical problems of poverty and oppression; at least, however, supporters of TA would say that they can be helped to avoid oppressing themselves. Finally, it can be argued that it is a shallow technique, giving superficial accounts of behaviour in a jargon which might make some people feel that they are not being treated with respect, rather than permitting a thoughtful analysis of behaviour. For some people, on the other hand, its entertaining and unportentous terms can help them look at their behaviour in a new easily-grasped way. This is enhanced by a diagrammatic technique, shown in Figure 3.1 which shows each personality in a transaction in terms of their parent-adult-child ego states and how these are interacting with one another.

Therapeutic environments: an application to residential care

Psychodynamic theory has been applied to residential care work through a variety of theoretical developments. Righton (1975) shows the theoretical relationships between:

- *planned environment therapy* (Franklin, 1968, Wills, 1973) based on work with maladjusted adolescents originally in the Second World War, and with its roots in psychoanalytic theory, and radical education, including the work of Homer Lane (Wills, 1964), A. S. Neill (1964) and G. A. Lyward (Burn, 1956)

- *milieu therapy*, a mainly American concept, used in the work of writers such as Polsky (1968), applying psychodynamic groupwork with maladjusted young people, using the ideas of Lewin (1951) on field theory and life space as a way of understanding interactions between individuals and within groups, particularly those in residential care (Redl, 1959), and applying ego psychology
- *therapeutic communities*, which derive from the work of Maxwell Jones in psychiatric hospitals; his work has also been applied in a variety of community settings including day hospitals (Whiteley, 1979), and hostels and housing schemes of various kinds through the worldwide work of the Richmond Fellowship (Jansen, 1980).

The psychodynamic groupwork of Bion (1961) has influenced some of this work. Perhaps the most widely influential of these models of residential care practice is the therapeutic community, and so Kennard's (1983) account of its main principles offers a useful summary of the practice of all three forms of work:

- informal and communal atmosphere
- group meetings are used as central aspect of therapy
- all participants share in the work of running the community
- residents are auxiliary therapists
- authority is shared between staff and residents
- basic psychodynamic principles are accepted
- basic equality of all members
- the community is a 'closed order' whose basic values cannot be disputed – a strong moral and ideological component.

Conclusion

This chapter demonstrates the wide range of applications that psychodynamic theory has had in social work, and its comprehensiveness as a theory. Moreover, it has had a special and powerful influence throughout the history of social work, and in earlier

Chapters we saw how some of the basic features of social work, such as relationship, individualisation and use of evidence in a scientific way have their origins in, or have associations with psychodynamic theory. All this made it particularly important and influential both in its day and today. Future chapters show how its ideas are the explicit or implicit basis for many other aspects of social work theory, or can be used within them.

4

Crisis Intervention and Task-Centred Models

Connections

These two models of social work have some features in common, so it is useful to present them together for comparison and contrast. Both stress brief interventions, though these may be strung together in a series. They are both structured, so action is planned and fits a pre-ordained pattern. 'Contracts' or other explicit agreements between worker and client are used. The sorts of circumstances in which each may be used are specified.

Many of these factors may suggest a relationship with behavioural approaches, as Howe (1987) proposes for task-centred work. Some suggested links include the use of contracts, but in fact these are widely used outside behavioural work (Corden and Preston-Shoot, 1987a; Hutten, 1977). Neither approach is in fact connected with behavioural approaches. Crisis intervention is explicitly based on psychodynamic ego psychology. Task-centred casework rejects any specific psychological or sociological base for its methods. It is derived entirely from pragmatic research, which arose from dissatisfaction with long-term psychodynamic casework in some agencies in the USA. This then led to an attempt to replace it with a 'planned short-term therapy.' Many basic behavioural ideas such as conditioning play no part in task-centred work, and it deals with broader classes of behaviour than behavioural work normally covers.

Both the circumstances in which crisis and task-centred work should be used and the focus of work differ. Crisis intervention is, classically, action to interrupt a series of events which lead to a

101

disruption in people's normal functioning. Task-centred work focuses on defined categories of problems. Both try to improve people's capacity to deal with their problems in living. Crisis intervention uses practical tasks to help people readjust, but an important focus is their emotional response to crises and long-term changes in their capacity to manage everyday problems. Task-centred work focuses on performance in practical tasks which will resolve particular problems. Emotional problems are helped by success in achieving tasks. Crisis intervention has a theory of the origin of life difficulties. Task-centred work takes problems as given, to be resolved pragmatically. In spite of these formal differences, social workers have tended to see the approaches as allied, because of their alliance as short-term, structured treatment approaches, and because of the usefulness of research into task-centred work as practical guidance for implementing crisis intervention (Golan, 1986, p. 309).

Task-centred work is as distant from psychodynamic ideas as from behavioural approaches, and this is another difference with the ego-psychological base of crisis theory. It rejects long-term involvement between worker and client assumed by insight-giving and supportive therapies, and concentrates on exposed problems rather than their underlying causes. Reid and Epstein (1972, p. 26) specifically distinguish the approach from crisis intervention because they say task-centred work deals with a wider range of problems, and emphasises clear definitions of target problems, tasks and time limits. They stress links with functional casework with their emphasis on time limits, client self-direction and having a clear structure and focus in the process of work. They use Hollis' classification of casework procedures (see Table 3.1).

The classic formulation of crisis intervention as a technique is that of Caplan (1965). This draws attention to the origins of the method in mental health work, and its emphasis on prevention rather than treatment of illness. Lindemann's early (1944) paper dealing with the grief reactions in various groups of patients, especially in the unexpected emergency of the Boston 'Cocoanut Grove' fire draws attention to how people coped with the crisis of bereavement in their lives. They managed better if they had coped with previous crises in their lives, less well if past problems had not been fully resolved.

A group of mental health workers around Lindemann and

Caplan constructed the ideas of crisis intervention while working with a variety of community mental health problems. The main writers are represented in the book which introduced the techniques to the social work literature (Parad, 1965a). Caplan and his colleagues continued their work in preventive mental health, particularly emphasising the support of social networks in the community in preventing breakdown (see Chapter 6). Crisis intervention can be usefully combined with support systems work and networking (Mor-Barak, 1988).

In social work, crisis intervention may be seen as a general technique for dealing with clients' problems. Parad (1965b), for example, argues that people approaching agencies do so when they experience crises in their capacity to manage their lives. The crisis is what motivates them to come, or leads other agencies to refer or require them to seek help. Thus, all clients can be seen as 'in crisis', so that crisis intervention is relevant to all social work.

Crisis intervention has been used in mental health services. It became associated with the idea of using multi-disciplinary teams of doctors, nurses and social workers to visit clients at home in an attempt to avoid damaging and unnecessary admissions to psychiatric hospital. Helping people to deal with severe reactions to loss and bereavement on death, for example, or when divorce or child care problems lead to the break-up of families is another common use of the techniques.

In the UK, 'crisis intervention' is sometimes misused to refer to '. . . a crisis for the worker or the agency . . .' (Browne, 1978, p. 115). O'Hagan (1986) treats crisis intervention as an overall term referring to work in emergency and night duty teams and some intake teams in the local authority social services. The classical usage of crisis intervention is retained in several services designed to respond to mental health emergencies (Davis, *et al*, 1985) and the emotional aftermath of major public disasters.

Crisis intervention – Naomi Golan

Golan (1978) offers one of the best articulated accounts of crisis intervention theory, and the following summary is based largely on her book. She outlines the main points of the theory as follows:

- every person, group and organisation has crises during their lives
- *hazardous events* are major problems or a series of difficulties which start crises off
- hazardous events may be *anticipated* (e.g. adolescence, marriage, moving house) or *unanticipated* (e.g. death, divorce, redundancy, environmental disasters such as fires)
- *vulnerable states* exist when hazardous events cause people to lose
- their *equilibrium* which is their capacity to deal with things that happen to them
- when equilibrium is disturbed, we try out our usual ways of dealing with problems; if these fail we try new problem-solving methods
- *tension and stress* arise with each failure
- a *precipitating factor* on top of unresolved problems adds to the tension and
- causes a disorganised state of *active crisis*
- precipitating factors may be presented to the worker as the client's main problem but these are *not* the crisis, only a point in the sequence; the clue to this is often immense emotion associated with apparently minor events
- stressful events may be seen in one of three ways, each with its own typical response, as shown in Table 4.1

Table 4.1 *Stressful events and responses in crisis intervention*

Stressful events	Response
threats	anxiety
loss	depression
challenges	mild anxiety, hope, expectation and more attempts at problem-solving

Source: Golan (1978).

- the more problems successfuly dealt with in the past, the more problem-solving strategies will be available, so states of active crisis are less likely; unsuccessful problem-solving in the past leads to people falling into active crisis often and finding it hard to escape
- all crises reach resolution in 6–8 weeks
- people in crisis are more open to being helped than those

who are not; intervention in crisis is more successful than at other times, and

- in 'reintegration' after active crisis, people become set in their newly learned ways of solving problems, so learning effective problem-solving during the crisis improves coping capacity in the future

Presented with a client, the worker needs to work out whether crisis is a relevant concept to use and the point within the crisis process that has been reached. The whole situation in which the client exists and its interaction with psychological issues in the client's life should be considered; what Lukton (1982) calls, adapting the term from the conventions of psychosocial casework, the person-in-crisis situation. Charles, for example, came to see a social worker two weeks after his father had died, feeling very distressed. It is tempting to see the death as the crisis, but in fact it was the precipitating event, since when looking into his story, the worker found that he had recently moved away from his father for the first time to another town to take up a new job – this kind of social change can be very stressful and formed a hazardous event. He had already lost his equilibrium and was in a vulnerable state because he felt lonely and without support in the new town. He had tried to deal with this by going out with some new friends and joining a social club, but he did not feel part of group in either situation. On one or two occasions he had drunk too much and this had been embarrassing. He had thus made a number of attempts to deal with his problems, but failed, and was suffering from increasing stress and tension as a result. He had been going back to his father's home at weekends, and his father's sudden death, once he had dealt with the immediate practical and emotional consequences, had emphasised his loneliness even further. Too strong a focus on the death as a crisis would fail to deal with the underlying problems that had created the state of active crisis from an event which he might have coped with if he had not already been facing this series of problems.

It follows from this set of ideas that people who suffer a lifetime of stresses will be more quickly incapacitated by problems and find it harder to cope with them than others who have the chance to deal steadily with their problems. Also, people who can be helped to deal with problems effectively now, will learn strategies which will prevent states of active crisis arising so easily in the future.

The steps in *reintegration* are:

● *correct cognitive perception* as clients gain a more accurate and complete view of the events which have affected them
● *managing feelings* involves getting the client to release extreme emotion and the worker accepting it (e.g. it is acceptable to grieve for a dead relative)
● *developing new coping behaviours*.

In the case of Charles, the worker's exploration of the sequence of events helped to disclose to him that he was not assailed by a series of unconnected disasters, but all these painful experiences fitted together in a pattern which could be dealt with as a whole. Aside from releasing a good deal of emotion around his grief for his father, which he was in the process of doing anyway, he was also able to release, for the first time away from the responsibilities of his job, his intense fear of failure and mental illness due to loneliness and depression. He was also able to study some fairly elementary ways of building up social relationships, and went to a class on making friends and social contacts.

Rapoport (1970) presents an approach to crisis intervention which is rather more psychodynamic than Golan's more modern cognitive approach and concentrates on exploring the history of the crisis and its emotional origins. Conflicts in emotions is more important in her account. She defines two levels of intervention:

● At the *first level*, workers
  – relieve symptoms
  – get the client back to previous levels of functioning or improve upon them
  – help the client gain understanding of the lead-up to the crisis, and
  – help family and community to support the client.
● at the *second level*, intervention is more complex:
  – help clients understand connections between present and past crises and 'conflicts', and
  – start new ways of thinking and coping.

Similarly, Sifneos (1967, 1972) argues that clients who are poor at coping should have their anxiety suppressed by the worker, using reassurance, support and practical help. Stronger clients can have anxiety provoked to help them use skills and see problems as a challenge (see Table 4.1, p. 104).

Golan thinks tasks are important in crisis treatment (pp. 73–6), but she does not use 'task' in the same way as task-centred theory does. Here, it is an emotionally or socially necessary role or series of actions in the client's life – something that must be gone through in order to achieve reintegration. However, she proposes a rather similar process to that put forward by Reid for task-centred work:

- explore the various options
- help select a solution
- apply for a service
- test the service
- get used to and gain skill in using the service.

The worker offers support and help throughout this process.

Golan also distinguishes these *instrumental or material-arrangement* processes from dealing with psychosocial tasks which involve:

- coping with feelings of loss and threats to security, self-esteem
- trying new coping mechanisms as a way of managing anxiety
- offering support during the stressful period of seeking new services
- helping the adjustment to using the service
- helping the client to realise what has been achieved, or to feel OK about a loss.

Golan then presents a model for treatment which is described in extremely truncated form in Table 4.2. Treatment strategies are analysed along the lines of Hollis' (see Chapter 3) and families and groups are seen as effective places for treatment. There is also an extensive categorisation of different kinds of crisis. The work of Erikson (also mentioned in Chapter 3) is important because he defined personal development as a series of crises, and it is argued that crisis intervention can be used preventatively to avoid some of the emotional consequences of such life crises.

Table 4.2 *Golan's model of crisis intervention*

Beginning phase: formulation (1st interview)	Middle phase: implementation (1st–6th interviews)	Ending phase: termination (7th and 8th if necessary, interviews)
A: focus on crisis state concentrate on 'here and now' get client to express emotional responses as emotions reduce, explore hazardous event discover type and effects of vulnerable state assess disturbance caused by crisis state	*A: Data collection* get missing data check inconsistencies select main themes (loss, anxiety, challenge)	*A: termination decision* check period since referral and remind client propose spacing of contacts and finishing deal with resistance to termination
B: evaluation decision statement – account of circumstances and priority problems check client's priorities decide main problem	*B: behaviour change* check client's coping mechanisms in problem area set realistic short-term goals set overall tasks jointly work out practical tasks jointly work out 'thinking' tasks	*B: review progress* summarise progress review main themes reminder of tasks covered, goals reached, changes, incomplete work
C: contract define goals, tasks, for client and worker		*C: plan future* discuss present problems discuss client's plans help client feel that process is ended help client feel OK about returning with other problems

Source: Golan (1978).

Task-centred casework: Reid and Epstein

The definitive statement of task-centred casework is in Reid (1978) with a more practical and accessible version in Epstein

(1978). The pioneer statement is in their joint *Task-Centred Casework* (Reid and Epstein, 1972) and the model originates from research into brief casework in the 1960s by Reid and Shyne (1969). The model has been extensively validated in research in a variety of settings and countries (Reid and Epstein, 1977; Reid, 1985). It has been explicitly applied to groupwork and family work (Reid, 1985).

In task-centred work, social workers resolve problems presented by clients. Any theory of social work should, therefore, show how problems arise, what they are and how they may be dealt with. Brief work with explicit time limits is an essential feature of the approach, and has been shown to be more effective than longer-term, less focused work. British studies, for example have shown its effectiveness in inner-city intake teams, in the probation service and with parasuicides (Goldberg *et al*, 1985). There is no specific psychological or sociological base (Reid, 1978, p. 14) since no theory adequately explains the range of problems that social workers deal with. Appropriate theories would therefore be selected from those available. The 'problem-solving' element has connections with Perlman's problem-solving casework (see Chapter 3) which task-centred work has largely supplanted.

Task-centred work is concerned with problems that:

● clients acknowledge or accept
● can be resolved through actions to be taken outside contacts with workers
● can be defined clearly
● come from 'unsatisfied wants' of the client rather than being defined by outsiders (note this particular view of need which somewhat excludes unwilling clients, although task-centred work has been proposed by Reid as suitable for unwilling clients)
● come from things that clients want to change in their lives.

Some problems are shared by clients with others in their lives, who may acknowledge and define the problem in the same way. Agreement does not always exist about shared problems; people other than the client may see them differently. For example, in the case of Joan, a teenage girl, the worker in discussion with the client discovered that her inability to find a job was worrying her most, and began to work out a plan for undertaking a series of tasks to share the task of finding one. Before completing this, however, she visited the home to find that Joan's mother preferred her to remain at home to help domestically with the elderly grandparent who was also living with her. Also, Joan's father felt that the idea of working in a shop, which she preferred, was not socially acceptable, and he wanted her to go to the college to learn office skills. The worker had first to take on the task of resolving the different perceptions of Joan's family duties with her own wishes before being able to proceed with job-finding.

Reid (1978) classifies the types of problems that task-centred work is effective with into eight categories shown in Table 4.3.

Table 4.3 *Problems with which task-centred work is effective*

Interpersonal conflict
Dissatisfaction in social relationships
Problems with formal organisations
Difficulty in role performance
Decision problems
Reactive emotional stress
Inadequate resources
Psychological and behavioural problems not otherwise categorised, but meeting the general definition of problems in the model

Source: Reid (1978).

Workers should try to understand clients' problem-solving behaviour, especially where explanatory theories account both for how problems are caused and resolved. The *direction and strength of clients' wants* should be assessed. Some wants support each other while others are in opposition. Wants start action off, but clients' *belief systems* shape the wants and acceptable ways of fulfilling them. In Joan's case, for example, the desire for a job was enough to start her seeking the worker's help, but the type of job that she believed was possible – shop work – and her lack of desire to spend time in college to gain qualifications for office work meant that the direction of job-seeking had to be changed from the father's preference.

Beliefs guide action and are changed by interactions between the worker, client and others. Such beliefs are *points of leverage* which can help change beliefs, along the same lines as in cognitive therapies. Points of leverage are:

- *accuracy* where workers help clients understand how accurate their beliefs are
- *scope* where workers help clients see the implications or range of beliefs which clients think are more limited
- *consistency* where distortions due to dissonance between one belief and another can be removed by the worker.

Again in Joan's case, the worker found it useful to explore whether her assessment of her capacity to get better qualifications was accurate, by discussing the different perceptions of father and daughter. She also explored with Joan how she might limit the scope for moving on to more interesting jobs in the future if she failed to take qualifications now, since she might get used to having a wage coming in and be loath to return to college. Joan and the worker also explored the mismatch between Joan's desire to do something interesting (as shown by her wish to find a job more interesting than her domestic responsibilities and her wish for the independence deriving from having a job and a wage) and the likelihood that a low-grade job would prove boring very quickly.

Emotions arise from the interaction between beliefs and wants. Fear or anxiety arise because a client believes that a want is lost or threatened. Unconscious motivation may affect beliefs or wants but not (directly) behaviour. Joan, for example, was afraid of getting stuck at home and was reacting too quickly and to her disadvantage as a result.

Action is behaviour carried out with intent, so understanding actions involves understanding intentions. *Plans* are descriptions of intentions formed by the interaction of beliefs, wants and emotions. Planning means assessing alternative options, preferably away from the situation in which action is needed. When a plan is acted upon, the outcome gives feedback to the actor. Actions often occur in *sequences* and the problem may lie early in the sequence. For example, if my son misbehaves, I might slap him, and then feel guilty because I believe that slapping a child is wrong. Is slapping appropriate to stop the misbehaviour? This may be so if he is overactive today and needs a warning and reminder to think about and moderate his behaviour. But suppose that the problem is that I ignored him, causing him to misbehave to gain attention. Deciding not to slap him would not be effective as a resolution of the problem of inappropriate slapping, because this plan mistakes the problem, and he would probably misbehave more to get attention which the early misbehaviour did not achieve. A better way to solve the problem of inappropriate slapping would be to play with him and show him that I have more time for him.

Clients may not have *skills* to perform actions which may be needed in particular circumstances. Skills may be learned directly or generalised from other situations. Going through a series of small steps may help such learning.

Some *social systems* may generate or affect clients' beliefs or respond to actions providing feedback in such a way that distorts further actions, whether for good or ill. The environment surrounding clients may therefore be important. Action sequences may in this way become *interaction sequences* so that actions affect one another in circles or spirals. This idea comes from communication theory. *Organisations* may form a context for actions, labelling or categorising people or generating 'collective beliefs' about certain sorts of people. For example, staff in a school may come to believe that children from a particular housing estate are disruptive. This may in turn affect what the children believe about themselves, and what their parents and other agencies think about them. Going further, this may then affect how people involved act towards one another.

The *intervention strategy* has two aims:

- helping clients to resolve problems of concern to them
- giving a good experience of problem-solving so that clients improve future capacity to deal with difficulties and are more willing to accept help.

Worker and client identify *target problems*, carry out *tasks* outside the agency setting and *rehearse and review* achievements.

From this account of general principles, it will be evident that the ideas in the model come from a variety of psychological and sociological sources. Social learning theory seems to influence the mode of action, identifying targets and tasks and rehearsal. Communication theory is present in the concern for sequences and interactions of behaviour. The emphasis on belief seems to show a cognitive element. The identification of influence from the environment and particularly organisations within it suggests some ideas borrowed from systems theory.

Task-centred practice

The aim of *assessment* is not, as in psychodynamic theory, to study clients' emotional responses or life history, but to identify:

● action requirements
● obstacles to action
● unchangeable constraints.

Clients wanting less formal, more friendly or more personally involving relationships should seek alternative forms of therapy. Where clients cannot maintain a focus on a limited range of problems, less structured or more exploratory methods such as crisis intervention should be used. Task-centred work helps in protective work (e.g. with the parents of abused children) but should not be used where authoritarian protection or social control are main priorities. Some physical and mental illnesses will not change by any client actions, so task-centred work can only be a part of intervention here, but it may help in dealing with the social consequences of illness of disability.

Problem specification is the first step, taken early on through agreement with the client to undertake a short period of assessment. The social context of the problem and others' responses to it are important. The process is as follows:

● identify potential problems by helping the client to describe difficulties in their own way, then summarising and testing out the worker's perception of the problems
● reach a tentative agreement on how the client sees the main problems
● challenge unresolvable or undesirable problem definitions (e.g. where the client unreasonably wants the return of a deserted spouse)
● raise additional problems, having first accepted the client's

definition of priorities, to present additional problems not
accepted or understood by the client
- seek others' involvement if necessary
- jointly assess the reason for referral if client is compelled to
attend by someone else
- get precise details of when and where problems arise
- specify the problem, usually in writing
- identify clear baselines of the level of present problems (see
Chapter 5 for further discussion of baselines)
- decide on desired changes.

In the phase of *contract creation*, worker and client reach specific
agreements on action. The process is as follows:

- agree to work on and specify one or more client-defined
problems
- rank the problems in order of priority
- define the desired outcome of treatment
- design the first set of tasks
- agree the amount of contact and time limits.

Reid prefers oral contracts to written ones because they are less
frightening, unless several people are involved or the problems are
complex.

Task planning takes place in regular sessions with the client.
Tasks must be explicitly planned, practicable for the client to do
outside the sessions and agreed between worker and client. They
may involve mental or physical action (e.g. to decide this or do
that). *General tasks* set a policy for the treatment process, and
operational tasks define what the client will do. Tasks may be
unitary, involving just one action or a series of actions, or *complex*
involving two different actions (e.g. to seek a new flat and take
part in occupational therapy). They may be *individual*, undertaken
only by the client; *reciprocal*, so that if the client does this, the
worker or a relative will do that; or *shared*, so that the client and
another important person will do it together.

The *task planning process* is as follows:

- possible alternative tasks are identified
- an agreement is made

- implementation is planned
- the task is summarised.

Task implementation then takes over the sessions between worker and client. This involves:

- setting up a recording system, especially where a sequence or repetition of actions is required
- identifying strategies (e.g. a series of increments, setting limits, setting precise targets, mental tasks, use of paradox, tasks to be done by client and worker concurrently, involving other people)
- agreeing incentives for finishing a task if these are not built in
- making sure the client understands the value of the task and how it helps to meet the treatment aims
- practising relevant skills whether by simulation (e.g. the worker acts out an employment interview) or by guided practice (e.g. helping a person with disabilities try out a new adaptation to their home in a day centre)
- analyse obstacles
- plan the worker's tasks that will contribute to the success.

The *worker's tasks* may involve:

- working with people other than the client to help the client to complete their tasks (e.g. preparing the way with another agency
- arranging for rewards and incentives for success
- sharing tasks with clients where they have insufficient skills or resources to do them alone.

Worker and client review achievements jointly in each session.

Mr and Mrs Knowles were an example of some of these processes. They were referred to a mental health advice service, with the problem that Mrs Knowles had become slightly agoraphobic, and now was unable to go out, except with her husband in the car. She was, for example, unable to do the shopping or go out on her own to see friends. She felt a little embarrassed by this. There were no resources to carry out a behaviour modification programme involving the worker, but he explained the basic principles of doing things in stages, having Mr Knowles alongside for support, and the idea of getting relaxed before moving on to the next stage. They then discussed a series of events in which they would go out in the car and Mrs Knowles would get out of the car, then later would go part of the way to a small shop, all the way, later still buy some things, and then progress in stages to going to the super-market. The contract included the worker being available on the phone if any difficulties arose. This programme seemed to work quite effectively without any further interventions from the worker.

The *ending phase* involves client and worker in:

- describing the target problem as it was and as it is now
- assessments by the worker, client and others involved of any changes
- planning for the future (e.g. how the client will use any skills learned or adapt to changed circumstances)
- additional contracts, to extend the process to finish off properly, or to establish new problem and task definitions
- an explicit end where (as in residential care or continuing supervision of a client subject to legal requirements) contact with the worker or agency continues
- movement to a long-term treatment process
- referral to another agency for additional or alternative help

Commentary

Both task-centred and crisis intervention approaches to social work have proved popular with social workers, the former in many different settings, the latter in more specialised ones. While the research validation shows that task-centred work can be valid in many kinds of work, its aims are limited. Both theories represent a trend in social work to clearer, more focused activity than the long-term, non-directive, insight-giving methods of psychodynamic work but they are in the traditional lineage of social work problem-solving, using a conventional social work, individualising, relationship with clients who are treated on a medical model with the aim of getting better. Crisis intervention, with its more psychodynamic roots offers a greater emphasis on emotional responses and irrational or unconscious behaviour than task-centred work which assumes greater rationality on the part of clients. In being more directive and in using contracts, the style of these interventions has some connections with behavioural approaches, which are considered in the next chapter.

The clear structure and specificity of these approaches may cause a problem because workers tend to use them inappropriately when an approach which offers a longer-term relationship aimed at improving personal functioning or dealing with emotional or psychological difficulties would be more appropriate. The idea of contract has also come in for some criticism. Rojek and Collins (1987, 1988), using concepts from discourse analysis, argue that it offers a false sense of equality between workers and clients; false because it neglects the radical analysis of the position of social workers who have all the power and authority of the state, and their profession and class to impose their will upon clients. They propose that in using terms like 'contract', workers imply to clients an equality which in a sense enables them to take greater power in the relationship. The fact that this power imbalance exists makes it difficult to use contracts in the way proposed by activities such as task-centred work; it prevents the mutual co-operation which the model assumes and which is said to be at the bottom of its success as a technique. In reply to this view, Corden and Preston-Shoot (1987, 1988) argue that the contract can benefit client-worker relationships by helping to make these explicit, and at least more specific so that each knows more clearly what is going on. In fact, also, it can be shown that contract work does achieve results in allowing clients to attain desired ends.

5

Behavioural Models

Connections

Behavioural approaches to social work derive from the work of experimental behavioural psychologists. Thomas (1968, 1971) in the USA and Jehu (1967, 1972) in the UK were the first significant interpreters of the psychological literature within social work. Hanson (1983, pp. 142–3) maintains that although therapeutic uses were being made of the basic psychological theories in the 1950s, it was not used in social work until the 1960s when traditional social work came under radical attack.

Behavioural social work is surrounded by controversy, because it is the most positivist of social work theories (see Chapter 2) and it has been at the centre of the positivist debate. There are also objections on ethical grounds, since behaviour is manipulated by the worker rather than being under the control of the client. This could lead to behaviourist techniques being used to impose a worker's wishes on an unwilling client, and if used in pursuit of social or political policies could, at the extreme, be used for authoritarian political control. Behaviourists argue that consent of the client is ethically required and practically necessary to success. They also say that the most ethical treatment is the one that works best and behaviourist approaches can be demonstrated much more clearly than most others to be effective. All techniques can be abused in the wrong hands. Many other techniques are manipulative in a way which is hidden from clients; an example might be the use of paradox. Watson (1980, pp. 105–15) argues that this is not a sufficient answer to the ethical problem. Behaviourism inherently assumes that all behaviour is caused. If clients make decisions that they want changes which might be achieved by behavioural methods, then they are acting using their own reasoning freely in the sense of deciding without constraint on their decisions, and, as the behaviourists say, are being treated ethically. However, what happens if the client's behaviour is considered socially undesirable, by a court, or by people in a position to put social or other pressures on a client? They might be persuaded that their behaviour is right, good or adaptive to social conditions. In such cases, we are moving from unconstrained reasoning to decisions which are being made in pursuit of social goals. The only ethical position, which maintains clients' rights to self-determination, is to use the technique only where the clients' own purpose is to free themselves from behaviour (for example, where it is compulsive) and clients cannot, but wish to, control themselves.

Behavioural approaches in social work: Fischer and Gochros

The following account of behavioural approaches is based on the book by Fischer and Gochros (1975), because of its clear and comprehensive organisation of the theory; other texts provide something more like a manual of techniques. However, most books on behavioural social work cover the same ground since the contents are directly derived from psychological writing. Books by Schwartz and Goldiamond (1975), Sheldon (1982b) and Hudson and Macdonald (1986) have also been consulted, particularly on social learning methods. Each of these covers:

- respondent or classical conditioning (the stimulus-response approach; Jackson and King, 1982)
- operant conditioning
- social learning.

All are directly applicable in social work.

In addition, some writers extend into cognitive learning approaches (Jackson and King, 1982), and there is a debate about how justified this is (Hudson and Macdonald, 1986). In this book, I have treated cognitive learning in a separate chapter because, although cognitive approaches are direct developments of behaviour modification, they have developed independently enough to be seen as separate ideas.

Behavioural social work is based on learning theory which, unlike psychodynamic theory, concentrates on observable behaviour. It is considered unwise to use hidden thoughts or inferences about structures in the mind because they cannot be independently and objectively checked.

All behaviour whether it is abnormal (*maladaptive*) or normal (*adaptive*) is explained by the same principles. This rejects a disease model like psychodynamic theory which says that abnormal behaviour is a symptom of disturbance inside clients' minds which should be treated. In learning theory, abnormal behaviour has been learned just like any other behaviour, but it is not appropriate because it does not help us function well in our particular environment.

Looking at particular behaviours means that we do not label the whole person as abnormal. Different behaviours may be adaptive in different environments and cultures. So, behaviour which is appropriate to and comes from different genders and ethnic cultures is not assumed to need change in learning theory. In psychodynamic theory, behaviours are considered acceptable according to the theory's ideas of the origins of that behaviour, so behaviour which does not fit in with the dominant culture but might be acceptable in a minority ethnic culture or an oppressed gender comes to be disapproved of. While Fischer and Gochros note this point about learning theory, they do not note that the idea of adaptive behaviour still requires a minority or oppressed culture to align itself with the majority culture. There is still a risk that a therapy which seeks to change behaviour so that it adapts to an environment undervalues minority forms of behaviour and less dominant aspects of the culture.

Behavioural social work is often based on 'single case' experimental designs. Careful definition of target behaviours is followed by measuring in a planned way how often it occurs in a 'baseline' period. The intervention follows. Occurrences of the behaviour during and after intervention are also measured. Sometimes after one period of intervention, there is a 'reversal period' in which the worker returns to their own baseline behaviour and the target behaviour is again measured. Intervention then starts again. In this way, it is possible to test whether the intervention is indeed affecting the behaviour.

Respondent conditioning is concerned with behaviour (anything we do) which responds to (is produced by) a stimulus (a person, situation, event, or thing usually in the environment). *Conditioning* is the process by which behaviour is learned; that is, connected more or less permanently with the stimulus. When a response to a stimulus has been learned, the person's behaviour has been modified. Respondent conditioning is also known as *classical conditioning* because it derives from the first experiments in the field by Pavlov.

Many behaviours are *unconditioned*. They happen naturally. An unconditioned stimulus produces as unconditioned response. For example, people's eyes water in a high wind, they salivate when given food, they withdraw their hands sharply when burned, they are sick when they eat a noxious substance.

Behaviours are *conditioned* when responses become *associated* or paired with a stimulus that does not naturally produce the response, for example if our eyes were trained to water when we were given food. These are called conditioned stimuli and conditioned responses. *Extinction* occurs if the association between conditioned responses and stimuli is not kept up. The conditioned response fades away and becomes unconnected with the stimulus.

Some kinds of behaviour are incompatible with other behaviour. For example, someone who is completely relaxed cannot be anxious or violent. *Counter-conditioning* seeks to associate desirable responses with particular stimuli, in competition with undesirable responses.

The most commonly used counter-conditioning technique is *systematic desensitisation*. Client are taught the practical techniques of relaxation or are offered other means of personal support. Then they are slowly introduced to the unwanted stimulus, using the relaxation or support to fight against their anxiety. This is often used with agoraphobic or school phobic people. We saw a simple example of this in the case of the Knowles in Chapter 4. Here, relaxation and Mr Knowles' presence were used to counter-condition against Mrs Knowles' agoraphobic anxiety. *Assertiveness training* is another technique used where people are unconfident. They are helped to practice appropriate forms of behaviour in a supportive environment, and then enabled to use these in (ideally) increasingly difficult real life situations.

Counter-conditioning has been used in various forms of sexual therapy. Pleasant sexual responses are learned in supportive surroundings and are gradually introduced into more ordinary sexual situations which had previously caused anxiety. For example, a man who ejaculates prematurely learns to control ejaculation when stimulated by his partner when full sexual intercourse is not permitted until he feels confident of control. Transfer to full sexual intercourse follows later.

One example of these techniques is in conditioning children who are enuretic (that is, who wet the bed when they should have learned to avoid this behaviour). There is a loud buzzer or bell connected to an electrical contact placed within soft mats under the child. The buzzer sounds when some urine makes contact with the mats, and the child wakes and can complete urination in a toilet. This process has two effects. First, the child is conditioned to wake when the bladder is full, so avoiding bed-wetting. Second, the tone of the bladder muscle is improved, strengthening the capacity to get through the night without wetting. These responses are set up as a form of counter-conditioning to the natural process of reflex urination when the bladder is full (Morgan and Young, 1972).

Most behaviour does not develop from unconditioned stimuli and *operant conditioning*, the second major form of behavioural work, deals with a wider range of behaviours. It is concerned with behaviour which operates on the environment, and can be used with complex and thought-out behaviour. In contrast, respondent conditioning is mainly concerned with learned automatic responses.

Operant conditioning focuses on the consequences of behaviour. Something happens (an *antecedent* event: A) which produces a behaviour (B) which tries to deal with the event, and, as a result of that behaviour, consequences (C) arise. The worker has to manage *contingencies* which affect the relationships between the behaviour and the consequences which strengthen or weaken the behaviour. Consequences are called *positive reinforcement* if, when applied to someone undertaking a behaviour, they strengthen it. *Negative reinforcement* arises when a desired consequence is removed following a behaviour in order to strengthen it. Positive and negative here do *not* mean desirable and undesirable. Unwanted behaviour may well be positively reinforced. For example, if a child throws a temper tantrum and thus gains attention from their parents, the tantrum has been positively reinforced, even though it is unwanted behaviour. Negative reinforcement is not an unpleasant consequence, it is the *withdrawal* of a consequence. So closing a door to reduce the noise coming from the next room (removing a consequence) is a negative reinforcement increasing door-closing behaviour because it is found to be effective in giving us peace and quiet. Generally, however, negative reinforcers are unpleasant to the client. For example, a teenage boy disliked being taken to school by his social worker when he failed to attend. It was made clear that if he did not register each day, the worker would find him and take him to his class. One or two experiences of this made him realise that the peaceful enjoyment of his truancy would no longer be permitted. A desired consequence had been removed consistently, inducing him go to school on his own.

Punishment is used in operant conditioning to *decrease* behaviours. When unpleasant consequences follow, are immediately related to and reduce a behaviour this is called *positive punishment*. *Negative punishment* is the removal of a pleasant part of someone's life unless they perform a behaviour. For example, permission to stay out late is denied to a teenager whenever they refuse to do their homework from school.

In summary, reinforcement, whether positive or negative, strengthens behaviour. Punishment, whether positive or negative, reduces behaviour. Positive always means doing something, negative always means taking something away. Both can be used together.

Extinction is also an operant learning technique. It is different in principle from extinction in respondent conditioning. It means removing the relationship between behaviour and its consequence. In negative punishment, we may remove a consequence which has nothing to do with the behaviour, as in the example given above. Extinction might be used where avoiding homework led to arguments between child and parents. The arguments positively reinforce not doing homework, because they take up time and emotional energy which can then not be applied to the homework. Instead of arguing, parents could put child and homework in a room, thus withdrawing the reinforcing behaviour. Unlike extinction in respondent conditioning, this is not solely avoiding making a response, it is positively removing the relationship between a consequence and the behaviour which led to it.

Positive reinforcement is usually preferable to or should be used together with other techniques. For example, extinction gives no control over the behaviour which might replace the undesirable behaviour; it might be equally undesirable. Positive reinforcement allows the encouragement of favoured behaviour alongside extinction. Also, unwanted behaviour may increase temporarily to test out the new response and this is hard to cope with, so encouraging useful behaviour makes the process easier.

Different clients will be affected by different reinforcers, so each case must be carefully individualised. Therefore, assessment and definition of the antecedent events, the specific behaviours and detailed consequences are all important.

Reinforcers:

- work automatically so clients do not have to understand them
- should be applied consistently soon after the relevant behaviour in a way which connects them to the desired behaviour
- should be used as often and strongly as possible without going too far and satiating the client
- may be either *extrinsic* (outside the person) or *intrinsic* (internal feelings such as satisfaction and pride); intrinsic reinforcement is harder to use and define, but allying intrinsic with extrinsic factors helps to maintain behaviours.

Extrinsic reinforcers may be:

- *primary*, meeting basic needs such as food or avoiding pain, or
- *secondary*, which people have learned to value. These may be divided into five groups:
  - material, e.g. toys, money
  - social, e.g. approval, love
  - activity, e.g. hobbies, privileges
  - token, which are symbols of material or other reinforcers and can be exchanged at intervals for the original reinforcer
  - 'Premack' meaning that 'high probability behaviour can be used as a reinforcer for low-probability behaviour' (Fischer and Gochros, 1975, p. 63). People enjoy some things more than others (e.g. hobbies) which can reinforce behaviours they enjoy less (e.g. doing homework).

Any reinforcers may be used together, but social reinforcers are used because they are very powerful, widely available and help to change the client's social environment thus supporting desired behaviours over a longer period.

Large changes of behaviour should be divided into small steps. A schedule of reinforcement should be worked out:

- *continuous reinforcement* of every instance of the desired behaviour will work quickly. If the client does not use the desired behaviour, so that it cannot be selected by reinforcement, several techniques can be used:
  - *shaping* means reinforcing small steps towards the desired behaviour
  - *fading* means seeing where the behaviour is used in another situation and changing the environment into the new situation in which the behaviour is to be used
  - *modelling* means demonstrating the behaviour and is dealt with at length later in this Chapter
  - *prompting* means advising the client about appropriate behaviours
  - *physical guidance* means moving the client's body in the way required, rather as the piano teacher positions a pupil's body and hands correctly.

  Once a behaviour is established, reinforcement may be withdrawn and not given all the time, which is more economical.

- *intermittent schedules of reinforcement* are used where a behaviour is not always reinforced:
  - *ratio* schedules reinforce after a set number of occurrences
  - *interval* schedules after a set period of desired behaviour.

Ratio or interval schedules may be fixed (completely regular) or may vary around a typical period of time or number of behaviours. Variable schedules are most resistant to extinction (particularly variable interval schedules) and also more practical, since very consistent reinforcement may not be possible.

Social learning is the third general set of principles in behavioural work, and comes from the work of Bandura (1977). Most learning is gained by people's perceptions and thinking about what they experience. They learn by copying the example of others around them.

The main process by which this is done is *modelling*. Hudson and Macdonald (1986) describe it as follows:

- a person sees someone else performing an action and pays attention to it
- the observer 'forms an idea' or codes in their mind how the behaviour is done (including some rehearsals in practice or in their mind)
- the observer identifies circumstances in which the behaviour occurs and has its consequences
- when an appropriate situation arises the observer repeats the behaviour according to the 'idea' of it which they have formed.

Many clients are helped simply by seeing a feared behaviour performed by a role model and to appreciate that there are no adverse consequences. It is better if the modelling contains the following features:

- the model should have standing with the client, thus attracting attention to the behaviour
- the model should be seen to have success with and to be reinforced for the behaviour in other ways
- clients should see some points of similarity between themselves and the model
- clients should be able to practice the behaviour quickly after seeing it
- reinforcing the behaviour helps establish it.

In practice, according to Hudson and Mcdonald (1986), p. 141) the worker should:

- define the behaviour clearly and ensure that the client pays attention to it
- give or arrange a demonstration
- get the client to copy and practise the behaviour
- give feedback and reinforcement with, if necessary, further practice.

Behavioural social work practice

The main aims of behavioural social work are increasing desired behaviours and reducing undesired behaviours, so that people who are affected by social events act appropriately. This increases their capacity for leading a full and happy life. Insight into the client's problems often helps because it speeds learning, but there is no evidence that it is necessary or that it is enough to get people to change. Warm personal relationships between worker and client help in behavioural work as in other forms of social work. Behavioural social work can be used very widely in many social work situations. Gambrill (1981), for instance, demonstrates its use in working with child abuse situations with both children and parents; it is helpful for its clarity in setting goals for behavioural achievements. Herbert (1987) describes the use of behavioural techniques in a very practical way with a wide range of children's problems.

Recording is an important part of behavioural work, because it relies on such detailed observation. The target behaviours, both desired and undesired must be counted as a baseline and then checked during interventions. Common recording techniques are:

- diaries
- cards to be ticked in columns
- coins, tokens or slips of paper to be shifted (e.g. from one pocket to another, or put on a shelf where food is taken from, or into cigarette packets every time one is smoked as a reinforcer)
- automatic counters (e.g. some digital watches offer counting mechanisms or signs of time periods elapsed).

Counting is often plotted on graphs which are then displayed to give reinforcement. These techniques may be useful to make other forms of social work clearer to clients.

Assessment is an important feature of behavioural work. The emphasis is on the present. Lengthy social histories are not needed. Initial assessment involves interviews to discover:

- what those involved see as the problem
- who, precisely, is complaining or suffering

- who is part of the problem behaviour (since it may be more than one or not the person first presented as the problem)
- the antecedents; the precise times and circumstances of the problem's occurrences
- whether the problem is about behaviour being too common or too infrequent or inappropriate
- who could be the mediator
- how the client would like to change
- likely reinforcers and their availability

Herbert (1987) summarises the process as finding out about 'persons, places, times and situation.'

Then the selected problem must be assessed. Is the change being sought a sensible one? Are expectations too high or too demanding? Changes should fit well with legal and social expectations of the client. They should be amenable to behavioural methods. Poverty and social dislocation are not appropriately dealt with in this way. Herbert (1987) offers a useful acronym for remembering the factors which should be assessed when looking at problem behaviour: 'FINDS' – the *F*requency, *I*ntensity, *N*umber, *D*uration and the *S*ense or meaning given to these factors by the people involved.

Helpful and unhelpful aspects of the client's behaviour in their life circumstances should be assessed. Action may need to be tempered by their limitations, of intelligence or of handicapping illness, which would make the changes unreasonable.

Target behaviour should be specified and put in order of priority – annoying but easy-to-change behaviour first. Early treatment should be in small steps with a high chance of success. Behaviours which are important to the client in social life should have a high priority, especially if they affect a wide range of situations. All these will prove good motivators towards change.

The stages of action should then be:

- assessing mediators (see below)
- deciding the best place to intervene
- checking and analysing baseline data
- defining important antecedent events and consequences
- final and intermediate aims
- plan and techniques to be used

- selection of reinforcers
- collection of data to check on success and modify action accordingly.

Much behavioural work is through *mediators*, such as clients' family or friends, rather than directly with clients. Mediators must first be found from the client's surroundings. They must be reinforced, either directly, or by seeing the achievements of what they are doing. Buchanan and Webster (1982) used a range of behavioural techniques through parents as mediators to help them manage young children who presented difficulties when it was time for them to go to bed. Parents from a range of social backgrounds found that after about four weeks, there had been a significant improvement in their problems, which continued for 6–8 weeks afterwards.

Someone will be useful as a mediator if:

- they are present when the target behaviour occurs
- they can use important reinforcers or aversive stimuli (which some people cannot bring themselves to do)
- they will be reinforced by improvements in the client
- they are willing to take part.

Work with mediators begins with assessment of how they can do their work. The mediator's aims should be connected with the client's behaviour, and then the process of work is as given above.

Group behavioural techniques

Both Fischer and Gochros (1975, pp. 115–19) and Hudson and Macdonald (1986, pp. 165–6) quote a variety of studies to show that behaviourial approaches can be effectively used in group-work. This may be by using a conventional group as a supporter and reinforcer to individuals undertaking behavioural programmes or by undertaking interventions with several people at once in the group. Such arrangements may help people with similar problems, for example alcoholics, or those who come from the same background, for example a local group of teenagers with offending problems, or who are within the same family or social group.

Typically, according to Hudson and Macdonald, the group works together on problem assessment, goal-setting, discussing and deciding on strategies, and in modelling and rehearsal. One of the most useful methods in groupwork is social skills training. Rose (1981) discusses behavioural groupwork with a cognitive approach using social learning about 'self-defeating' and coping cognitions.

Burgess *et al.* (1980), a group of students on placement, describe the use of social skills training with a group of sex offenders in prison, which gives a good example of the range of techniques which may be applied. Three techniques in varying combinations were used. Microteaching of small elements of skills in interactions with others was one element, such as use of voice, eye contact, posture. A number of simple exercises on these elements of behaviour started off the process. Assertiveness training to help prisoners express their opinions and seek their interests without interfering with others was another aspect. Role playing of increasingly complex events which might occur in the prison developed this aspect of the group. It then moved on to situations which might arise outside the prison. Also, the use of operant conditioning to focus on individual problems and how prisoners behaved with others in groups was tried, based on the work of Liberman *et al.* (1975). Workers reinforced interest in the group by having a written contract, emphasising the aims of a particular piece of behaviour and using a range of activities. The group was divided up for practical work on prisoners' individual problems. Workers' modelling of skills was important, and prisoners were given homework to practice with. At the end of each group meeting, a winding down session of social conversation was arranged.

Residential work

Behavioural approaches present the second major grouping of theories of residential work (Hudson 1982; Ryan 1979). The most common approach is the use of *token economies*. These are systems for managing the total programme of a residential establishment, in the same way that therapeutic environments, discussed in Chapter 3, attempt to manage the total experience of residence. Thus, they are not treatment programmes for individuals which happen to be carried out in residence, but represent a genuine theoretical approach to residential work.

Token economies have been used in schools and residential homes for adolescents with behaviour problems and offenders. They have also been used with mentally ill and handicapped people (Birchwood *et al.*, 1988). Token economies are fundamentally an operant conditioning system using interval (or sometimes intermittent ratio) reinforcement. Staff in the establishment agree (according to Sheldon, 1982b, p. 156) a list of behaviours to be strengthened, and tokens are given for continuing these behaviours for a certain period or for performing behaviours a set number of times. Clients collect the tokens and exchange them for desired goods and for privileges. There is, in effect, a price list of rewards, each reward requiring a specified number of tokens. Relatively unskilled staff can be used to maintain the system (Fischer and Gochros, 1975, pp. 288–9).

Token economies are useful for *discrimination training* (Sheldon, 1982b, p. 156; Fischer and Gochros, 1975, p. 287). This helps people learn what sorts of behaviour are appropriate to particular social circumstances.

Pizzat (1973) gives an extended account of a residential programme using a variety of reinforcers. He shows that in the early stages, or when clients are first admitted with extreme behaviour difficulties, they need a phase of immediate reinforcement to gain quick improvement. This can then be backed up by a system giving tokens at specified times of day. Later still, the establishment offered a weekly allowance unconnected with specific behaviours for good conduct. Otherwise social and self-reinforcement was adequate at this stage. This is a helpful account of a range of behavioural techniques used in a residential setting, and demonstrates the importance of developing the various forms of reinforcement carefully.

Sheldon (1982b, pp. 156–7) notes that while token economies have been shown to be successful in changing behaviour, there are problems in maintaining them over a period. In most residential establishments, clients are not carefully selected, and most are not large enough to offer several fairly separate stages, as Pizzat's was. As a result, staff have too wide a range of problems to deal with. It may also be hard to ensure that staff and others who are present impose the system uniformly, and not all may believe in it sufficiently. It is important to support staff adequately. Outside pressures such as courts, health authorities or local authorities may limit the degree of control necessary to impose a consistent system. Birchwood *et al.* (1988) in a recent review of the research support these comments and claim that social modelling may be an equally effective form of treatment in many instances.

The sum total of these difficulties may lead to excessive rigidity, or to residents being rewarded for acquiescence rather than progress in appropriate behaviour. It may be useful to institute behaviourial systems for part of an establishment, or during a phase of particular difficulty, to get quick results.

Commentary

Behavioural approaches are clearly a valid and widely applicable form of treatment, whose effectiveness is supported by research, but whether the good results can be maintained over time is more variable. In spite of this demonstrable effectiveness and the energetic promotion by their supporters, behavioural approaches have not made an impact on general social work, although they have been heavily used in specialist settings for limited purposes. Patterson (1986), in relation to counselling, asserts that the use of conventional behaviour modification is receding, although social learning methods are being more widely used. This is true of social work, where in particular social skills and assertiveness have had some application. McAuley and McAuley (1980) discuss their experience of behavioural methods in fairly ordinary social work in a hospital setting, and consider that they were least successful where children had a long history of behaviour problems, where the family had multiple problems, was socially isolated and poorly motivated to change, where parents of children had longstanding personality problems, and where co-ordinated involvement from a variety of agencies was necessary. B. Hudson (1978) reported the early stages of a project to help schizophrenic patients in the community using behavioural techniques, and found it to be effective in achieving objectives with patients who were actively involved, but, in many cases, was unsuccessful because patients' families could not take part. This practical experience suggests that the most complex cases of many official agencies may not yield easily to techniques which are clearly effective in more limited situations. Hanson (1983) argues that behavioural work applied unsympathetically can be 'linear' and restrictive rather than interactive and imaginative. He proposes that using the model within an eco-systems approach (see Chapter 6), with an emphasis on the surrounding environment, avoids this tendency.

The reasons for the lack of impact of these techniques seem to be threefold. First, the explicit attack on the conventional psychodynamic form of social work combined with the adoption, by the behaviourists, of the positivist critique of the effectiveness of social work seems to have led to a degree of defensiveness. Second, the specific techniques are distant from the standard non-directive approach of social workers, and have a mechanistic terminology and procedure which they may feel uncomfortable with. Third, there have been some ethical criticisms which, while not wholly valid, have tended to reinforce the reserve of social workers and the feeling that this is not in the style of social work.

Behavioural approaches were the first major attack on the conventional psychodynamic mode of social work, and seem to have made relatively little impact on everyday social work, although they have been effectively used in limited circumstances. Social skills techniques have been the most promising development, and have been used in many different situations. However, an alternative critique came from a sociological perspective, systems theory, and it is to this that the next Chapter is devoted.

6

Systems and Ecological Models

Connections

Systems theory has had a major impact on social work since the 1970s and has been a subject of controversy for almost as long. It is conventional to distinguish two forms of systems theory in social work:

- general systems theory
- ecological systems theory.

There are also attempts to distinguish a third and separate stream of social systems theory based on Parsons' sociological analysis of systems in society (de Hoyos and Jensen, 1985).

Mancoske (1981) shows that important origins of systems theory in sociology lie in the social Darwinism of Herbert Spencer. Siporin (1980) argues that the social survey research of the late 19th century in England (e.g. the work of Booth and Rowntree), information theory, and the ecological school of Chicago sociologists in the 1930s were also antecedents.

Hearn (1958, 1969) made one of the earliest contributions applying systems theory to social work. The greatest impact came with two simultaneously published interpretations of the application of systems ideas to practice (Goldstein, 1973; Pincus and Minahan, 1973). These gained considerable influence in the UK through interpreters such as Vickery (1974; Specht and Vickery, 1977) and Olsen (1978). The later development by Siporin (1975) and Germain and Gitterman (1980; Germain, 1979a) of ecological systems theory has had considerable impact in the USA.

Systems ideas in social work have their origins in the general systems theory of von Bertalanffy (1971). This is a biological theory which proposes that all organisms are systems, composed of sub-systems and are in turn part of super-systems. Thus, a human being is part of a society and is made up of circulation (for example) systems, cells and these are in turn made up of atoms which are made up of smaller particles. The theory is applied to social systems, such as groups, families and societies, as well as biological systems.

Systems theory – basic concepts

The main concepts are as follows:

- a *system* is an entity with *boundaries* within which physical and mental energy is exchanged more than it is across the boundary
- a *closed system* is where there is no interchange across the boundary, as in a closed vacuum flask
- an *open system* is where energy crosses the boundary which is permeable, rather like a tea-bag in a cup of hot water which lets water in and tea out but keeps the tea leaves inside.

The way systems work and how they may be changed are understood by another set of concepts (Greif and Lynch, 1983):

- *input* – energy being fed into the system across the boundary
- *throughput* – how the energy is used within the system
- *output* – effects on the environment of energy passed out through the boundary of a system
- *feedback loops* – information and energy passed to the system caused by its outputs affecting the environment which tell it the results of its output
- *entropy* – the tendency of systems to use their own energy to keep going, which means that unless they receive inputs from outside the boundary, they run down and die.

A simple example of these processes is if you tell me something (input into my system). This affects how I behave (throughput in my system), my behaviour changes (output) and you observe this change. So you receive feedback that I have heard and understood what you said (a feedback loop). The system in this case is a 'black box'. You can see the input and the output that results, but you cannot see what happens within the system. The feedback allows you to infer what happened.

The state of a system at any one time is defined by five characteristics:

- its *steady state*, how it maintains itself by receiving input and using it
- its *homeostasis* or *equilibrium*, the ability to maintain its fundamental nature, in spite of changing as it receives input, throughputs it and issues output; so that I may eat cabbage, but I do not become cabbage-like – I remain me, while the cabbage is digested, gives me energy and nourishment and part of it is output through heat, activity and defecation
- *differentiation*, the idea that systems grow more complex with more different kinds of components over time
- *nonsummativity*, the idea that the whole is more than the sum of its parts
- *reciprocity*, the idea that if one part of a system changes, the change interacts with all the other parts which therefore also change.

As a result of reciprocity, systems exhibit both *equifinality* (you can reach the same result in several different ways) and *multifinality* (similar circumstances can lead to different results because the parts of the system interact in different ways). Social systems may possess *synergy* which means that they can create their own energy to maintain themselves. So, human beings interacting in a marriage or in a group often stimulate each other to maintain or strengthen relationships which build up bonds within the group and make it stronger; this is an example of nonsummativity, because these bonds could not be achieved without the interaction within the system. Without creating synergy, the group or marriage would have to be fed by outside energy or entropy would occur; thus, synergy negates entropy, which is why it is sometimes called *negentropy*.

Applying systems theory to social work practice: Pincus and Minahan

Pincus and Minahan (1973) offer an approach to social work which explicitly applies systems ideas. The principle of their approach is that people depend on systems in their immediate social environment for a satisfactory life, so social work must focus on such systems. Three kinds of system may help people:

- *informal or natural systems* such as family, friends, the postman or fellow workers
- *formal systems* such as community groups or trade unions
- *societal systems* such as hospitals or schools.

People with problems may not be able to use helping systems because:

- such systems may not exist in their lives, or have the necessary resources or be appropriate to their problem (e.g. an elderly lady may not have relatives or friendly neighbours, and so is without that kind of informal system)
- people may not know about or wish to use them (e.g. a child who is being abused by their parents may not know where to go for help, or may fear to go to the police or social services in case they are taken away from their parents, whom they love in spite of the abuse)
- the system's policies may create new problems for users (e.g. dependence, conflicting interests)
- the systems may conflict with one another.

Social work tries to see where elements in the interactions between clients and their environment are causing problems. Neither client nor environment are necessarily seen as having problems; it is the interaction between them that may be difficult. The aim is to help people perform life tasks, alleviate distress and achieve aims and value positions which are important to clients. 'Life task' means here activities in our lives which have meaning and importance for us, as it was in crisis theory (see Chapter 4).

Social workers are concerned with the relationship of 'private troubles' to 'public issues.' They look for and work on the general consequences of personal problems and the effect on individuals of more general issues. Social work tasks are:

- helping people to use and improve their own capacities to solve problems (e.g. learning new child-care skills to improve relationships in the family)
- building new connections between people and resource systems (e.g. helping a newly disabled man to feel happy about going to a local social centre, by introducing him carefully, and making sure he is welcomed and not rejected because of his disability)
- helping or modifying interactions between people and resource systems (e.g. helping a social security claimant present their case in such a way that it has a greater chance of success)
- improving interaction between people within resource systems (i.e. families, other agencies)
- helping develop and change social policy
- giving practical help
- acting as agents of social control.

Pincus and Minahan define four basic systems in social work which are set out in Table 6.1. Social work gains in clarity if workers analyse which system the people they are dealing with at any one time fall into.

Relationships between workers and others may be:

- *collaborative* where there is a shared purpose
- *bargaining* where agreement needs to be reached
- *conflictual* where their purposes are in opposition.

Again, it helps clarity to analyse the nature of the relationships with each of the systems, and to engage in relationships appropriately and honestly.

The social work process is seen as a series of phases with associated skills, and these are summarised in Table 6.2.

Ecological systems theory: the life model

Germain and Gitterman's (1980) 'life model' of social work practice is the major formulation of ecological systems theory;

Table 6.1 *Pincus and Minahan's basic social work systems*

System	Description	Further information
Change agent system	social workers and the organisations that they work in	
Client system	people, groups, families, communities who seek help and engage in working with the change agent system	*actual* clients have agreed to receive help and have engaged themselves; *potential* clients are those whom the worker is trying to engage (e.g. people on probation or being investigated for child abuse)
Target system	people whom the change agent system is trying to change to achieve its aims	client and target systems may or may not be the same
Action system	people with whom the change agent system works to achieve its aims	client, target and action systems may or may not be the same

Source: Pincus and Minahan (1973).

Germain has edited a collection of articles demonstrating its application across a range of social work (1979a). She argues that there are close parallels with ego psychology in the importance given to the environment, action, self-management and identity (Germain, 1978), although both sets of ideas are conceptually distinct and can be used without each other.

The life model sees people as constantly adapting in an interchange with many different aspects of their environment. They both change and are changed by the environment. Where we are able to develop through change and are supported in this by the environment, *reciprocal adaptation* exists. Social problems (e.g. poverty, discrimination, stigma) pollute the social environment reducing the possibility of reciprocal adaptation. Living systems (people individually and in groups) must try to maintain a good fit with their environment. We all need appropriate inputs (e.g. information, food, resources) to maintain ourselves and develop.

Where transactions upset the adaptive balance, stress results

Table 6.2 *Phases and associated skills in social work practice*

Phase	Activities	Skills and methods
Assessing problems	stating the problem	each problem has three parts, which should all be stated: social circumstances, people deciding that the circumstances are a problem, and the reasons for their decision
	analysing the systems	consider how they affect the social situation
	setting goals	include steps leading to the main goal; decide on feasibility and priorities among goals
	setting strategy	who is to be involved from each of the four basic systems?, points of entry to those systems and resources, relationships needed and difficulties expected
	stabilising the change effort	check on problems for client arising from changes and try to prevent them
Collecting data	questioning	verbally, in writing or using projective tests
	observation	watching client at home, in simulations, or using stimulating techniques (e.g. playing with anatomically correct dolls in child abuse cases)
	checking records	written, other formats, verbal
Making initial contacts	availability	being available to people in the client system
	contacting	get in touch with other parts of a system, having met one
	overcoming ambivalence	remove resistances to being helped
	promoting	demonstrate the value of the agency's work to the client system's aims
Negotiating contracts	primary	between worker and client system
	secondary	between worker and other systems
	defining content	important aims of each party, tasks each will perform; describe change process
	setting up good relationship	explain purposes of contract, make its terms clear, work out disagreements

Phase	Activities	Skills and methods
	dealing with resistance	involve other members of system or other systems (e.g. to remove fears about their reactions or prove that they will help), accept and acknowledge resistance, offer new information, encourage hope, set trial goals, use groups for collective influence
Forming action systems	deciding size and composition	e.g. client and worker only, client and family with worker, worker and other agency, client and worker with other agency
	operating procedures	length of contacts, time of meetings, frequency, place, rules of behaviour (e.g. permissive or controlled)
Maintaining and co-ordinating action systems	avoiding entropy of system	build up relationships well; make roles, communications, power, loyalties, attitudes, values and aims consistent; avoid changing roles, operating procedures, system activities, system changes, or else be explicit about such changes
Influencing action systems	affecting any parts of systems affects all other parts – multifinality	use knowledge and experience, material rewards and services, legitimate authority, established relationships, status, charisma and personal authority, control over information
Terminating the change effort	concluding evaluation	draw together evaluations of progress made during above activities
	separating from relationships stabilising change effort	

Source: Pincus and Minahan (1973).

and this produces problems in the *fit* between our needs and capacities and the environment. Stress arises from:

- *life transitions* (developmental changes, changes in status and role, restructuring of life space)

- *environmental pressures* (unequal opportunities, harsh and unresponsive organisations)
- *interpersonal processes* (exploitation, inconsistent expectations).

As in crisis theory, not all stressful events lead to actual stress. Whether they do so depends on personal and environmental circumstances and especially perceptions of the events (in this sense the life model stresses the importance of cognition and capacity to control the outside world).

The main aim of social work is '. . . to strengthen the adaptive capacities of people and to influence their environments so that transactions are more adaptive.' (Germain and Gitterman, 1980, p. 10) While this does include environmental change, the emphasis on adaptiveness illustrates the way ecological theories assume a fundamental social order, and rather play down possible radical social change.

Problems arise from transactions in people's life space being maladaptive. The client's view of the problem and the transactions should be considered. Empathy is important in entering the client's world. Each of the three areas of life problems may be dealt with simultaneously, but one may gain priority. The worker-client relationship is a transaction to which each brings other transactions (e.g. the worker-agency relationship; client relationships in the family). Three areas of transactional problems often arise in worker-client relationships:

- social definitions of role and status (e.g. the client's fear of the worker's class or official status)
- agency structure and functions (e.g. policies)
- professional perspectives (e.g. ethics).

The three phases of practice are initial, ongoing and ending. Assessment involves identifying objective and subjective facts, making hypotheses to be tested while remaining open to further information and responsive to the client's wishes. A wide variety of methods is used, directed towards improving adaptive capacity in people and the environment and improving interactions. There is an emphasis on the client's own capacity, self-direction and action.

In the *initial phase* the worker prepares by thinking over and researching theoretical understanding of the problem and by gaining emotional contact with the client's feelings and responses. Role-playing incidents leading to problems can help in empathic understanding, so that workers can identify with and incorporate the client's view into their understanding. Reverberation (remembering similar experiences in the worker's life) and awareness of personal feelings and reactions to the client are important. These emotional responses must be integrated with objective assessment.

For example, Harriet came to a social work agency complaining about her husband's violence towards her, and an interview was fixed with a specialist worker, with experience of these difficulties, thus delaying the initial response to her difficulties but ensuring that the first response would be well-informed and understanding. Harriet described in general terms her fear of the husband, but the worker could not get an idea of how these events arose, and acted out with her two or three events, to see if a pattern of interaction was apparent. This also gave her a clear picture of Harriet's distress. Details of the family and its children's needs were collected, as was information about income and possible help from Harriet's family and friends.

Different interactions may arise depending on whether the service is sought, offered or imposed. Where it is the latter, some degree of acceptance by the client is needed, and the early stages involve finding common ground. Clienthood only begins when the service is accepted and the agency agrees to give it. Where clients seek the services, workers provide a welcoming, courteous, supportive environment and encourage clients to 'tell their story'. Where the service is offered, it should be clearly explained and confusions of questions dealt with, before moving into how the agency may help.

Worker and client then reach agreement about the problem and what each is to do. They both contribute; reciprocal accountability should be defined. Concerns should be divided into:

- problems
- priorities
- commitments

Children may need a more responsive approach 'tuned' to their rhythm and enthusiasms. Adults often require more structured, cognitive work. The timescale and time structure of the process should be explored; people experience time differently, e.g. in attitudes to punctuality (Germain, 1976).

The *on-going phase* concentrates on change in one or more of the three areas of focus. Life transitions are experiences by everyone, corresponding with biological changes, and affected by social cultural expectations, constraints and opportunities. Transitions are often a source of stress but offer opportunities to stimulate *innate* adaptive mechanisms or learn *acquired* ones.

Cognitive development occurs in stages, and stress can arise from damage to or deprivation of cognitive development, or from conflict in cognitive styles (e.g. between the worker's and client's ways of thinking). Status changes and role demands also cause stress arising from different expectations among friends, family, organisations and institutions. Crisis events also cause stress because normal coping mechanisms cannot manage.

The worker's aim in working with *transitions* is to help people progress through them with undamaged or improved adaptive mechanisms. The worker's three roles are:

- *enabling* (e.g. strengthening the client's motivation, validating and supporting the client, helping to manage feelings)
- *teaching* (e.g. helping clients learn problem-solving skills, clarifying perceptions, offering appropriate information, modelling behaviour)
- *facilitating* (e.g. maintaining client's freedom of action from unreasonable constraints, defining the task, mobilising environmental supports).

In Harriet's case, for example, the worker discussed with her the various options and explored what each of them would be like; this disclosed Harriet's fear of confronting her violent husband, but also her anxiety about leaving and coping with the children on her own. The worker helped Harriet to work out precisely what she would do, and this enabling approach made Harriet more confident about taking on either option. Before deciding whether she would confront her husband, Harriet accepted some teaching through role play of ways in which she could do so appropriately, and the worker also acted to facilitate Harriet's decision by making tentative arrangements for her to retreat if need be to the local women's refuge.

In working with *environmental problems and needs*, the field of concern is the social and physical environments, including political and economic structures. The power of bureaucratic organisations, their system of status definition and structures and their socialisation of people into unhelpful attitudes can all obstruct clients' adaptation to their environment. Social networks are also important aspects of their environment. The physical environment includes the *natural* and the *built* worlds which affect opportunities and obstacles in our lives. For example, one elderly client of mine lived in a rural area some miles from the nearest shops in a small group of cottages with very uneven access roads. Although she was not particularly immobile, this isolation prevented her from managing as well as she would have been able to closer to town. Fortunately, there were several empty houses near her daughter, and we were able to arrange for her to rent one so that, although the move was difficult, she was able to manage again, being nearer the shops and her daughter's help.

Life experiences can often make clients feel that the world is unresponsive to their needs. In one case, two elderly clients discharged themselves from hospital in spite of considerable and life-threatening disabilities. On investigation, it was discovered that they were in different wards of the hospital which was divided into male and female wards, and they had not felt that it would be acceptable to trouble staff to arrange for them to visit each other and they wanted to be together. It proved possible to guarantee a daily period together, and they agreed to be readmitted. The worker must concentrate on the interface between clients and organisations and social networks and on aspects of the physical environment which cause stress. In this area of work the worker's roles are:

- *mediating* (e.g. helping the client and the system meet and deal with each other in rational and reciprocal ways, as in the hospital example above)
- *advocating* (e.g. pressurising other agencies or individuals to intervene, including taking up social action)
- *organising* (e.g. putting the client in contact with or creating new social networks).

In dealing with *maladaptive patterns of interpersonal relationships and communications*, the worker is dealing mainly with families, which organise a network of statuses and roles, and are also the place where basic survival needs are met (e.g. shelter, food, sex). Families have to develop communication mechanisms internally and with the outside world. The nuclear family and the structure and role of families in our lives applies many stresses. Similar issues arise in *formed groups* where clients come together in the agency to share work on a life task which they have in common.

In the *ending phase*, client and worker may be affected by a painful separation, and may need preparation and careful work to end successfully. The process is affected by time factors (e.g. if a client of a hospital worker is discharged suddenly), type of services (e.g. individual casework often leads to more intense relationships), and relationship factors (e.g. where the worker has played a parental role). Separation may also be affected by the worker's and client's previous experience of relationships and losses.

The worker should prepare by reviewing the client's previous experience of loss, and may need to work through stages of denial, negative feelings, sadness and a feeling of release and having made progress. An evaluation of progress by client and worker, sometimes as part of an agency review system, should be part of the ending phase.

Social workers should take responsibility for using information from their casework to take up social issues that arise from their cases with their agencies and more widely.

Networking and social support systems

One of the important developments of systems theories of all kinds is the analysis of networking in social support systems. This focuses on both planned formal support groups and on enabling 'informal' or 'natural' carers to help friends, neighbours and family members who are in need (Garbarino, 1983; Walton, 1986). Such work, according to Garbarino, can be either *personal* or *social*. Personal work uses the psychological strength and skills of clients, aiming to improve their competence by enabling self-help and empowerment. In this direction, networking has connections with social skills training and radical empowerment approaches (see Chapters 5 and 11). Social helping uses nurturing and feedback to stimulate clients' support systems. Both personal and social help seek to invest in clients who are enabled to become involved with a network and thus offer resources to others while being helped themselves. In conventional social work, clients are helped, and then move out of the helping system; in this approach they stay in the helping system to help others. The worker's role is as an intermediary between people, rather than concentrating on a relationship with the client and a few others. The aim is interdependence among the client and others rather than the independence of the client. The worker acts as a consultant rather than as a clinician and is empowering rather than being a simple provider of services.

Caplan's work (1974; Caplan and Killilea, 1976) in the mental health field used support systems for people coming out of institutions and is an important source for these ideas. It led to an influential study by Collins and Pancoast (1976) of attempts to support informal helpers of former mental patients. A variety of studies exist explicitly using general systems theory in relation to volunteer projects in local schools (Davies, 1977), ecological systems theory in several different projects (Whittaker and Garbarino, 1983), and competence in dealing with the environment (Maluccio, 1981).

Specht (1986) shows that social support applies to a wide range of social relationships and organisations, whereas social networks refer to a specific set of interrelated people. He argues that there is little evidence that there are untapped resources available in the community to support people with problems in the USA, and there is empirical support for this view in the UK (P. Abrams, 1980; Bulmer, 1987). E. Timms (1983) and Allan (1983) suggest that a supportive service to existing social networks is appropriate, but attempting to replace formal provision with informal care or to change the existing patterns of informal care is likely to be unsuccessful. This is confirmed by Cecil *et al.* (1987) in a study in Northern Ireland.

Commentary

Systems and ecological theories, with their attempts at structuring and their technical terminology, form a very different style of theory from traditional social work practice which emphasises individualisation and psychology. They are among the few comprehensive sociologically based theories of social work. Advantages of the systems approach are:

- a greater emphasis on changing the environment than psychological approaches
- it is interactive, concentrating on effects of one person on another, rather than on internal thoughts and feelings
- it alerts social workers to the possibility of alternative ways of achieving the same object (equi- and multi-finality) and reducing the stigma arising from diversity of behaviour and social organisation which some psychological theories – which concentrate on normality and deviance – tend to create (Leighninger, 1978)
- it is unitary (Goldstein, 1973), integrated (Pincus and Minahan, 1973) or holistic (G. Hearn, 1969, Leighninger, 1978), including work with individuals, groups and communities, and does not emphasise any particular method of intervention; instead it provides an overall way of describing things at any level, so that all interventions can be understood as affecting systems, and particular explanatory theories form part of this overarching universe; workers choose theories appropriate to any particular level of intervention with which they are involved and thus avoid sterile debates about whether social work should be concerned with individual change or social reform
- it avoids linear, deterministic cause-effect explanations of behaviour or social phenomena, because equi- and multi-finality show how lots of energy flows can affect systems in a wide variety of different ways; patterns of relationships and how boundaries are shared or *interface* with one another are important ideas.

There are, however, problems with such claims:

- it is expository rather than explanatory (Forder, 1976) so it sets out ideas in a novel way which makes them easier to grasp and it makes connections between different levels of society and individual behaviour, but it does not explain why things happen and why those connections exist; it is therefore hard to test empirically

- it is not prescriptive (Germain, 1979b, p. 6), so it does not tell us what to do, where or how, in order to affect systems (Mancoske, 1981); it also does not allow us to control the effects of interventions in a system, because we do not know how each part of it will interact with the others; it assumes that affecting one part of a system will affect other parts, but in practice this does not seem to happen (Siporin, 1980)
- it is over-inclusive; not everything is relevant and it does not help to decide what is; many things may not fit into a general schema, deciding on boundaries may be complex or impossible, and it may be assumed that things are related together in a system without checking to see if they actually are (Leighninger, 1978); in encouraging social workers to concentrate on the wide scale issues, it may lead to the neglect of the small scale and the personal (Siporin, 1980)
- systems (particularly ecological) theory may overstate the importance of integrating parts of the system and assume that all the parts of a system are needed to maintain it, and are or should be interrelated; it thus tends to assume that systems are or should be conserved, and should maintain equilibrium rather than change or be changed; also, systems theory tends to assume that conflict is less desirable than maintenance and integration, which may not be true in practice (Leighninger, 1978)
- the idea of feedback implies slow and manageable change, but what if radical change is needed? systems theory makes little provision for this and does not deal with the problem that feedback sometimes amplifies deviance rather than reduces it (Leighninger, 1978)
- the ideas of entropy and survival as aspects of systems are analogies with the behaviour of physical systems, and like many of the biological and physical analogies in systems theory, may not have a general application to all social systems (Leighninger, 1978); should all systems (e.g. families torn by strife) seek to survive? do they? should entropy be exported to the environment, or cause a system to leach energy from what may already be an environment poor in energy (e.g. should a poor family make demands on the resources of a poor neighbourhood, or should resources be redistributed from richer neighbourhoods?) Such questions

raise political issues that the model does not deal with, and it
seems to assume a local, non-political resolution when
applied to the daily round of social work

- it has a complex and technical language which does not fit
well with a human activity like social work (Germain, 1979b,
p. 6), and often alienates workers as a result; this is a
common criticism of borrowed technologies which systems
theory shares with behaviour modification; by contrast the
ideas of conflict, need and drive in psychodynamic theory, or
genuineness and alienation of humanist theory seem much
more attractive
- because it is a very generalised theory it is hard to apply to
any specific situations (Germain, 1979b, p. 7; Leighninger,
1978) and, on the other hand, applications might be very
variable; one worker might interpret a situation in one way,
another worker in another and it would be hard to judge
which is right.

As well as these practical criticisms, there are also ideological
doubts about systems theory. Many of these stem from criticisms
of social systems theory in sociology because of its structural–
functional perspective on society, and particularly that of Parsons
(Evans, 1976). Mancoske (1981, pp. 714–15) summarises these
criticisms as follows:

> Critics claim that Parsons' action theory is less a systems theory
> than a statics theory, it is not empirically verifiable as developed,
> and is so abstract and vague that concepts are undefinable. The
> emphasis of action theory is on function, not process of inter-
> action, and this negates the meaning of systems.

Mancoske argues that in its social work formulations, the criticism
of systems theory as static are weak, because usually considerable
attention is given to change, both individual and social. Evans
(1976) suggests that there is no logical connection between *social*
integration, which is about whether there is social harmony or
conflict in society, and *system* integration, which is about causal
links between different social structures, which may be conflictual
or change-oriented. In social work interpretations of systems
theory, however, and particularly that of Pincus and Minahan, he

argues that there is a hidden assumption that all systems are interdependent. This is only true of closed systems; open systems are much more flexible, and it is important to make the distinction clear. Leonard (1975a p. 48) writing from a Marxist perspective, argues that systems theory can help in understanding institutions, their interaction with one another, and how change might be brought about in a radical way, provided that the theory is not used simply to suggest that systems maintain themselves wholly stable. Siporin (1980) points to Marxist criticisms of systems theory which claim that it does not take account of the incompatibilities of class interest in capitalist societies and how these prevent any integration in such a society.

Germain and Gitterman's life model presents a fairly conventional mode of social work, with an unusual emphasis on adaptation, and is typical of recent developments in social work theory in being interactive or transactional in its approach, so that it deals with interactions between clients, workers and the environment rather than just personal change. Unlike Pincus and Minahan, the terminology and ideas of systems theory are much less evident, but clients and their worlds are treated as systems. It is less structured and comprehensive than Pincus and Minahan's work, and gives an impression of being more balanced between emotional, interpersonal and environmental factors. However, it is still subject to many of the criticisms of systems theory, and in particular its emphasis on adaptation may lead to assumptions that individuals should adapt to environments rather than vice-versa, so like behavioural approaches it can be criticised ethically that it tends to accede to social pressures on unwilling clients.

A competing model is the *eco-systems perspective* (Meyer, 1983). This is claimed to be more flexible than the life model, since it explicitly sets out to provide a framework for other explanatory theories, rather than creating its own problem categories, such as life transition, environmental obstacles and interpersonal processes. Greif (1986) claims that it has particular value as a widely applicable assessment tool. It also gives a greater emphasis to general systems theory than to ecology.

Devore (1983) argues that the life model is better at dealing with social class, ethnic and cultural differences and life style than many other theories, but still lacks specificity in dealing with issues affecting black people.

Siporin (1980) criticises Germain for trying to distinguish between ecological, ego psychology and exchange theory, when he considers that an integration of these perspectives which have relationships should be attempted. He also complains about Germain's adherence to a medical model of social problems and social functioning which is inappropriate in ecological theory, which offers multiple causes and interactions as the origins of clients' difficulties. It also fails, he considers, to concern itself with social reform.

Radical, advocacy and empowerment theories are the other major sociological theories of social work, but social psychological, role and communications theory offer a more social psychological approach to social work activity, and the next chapter is concerned with these.

7

Social Psychological and Communication Models

Connections

A number of ideas which are well-used in social work originate from sociological and social psychological theories. Particularly important are concepts from role theory, the idea of labelling and the whole area of social psychological research into human interactions. Breakwell and Rowett (1982) propose a social psychological approach to social work which emphasises in particular material on social and personal change, how relationships are formed and managed by people in social situations and how issues of identity are related to matters such as stigma, group behaviour, the effects of environments, territory, and the need for personal space. The ideas of Kelly's personal construct theory propose that people manage their behaviour according to 'constructs' in their mind about how to behave, which have been developed from past experience; we construct events differently from each other and looking at and changing people's constructs may help to change behaviour. This approach may also be a useful way of understanding social interactions (Tully, 1976), and has relationships with phenomenological and existential ideas, considered in the next Chapter, which proclaim the variety of interpretations that are possible of the personal and social world.

An important range of ideas have also come from microteaching of personal and social skills (Kurtz and Marshall, 1982) which we have already encountered in relation to social skills training in behavioural approaches to social work. Similar ideas have also grown up around the development of counselling through the work of Rogers and Carkhuff (see Chapter 8) using experiential techniques; these give clients a better chance of practical learning of some of the skills that counsellors are helping them acquire. Microtraining grew up to offer a practical basis for using such techniques among helping professions. It includes the use of video for viewing actual behaviours, and detailed attention to feedback on specific behaviours. (Kurtz and Marshall, 1982).

Role theory

Writers such as Strean (1971) and Davis (1986) stress the contribution of sociological and social psychological insights for social work, while Perlman (1968) considers that 'social role' is a useful concept for understanding relationships and personality with which social workers are concerned. Because role theory is about our interactions with others and how their expectations and reactions cause us to respond in characteristic ways, she argues that it is a form of social explanation which complements psychological understanding of personality. Perlman emphasises work, family and parental roles as determinants of personality and behaviour, showing how traditional social work theory emphasises these social institutions. Biddle and Thomas (1979) forms an extensive collection of useful articles on role theory and research.

Role theory is related to and part of structural-functional theory in sociology. It assumes that people occupy positions in social structures and each position has a role associated with it. The role is the set of expectations or behaviours associated with a position in the social structure, and the idea implies that roles are always to be considered in the context of relationships, since it is only in relationships that roles can be identified (Munson and Balgopal, 1978). In some sense, roles create our identity as others see it, and because of this they tend to build up our own concept of our identity (Ruddock, 1969). Roles may derive from our own expectations or those of others. They may be *ascribed* to us as a result of some circumstance (e.g. being a woman or black or disabled) or *attained* by us through something that we have done (e.g. being a writer or Member of Parliament). A *role-set* is a collection of roles which go together with a particular social position; you cannot occupy that position without having some or most of those roles. So if you are a father, you are often expected also to be the main wage-earner in a family, the disciplinarian of your children, and you are usually also a husband, son-in-law, and may well be a brother-in-law and grandfather as well. How we see our roles affects how well we manage change. Howard and Johnson (1985) give the example of single-parent families, where American research has found that people with traditional assumptions about the role that they will play in marriage find it harder to adjust to being a lone parent than those who have experienced role flexibility in their marriage.

Role *complementarity* exists when roles, behaviour and expectations all fit together well with the expectations of surrounding people. Role *conflict* exists when one role is incompatible with another role. *Inter-role* conflict occurs when different roles held by one person are incompatible. *Intra-role* conflict occurs when expectations from different people of the same role disagree. Role *ambiguity* arises when there is uncertainty about what a particular role entails. One of the difficulties of social work is that in order to maintain the special features of the professional relationship, workers separate to some extent their own personal attitudes and behaviour from the behaviour expected in a professional role, and there has been debate about how this may be balanced with a trend to greater equality and openness in relationships with clients (Munson and Balgopal, 1978). One of the problems is that this form of *role distance*, which may be professionally appropriate, may be mistaken by clients or other observers, for a distaste for occupying the role, which is a more common reason for people having role distance (Ruddock, 1969, p. 14).

The value of these ideas is that some behaviour can be understood as role conflicts and uncertainties. This is easy for clients to understand, it does not criticise them in a personal way, and so it is easy to intervene and create change. Moreover, role theory takes in a social perspective on behaviour, so it is a useful link between behaviour problems and social environment.

For example, Clare, a middle-aged woman, was working as a secretary, having been divorced by her husband and having brought up her two children successfully alone. Her elderly mother, also alone, suffered from failing sight, was registered as blind and later had a fall in her home. The doctor to both families suggested that they should live together, and Clare would provide greater care for her mother. This arrangement turned out to be stressful and difficult and a social worker was asked to help. Using ideas from role theory helped to explain that there was role conflict here between Clare's working role, which was important for her self-esteem (this is often the case with work), and her role as a caring daughter. This was both inter-role conflict, because work and daughter roles conflicted, and intra-role conflict, because it appeared that the mother's expectations about the role of a caring daughter conflicted with Clare's and, indeed, those of the doctor and Clare's daughter who still lived at home. Looking more deeply into the situation, Clare was suffering from role ambiguity; because she understood and appreciated all these views of what her role as daughter should be, she was herself uncertain about how she should behave.

In this example, we can see how role theory can clarify what is going on in a situation, without blaming individuals or criticising their behaviour or thoughts. However, proponents of more psychological ideas would criticise this approach for neglecting to deal with the strong feelings which might arise and prevent people from actually changing their behaviour or resolving the conflicts revealed. Ruddock (1969) argues that role theory is insufficient to explain particular behaviour on its own; many other forms of explanation are required alongside it. Nonetheless, it is a useful concept, in his view, for linking explanations of behaviour with social factors.

This approach can also be criticised from a radical perspective because it fails to emphasise wider social pressures leading to the oppression of women as carers, when social provision to help them accept their responsibilities is not available. Also, women's roles as carers, in a Marxist perspective, relates to their position as a reserve pool of labour in society, to be made available if there is not enough male labour, and as the centre of families reproducing oppressive capitalist social relations in which unsupported, exploitative expectations of daughters exist.

So, while role theory helps to explain how social patterns affect individual clients, its structural-functional approach tends to lead to the assumption that the roles exist and are a necessary part of the pattern of society, without leading us to question whether those patterns are appropriate and might be changed for the benefit of clients and society more generally. Moreover, role theory may not offer the means of intervention in the situation because it does not provide techniques for behaviour change and dealing with emotions and personal responses to role conflicts – it merely makes them apparent.

Another way of looking at roles exists, which is typified by the work of Goffman (1968b). In social interaction, people need to find out about others, and they do so by picking up signs from others' behaviour. This makes it possible for us to influence others' views of us by managing the information they receive from us; we give 'performances' designed to give an appropriate impression. Roles, in this view, are 'enactments' of the social expectations attached to a social status. We may have a number of parts (the dramatic analogy is intentional) in the performance of a role, and we may act different parts in different situations. Our performance is usually 'idealised' so that it includes common social expectations. Some aspects of the role are emphasised, others concealed. So, in another famous book, Goffman (1968a) is concerned with how stigmatised people manage the impressions other people get of that aspect of them which is socially disapproved, so that they can 'pass' as relatively normal. People often work together in 'teams' to share the responsibility, particularly in organisations, of enacting socially approved roles, and they can share behaviour which is not in role 'backstage' as a relief when they do not have to put up a front. In a series of books, Goffman (1972a, b, c) extends these ideas into a comprehensive analysis of how socially expected roles can explain many different forms of behaviour.

These ideas relate to symbolic interactionism (see Chapter 8); they emphasise how roles are formed by social expectations and *labelling*, and emphasise that we alter our behaviour in roles according to the situation we are in and the expectations of those around us. We are sometimes labelled with roles that we have occupied, whether or not we still actually occupy those roles. Thus, someone who is mentally ill comes to be treated as such even though they are fully recovered. These ideas are useful to social workers because many of their clients are stigmatised by having problems or physical and mental conditions which are disapproved by others. We shall see in the next chapter that writers such as Laing have extended such ideas as far as proposing that some mental illness can be understood as bizarre behaviour which is a rational, understandable response to unusual social pressures.

While such views are not supported by empirical evidence, they alert us to how significant social expectations may be in the creation of extreme behaviour difficulties.

Labelling originates from the work of Lemert (1972) and Becker (1963). According to Lemert, most people occasionally act in a deviant way, and the crucial issue is the response of the surrounding social environment to that act. Sometimes, people are put through a social system which labels them as deviant or criminal. Once labelled, they are likely to live up to the social expectations of their label, and to be encouraged to act in more deviant ways; this leads to an even stronger labelling process. Becker shows how social groups create deviance by making rules and deciding who they are applied to, labelling them as 'outsiders' to normal social life. 'Moral panics' (Cohen, 1972) about particular forms of deviance, such as hooliganism or rowdy behaviour at sports events, mean that social concern about that form of deviance rises and strengthens the labelling process which in turn imprisons people in the expectation that they will be deviant and encourages deviant behaviour.

For example, John was an adolescent boy from an inner-city area, who as a keen supporter of the local football team, went with a group of friends to a game, and was arrested for rowdy behaviour in the town centre. With a minor criminal record, he was encouraged by social pressures to show off in other ways, to live up to his 'criminal' standing in the eyes of his friends. This led to a number of other daring exploits, which came to the notice of the police, particularly because, being black, he was easily identifiable. Having gained a local reputation for being 'bad', he was excluded from the local youth club, and spent more time on the street, with others who had been similarly excluded. This led to further offending. Eventually, court proceedings led to social work involvement. By exploring this history, the worker could see the process by which he had become separated and alienated from a more conventional social background, and steps could be taken to reintegrate him into less deviant social settings, such as another youth club, and help him find acceptable and status-enhancing activities – membership of a local band.

This approach still suffers from the weakness of sociological theories of this type that, while it acknowledges rather better than many versions of role theory the alienating effect of oppressive interventions by authoritative agents of the state, such as teachers, youth leaders and the police, it does not help to change attitudes and patterns of behaviour which may be quite well-established. Also, it tends to accept conventional social responses to the behaviour, at the same time assuming that behaviour is in essence socially created, which, if it were true, would mean that conventions would have little force. These ideas thus fail to question the social circumstances which lead to deviance and alienation in the first place, and how the power of agencies such as the police and courts is crucial in creating deviance among some social (mainly working class) groups and not among others.

Their value as ideas, however, is that they draw attention to the part official agencies, such as the ones in which social workers operate, may play in the social creation of the problems they are set up to deal with, and the need to take care in assessing and providing services to avoid stigmatising systems and behaviour (Levy, 1981). There is some research evidence which suggests that social workers tend to label clients negatively (Case and Lingerfelt, 1974; Gingerich *et al.*, 1982).

Communication theory in social work

One type of social psychological theory which does help us to decide on appropriate direct interventions with clients is communication theory. It brings together a number of psychological studies, particularly of a group of psychologists and therapists in Palo Alto, California, of whom the best known is possibly Satir (1964, 1972) whose work is about the complexities of human interaction particularly through speech and in attempts to change patterns of behaviour; and the work of anthropologists and social psychologists such as Birdwhistell (1973), Scheflen (1972; Scheflen and Ashcraft, 1976) and Hall (1966) who are concerned with the micro-level of detailed physical movements associated with communication, and broader cultural issues such as territoriality, personal space and also proxemics, which is about how physical closeness and related factors affect relationships. Related to this work is the theory of neuro-linguistic programming (MacLean, 1986) which originates from the detailed study of the language interactions of therapists.

Nelson, (1980, 1986) argues that communication theory can offer a useful connection between many theories of social work. Much of the energy which maintains the equilibrium of a system, such as an individual, family or social group, consists of information and reactions to it. Many theories of personality which are used in social work, such as ego psychology, are concerned with how the individual processes reality, and this too relies on communication. Behavioural theories, similarly, rely on people's capacity to understand the patterns of their behaviour; cognitive theorists are concerned with how reality is perceived and interpreted. Nelson would say, therefore, that communication is an essential part of any social worker's understanding and communication theory and research has established knowledge and a framework for such understanding.

Nelson's (1980) book applies communication theory which has been developed elsewhere to social work in general, rather than, as with some family therapy texts, to a particular form of therapy. It is, therefore, used as the basis of the account given here. The starting point of communication theory, according to Nelson, is that when we take some action, we always do so in response to some information that we have received. Information might be facts, or other things that may have been learned, such as emotion, memories, bodily sensations or an idea about how someone feels about you. We perceive the information, and then we evaluate it; this is information processing. As we evaluate communications, we give *feedback* to the communicator, who thus gains some idea of how we have perceived and evaluated the communication. We came across this idea when discussing systems theory. We all have our own internal rules for processing information, which cause us to give importance to some things and not to others; this leads to *selective perception.*

So, for example, a young mother with two toddlers had found the younger child difficult to manage as a baby – he had cried a lot and disturbed her. She gained a perception of him as difficult, and interpreted behaviour from him which was aimed at getting her attention and love as a continuation of his disturbing early behaviour. Similar behaviour from her elder daughter was accepted. The boy responded to the rejection of his attention-seeking behaviour by becoming more demanding, thus reinforcing her perception of him, and she came to see all his behaviour as difficult, selecting out from his repertoire of behaviour the bad or difficult things and not noticing behaviour which would ordinarily have been acceptable. So, selective perception and the feedback from it reinforced a cycle in which his behaviour became more demanding causing her in turn to become more rejecting. While such understanding can be useful in practice by showing what is happening and how it might be possible to intervene, from a psychodynamic perspective, it might be argued that it fails to take into account what emotional or unconscious pressures caused her to have her initial selective perception. Therefore, from this viewpoint, action to interrupt the cycle of behaviour might not help because the psychological forces causing the inappropriate perceptions are not dealt with. This approach might also ignore important factors in the situation; a women-centred approach, for example, would undoubtedly look at the expectations of mother-hood, and the factor of the different sexes of the children.

Many people have problems with communication, because they perceive information badly or what they select is hard for others to understand, because their evaluation is poor, because they do not give feedback which others understand well or because they do not perceive the feedback that others give them very well. These problems, called an *information processing block*, often lead to difficulties in relationships.

Some communication is *verbal*; giving feedback to show that we are listening to verbal communication can be comforting to speakers. *Non-verbal* communication, such as how we hold our bodies or move, or how close we sit also gives information to others. *Metacommunication* is discussion about the nature of the relationship between people.

We are all always communicating; even silence or absence is communication, because someone else is interpreting it. All communication must be evaluated within its context; behaviour which is strange in one place at one time, would be perfectly normal at another. For example, I was once asked to see a client who was behaving in a disturbed manner by a doctor who had seen her in an emergency; he thought she was mentally ill. When I enquired into the events of the previous few hours, I discovered that her husband had declared his homosexuality and left her to live with a man and she was understandably distressed. Her distress mimicked the symptoms of mania, and by failing to explore the context the doctor had misunderstood the communication.

Learning and change come from communication. Early attempts at learning are by trial and error, and receiving feedback about our efforts. Poor feedback or poor perception and evaluation may mean poor learning. Also communicated to us in very complex ways is a whole culture about what we should perceive and how we should interpret it, and this forms a very important part of our lives.

Most communication forms *patterns*. People become accustomed to a fairly balanced and predictable way of communicating between those that they regularly have contact with. This forms the basis of their relationship. We saw this in the case of the mother and her 'difficult' son. Communication always has *content* which is its surface material, but in a relationship, the metacommunication may give added or different meanings to the apparent content. The way in which content is presented offers a proposal of a certain sort of relationship. So, the way a worker behaves towards a client says something about how the relationship between them is expected to be. Patterns of communication often express power, domination or subordination and when considering more radical forms of social work in later Chapters, it is important to note how communication theory may help us to identify oppression and inequality.

Communication theory is especially about control in relationships. *Symmetrical* relationships are equal, and the people concerned behave similarly towards one another. *Complementary* relationships are unequal, but each contributes a particular role within the interaction; as in an employer-employee relationship. Most relationships contain elements of both these types, but lean towards one or the other. Successful relationships vary between the two tendencies; this includes worker/client relationships since a worker should never be always in control. *Metacomplementary* relationships exist where one person lets go of power or forces the other to take it. This happens, for instance, when a social worker tries to get a client to make decisions in the process of their work together. *Symmetrical escalation* occurs when both sides of the relationship (all or several sides in a group or a family) keep trying to cap one another in an effort to gain or give up power. Understanding such behaviour helps workers to identify gender, ethnic, and other power inequalities.

All communication involves giving *messages* to which a *response* is given; both messages and responses carry content and relationship communications, usually at the same time. Responses may be *accepting*, *rejecting* of the content or relationship material in the message, or may be *selective*. Workers need to be aware of responses to their communications by clients; such responses may be verbal or non-verbal, and sometimes the messages given by one may conflict with those given by the other.

Much use is made in social work using communication theory of the idea of *paradox*. The idea of this is that some forms of difficult behaviour occur as people try to gain power in a relationship. If the power is given freely, the person giving the power gains the ascendency, so there is no point in using the difficult behaviour, which should then go away. So, if a client is aggressive, and the worker sits back and allows the aggression to be poured out in the worker-client relationship, the worker gains the power. Aggression does not work for this client any longer. This can be taken further by setting clients tasks using paradoxes. For instance, a man who constantly ignores his wife can be set the task of doing so every evening for an hour.

Similar points may be made about communication in small social systems such as groups and families. Patterns of communication give evidence of *operating rules* within the group. When some sort of upset in the equilibrium of the group arises, the rules (reflected in communication patterns) are brought into play. People newly in a group have to work out operating rules between themselves, and these then become patterns of behaviour and communication. So, one member may be the one who shows the anger, or takes the lead in making decisions. Workers dealing with established groups can affect how they work by trying to change the operating rules. In a system, giving information introduces energy which will affect the whole system, so persuading one group member to behave and communicate in a different way, or getting all or some members to agree about how they will act, should produce wider change as all the elements of the system become affected. Operating rules are often about sexuality, power, dependence, assertiveness and separateness. As with all systems theory, however, this approach can be criticised because it does not help us to be precise about what change will bring the desired result. We can see that some change will result from affecting the system, but with all the complex interactions, some unintended results may occur.

People often bring operating rules into groups and families that they have learned in relationships elsewhere. So, relationships in the past affect those in the present. The environment, culture and communication in a group affect relationships, which then affect other relationships, which go on to create a culture about appropriate behaviour in relationships. There is a cycle in which communication connects present, past, relationships and environment in a complex way. *First-order change* is the constant alterations in contacts and relationships between people as they go about their lives; it does not affect the system of culture and environment around them. *Second-order change* in the wider system only takes place as the operating rules change. If it is to happen, people in the system have to change their patterns of communication and relationship. If they find this difficult, the worker may have to attempt contextual changes to create the energy for progress to be made. First-order changes will not help if second-order changes are required. For example, if a father brings to a family a pattern in which he is unloved, and has an inappropriately sexual relationship with a daughter as a result, it might be possible to change the communication patterns so that he learns that this is inappropriate. However, if nothing is done about the acceptance in the family that he is unloved, and that his wife's communication of being loving is not enough for him, the pattern of sexual behaviour might repeat itself with another daughter.

Communication theory is particularly useful in *initial interviews*, where new relationship patterns are becoming established, and so communication is at a premium. Context is very important; as we saw in Chapter 1, clients often come with perceptions of what is appropriate in a social work agency gained from the social context outside. In particular, they often arrive assuming that they are inferior in a power relationship. Social contexts, such as a low-status office or scruffy waiting room may make them feel more inferior. The content of initial communications will be about gaining useful information, but there will also be proposals about suitable relationship patterns. Much of this will be about the power of the parties and it is up to the worker to establish the appropriate pattern. In group and family work these initial establishing proposals will be made among group members as well as with the worker.

In *assessment*, workers should consider the information that clients are using to decide on their behaviour, its sources, its communication and what blocks may have got in the way of processing that information appropriately. Clients are at risk when blocks exist. The blocks may be internal, such as immense emotions or poverty leading to hunger, or external, being concerned with social relationships in the present or the past. Likely patterns of relationship and communication in the client's environment must be examined, and the operating rules of their family or other systems may be relevant. The possible need for second-order change must be examined. One way of doing this is to look for the typical pattern of behaviour in operating rules when the worker proposes some change.

Sources of information should be checked against each other; they may be the client's answers to questions about specific events in the present, judgements about likely information affecting the client (such as knowledge of widespread racial prejudice), and information from theory, research and experience about things which commonly affect clients. How well the client processes information should also be checked as the worker gains responses from message given.

During the process of *intervention*, the worker operates at the content level in four ways:

- gaining information, using questions and an encouraging manner, and reframing clients' comments to show understanding of them
- giving feedback, showing how the worker evaluates what the client says – accepting, rejecting, neutral or selective
- giving information, including material which explains why the worker is acting as he is, so that waiting until the worker hears the full story is not seen as rejecting
- changing information coming to clients from elsewhere, to affect information which conflicts or is likely to be overwhelming or inaccurate.

Most communications are more acceptable and therefore likely to be more effective if they are fairly close to the client's expectations; work should proceed in small steps. This also applies to relationship proposals and negotiation; the style of relationship should proceed in stages from what the client finds acceptable. The relationship will be complementary with children, less so with adolescents and tend towards symmetry with adults. So, working with very young children in trouble with the police, I often treated them fairly directively, and, while consulting them, made active suggestions about things that they should do, or specific arrangements for activities which would avoid patterns of delinquent behaviour. With older adolescents, my approach was rather more to offer a series of acceptable options for intervention, and discuss the pros and cons of the alternatives. With adult offenders, I would help them construct their alternatives for themselves.

Sometimes blocks occur between worker and client, when either content or relationship information proposed by one is rejected by the other, and the first misses the response which shows that this has happened. This can be prevented by paying careful attention to both content and relationship information and verbal and non-verbal communications. When it happens both the missed response and the rejected information must be made apparent. Clients should be encouraged to make explicit when they disagree with or dislike a communication, thus learning to make appropriate feedback. Often, however, clients may not be clear about blocks, and workers must look out for uncertain or unclear responses. Over a period of working together, relationship operating rules should become (explicitly) more flexible and symmetrical. On several occasions, for example, I have found it useful to discuss with clients how we have gone about dealing with problems; how I have tended to behave towards them and why I think it is appropriate. I have found that when asked to describe the typical way I work, many clients have a fairly good idea from experience how I help interviews to progress, and what my reactions will be to certain things that they will say. This is typical of many social relationships, and, as we have seen, these expectations of patterns will condition how people respond. This may be unhelpful; clients can conceal information which will not be acceptable, for example. But it also sets a model of behaviour which, if it is useful, clients can follow.

Some blocks may arise from misunderstanding; those due to class or racial differences, for instance. Others come from either side having inadequate information. These can often be sorted out by careful information-giving. More difficult problems may arise where the client's information from sources who have powerful influences conflicts with the worker's communication; or when the worker offers communications which the client is not ready to receive or which do not help. Sometimes, for example, potentially useful information offered by the worker fails to help the client because help is also needed in processing it, by advising the client how it might be used in practice or how it could affect important relationships.

In these more difficult situations, workers must *withhold participation* in the blocking, but be neutral while discovering more about the issue, and then by *accepting negative responses* from the client, help the client to provide better communication by demonstrating that rejection is acceptable. It may be possible to compromise by accepting some of the client's negative response, and re-offering part of the proposal which led to it which would be acceptable. One of the best ways of dealing with blocks is to use metacommunication and to discuss the relationship consequences of the interaction. Paradox may also help. Another possible intervention is by changing the environment; changing from home visits or office interviews, or involving other members of the client's family or social groups. Communication theory can also be useful in *interprofessional practice*. Contacts with colleagues may be made more useful to clients by positive feedback, clear communication of content and appropriate metacommunication within professional relationships.

Commentary

The advantages of this model are that it is relatively easily understood, at least in general principle, universally applicable, and based on a long and fairly rigorous research tradition. It fits with many other theories of social work practice. Workers who would use other explanatory psychological or sociological theories could also use communication concepts. They may be applied either to assist in clarifying interactions in practice, or as a form of explanation for the minutiae of human problems. In the first case, the theories, and the research which lies behind them, give practical help in controlling interactions with clients and learning a technology of interviewing and interpersonal skills. A fairly extensive practice of 'microteaching' of intervention techniques has grown up, and this is widely used, even if it is not applied to interventions which rely on communications theory as a way of explaining where clients' problems originate from. The model encourages workers to pay attention to important aspects of behaviour which they otherwise might ignore or play down. It also offers fairly specific research backing for its information about communication behaviour, to set against more imaginative constructions about behaviour available in some psychological or sociological theories.

In the second case, workers who generally rely on broad-ranging theories of explanation appreciate having the fairly small-scale explanations of problems in interpersonal relationships to add to wider-range theories. Communications theory is relatively neutral in major ideological debates between, for example, behaviourists and psychoanalysts or Marxists and functionalists, for this reason. It accepts a role for environment, and also for internal thinking and emotions. We have seen, however, that it may not always emphasise sufficiently, and permit intervention in, the emotional and social origins of behaviour.

The problems with communications theory, however, lie in its concentration on the style and nature of the interactions rather than the content. While content is said to be important, how to assess it is not well articulated. It falls foul of the same sort of criticisms which might be made of psychoanalysis – that it encourages workers to look for inferred thoughts and problems behind difficulties expressly presented by clients. The worker is taken to be relatively competent, compared with the client, and may be seen as a manipulative and devious figure. One feature of the model, the use of paradox, particularly gives rise to this criticism. Compared with psychoanalysis, however, interaction with clients is relatively open in a communication model.

With the practical problems which many clients face, communication models have little to offer. Contacts with other agencies, and competence in everyday life may be enhanced for the client, but different techniques are presumably needed to gain social security entitlements.

8

Humanist and Existential Models

Connections

Humanism and existentialism are ways of looking at life. While they have specific philosophical meanings, in social work theory models of practice with certain features tend to be grouped together as humanist. These models have in common ideas that human beings are trying to make sense of the world that they experience, that social workers are trying to help people gain the skills to explore themselves and the personal meaning that they attach to the world they perceive and which affects them, and that their interpretations of their own selves are valid and worthwhile.

They are important because well-known systems of practice and writers in social work and related fields are regarded as humanist or existentialist and their ideas have filtered into more general use. Examples are Laing's views of mental health, Rogers' client- (more recently person-) centred therapy, and a variety of writers such as Brandon and Keefe on thought systems such as zen and meditation and the gestalt therapy of Perls *et al.* (1973). One writer in social work, Krill, has devised a model of practice derived from existential and humanist ideas, which is presented later in this chapter as an example of such approaches.

Some humanist influences on social work

Carl *Rogers* (1951, 1961; Rogers and Strauss, 1967) is probably the most important humanist writer on therapy to have an influence on social work. His impact is, however, indirect, since his greatest significance is in the related field of counselling, and it is social workers' involvement in counselling work and training that has moved his ideas into social work. Another significant influence is his formulation of the conditions necessary (and he would say sufficient but this is not supported by evidence according to Patterson, 1986) to successful therapy. These are that *clients should perceive* that workers:

- are *genuine and congruent* in their therapeutic relationship (i.e. what they say and do reflects their personality and real attitudes and is not put on to influence clients)
- have *unconditional positive regard* for the client
- should *empathise* with clients' views of the world.

These ideas have been adapted by Carkhuff and his associates (Truax and Carkhuff, 1967; Carkhuff and Berenson, 1977) into more general concepts of, first, honesty and genuineness; second, (sometimes non-possessive) warmth, respect, acceptance; and third, empathic understanding. Carkhuff's work proposes scales by which the extent of these in a therapeutic relationship may be assessed, and there has been empirical work confirming that these are the effective elements in therapeutic relationships. This has led to Rogers' influence on social work through development of understanding of the relationship and effective elements within it. Since, as I have argued in Chapter 1, this is a central and crucial aspect of social work, this impact is significant.

The worker's approach, according to Rogers, should be non-directive, nonjudgemental and, in later formulations should involve 'active listening', 'accurate empathy' and 'authentic friend-ship'. Rogers' early work is broadly psychodynamic (Rowe, 1986, quoting Hart), but developed a humanist perspective concentrating on the importance of the 'self' seeking personal growth. There is an emhasis on the 'here-and-now' rather than on the history of clients' problems, and because of the belief in clients' uniqueness, diagnosis and classification of conditions are not accepted. Everyone must be treated as an individual. Rogers' later ideas extended into taking up these humanist ideas in community work, in organisations and in political change. He proposes that people should be enabled to take up their 'personal power' which we all possess to achieve their objectives (Rogers, 1977).

In addition to Rogers' work, there are a variety of humanist psychologies and therapies which were influential in the 1960s and 1970s. Carkhuff and Berenson (1977) suggest that five ideas characterise them all:

- we can only understand ourselves in relation to others
- our main anxiety in life is losing others and being alone
- we are guilty because we cannot achieve a creative life
- we alone have responsibility to act on our own decisions
- therapy aims to help us act and accept freedom and responsibility in doing so.

Many ideas in humanistic psychology derive from Maslow's concern for 'self-actualisation' and the attainment of 'human potential.' (Maslow, 1970) Maslow's basic theory, like psychoanalysis, supposes that the motivation to act for such purposes comes from a need which derives from something that we are lacking. Frankl's logotherapy is typical in emphasising that we must each find our own meaning in life (Arnold and Gasson, 1979). Some writers (e.g. Keefe, 1986) have promoted meditation as a way of exploring oneself and one's potential, and in increasing workers' capability to be empathetic with and conscious of clients' needs.

Brandon (1976) offers zen ideas as a useful contribution to social work. His is an intense and personal vision in which workers should use all the elements of their personality to arrive at an authentic inter-relationship with people in distress. Unlike many humanistic approaches to therapy, which have been criticised as being therapies only for the mildly disturbed seeking greater personal fulfilment, he seeks to approach people in extreme difficulties. Work is directed towards self-understanding, enlightenment (the zen concepts is *satori*, a leap towards intuitive understanding) and self-growth for both worker and client. An important concept is 'hindering' the client's movement towards self-development, and enabling clients to avoid the many features of their environments which do so. Brandon's is an attractive approach relying on personal charisma and genuine sharing between clients and workers.

A number of writers, among whom England (1986) is recently pre-eminent, argue that social work should be seen as an artistic

endeavour rather than as an application of social science. Black
and Enos (1981) claim that phenomenological ideas validate this
approach, since phenomenology argues that human behaviour can
only be understood from the viewpoint of the people involved, and
methods are required to explore and understand individual view-
points. England extends this into a humanist theory of social work,
based around the ideas of 'coping' (a concept important in ego
psychology) and 'meaning.' Many of the problems presented by
clients are seen as being concerned with managing the interaction
between the client's internal and external resources and the world
whose pressures have to be coped with. Clients' coping capacity is
a major factor in social work assessments and attempts to change
clients' positions. Treating clients as individuals and understanding
them, among the important aspects of social work identified in
Chapter 1, are seen as a process of attaching meaning to the
client's experiences and ways of living. As in the personal construct theory, how we, clients, and others around them, attach
meaning to events crucially affects how they will deal with them.
An important way of understanding and attaching meaning to
aspects of clients' lives is our 'intuition', which involves using our
self in an attempt to 'make sense' of clients' experiences. He
claims that Curnock and Hardiker's work (1979), which we have
looked at in Chapter 2 in the context of showing that social
workers use theoretical concepts, but in an inexplicit way, also
shows that we create our own personal models of social work from
a heterogeneous collection of ideas, primarily formed around our
own sense of meaning. The idea of making sense, also relates to
the importance of advocacy, as considered in Chapter 1, as a way
of humanising and interpreting clients as worthwhile parts of
society.

Such approaches can be used to understand not only interactions and the needs of clients, but the organisations within which
social workers operate, and their own needs as workers. England
(1986) argues that social sciences as a means of understanding and
bureaucratic management as a way of organising are inadequate to
represent the full role of social work; effective explanations of how
social work should be undertaken using ideas of 'making sense'
could provide a basis for a clearer definition of organisational
needs. McNamara (1976) gives the example of a practical programme in a hospital setting using humanistic approaches to high-

light a multi-disciplinary team's self-awareness and sensitivity to clients' needs.

Laing (1965, 1971) explicitly uses existential ideas as well as psychoanalysis in his early work on theories of mental illness which have had some influence in social work, particularly in the UK. In later work he became more radical and mystical (Sedgwick, 1972). His important work is on schizophrenia, and argues that this major psychotic mental illness can be understood as a person's reaction to an incomprehensible or possibly damaging social environment. He gives great importance to the 'self' in his discussion of the 'false-self system' and self-consciousness. Later, he picked up the ideas of communication theories in the family, in particular the *double-bind* of Bateson *et al.* (1956), to propose that disturbances in communications within families lead to one family member being caught between conflicting demands from others, leading to disturbed reactions diagnosed as schizophrenia. Laing interprets their thought disorders as alienation and depersonalisation arising from their experiences in their environment and relationships which 'disconfirm' their own understandings of their experience, when we all need confirmation of our interpretations of what happens to us. From this brief account, it is evident that many of Laing's ideas reflect a phenomenological approach (Collier, 1977) in which how people understand and interpret the world is considered important to an analysis of their behaviour and its social importance. This, in turn, is related to phenomenological and symbolic interactional ideas in sociology which were current at the height of Laing's influence.

While Laing's interpretation of schizophrenic behaviour has not stood the test of time, and there is evidence that schizophrenia arises from a variety of origins several of which usually interact (Birchwood et al., 1988), many of these ideas have drawn attention to approaches to the study of problems which have been important to social workers. Particularly in psychiatric settings social workers have been taught by Laing's work to be cautious about medical diagnoses which fail to consider social and family factors as possible elements in the cause of problems. More widely, symbolic interactional and phenomenological sociology has influenced work in settings where other people who are often regarded as deviant (e.g. offenders) are dealt with.

Symbolic interactionism is a sociological and social psychological perspective deriving from the work of George Herbert Mead (1934) and Blumer (1969). The basic idea is that people act according to symbols (ideas that stand in place) of the outside world, which they hold in their minds. They create their symbols through interpreting interactions between themselves and the outside world, using language. Their self is similarly created because in order to have interactions with the outside world, they must have an idea also of the being which is undertaking the interaction. In order to think about the world, therefore, people have to have interactions with themselves. Such ideas have links with personal construct theory in which people's behaviour is seen as organised according to the internal constructs they hold about the external world.

These ideas extend beyond concepts which offer a theory about individual interactions, because they also imply things about society. If all behaviour is carried on through symbols and their interaction with each other, then people's development and socialisation derives from interactions that they have in society, and society can be seen as the interactions between human beings and their symbols. People can, therefore, manage and plan their own behaviour, and they do so as they go along in their interactions. The theory thus argues that people are in control of their thinking about their symbolisations of the world and, therefore, also capable of change and capable of influencing the world in accordance with their wishes. This aligns it with humanistic theories, and contrasts it with deterministic theories such as psychoanalysis and behavioural approaches which assume that people's behaviour is caused by past experiences and learning derived from in-built instincts or stimuli.

Chaiklin (1979) argues that symbolic interactionism offers an alternative for social workers to a purely psychological mode of understanding human behaviour, and that focusing on interactions and symbols may be less demanding emotionally for both client and worker than the traditional close relationship. Moreover, these ideas assume the basic normality and competence of most people, rather than assuming illness or maladaption and an inability to control their own destiny. One of the most important of these is the idea of labelling, which we met in Chapter 7.

Many of these ideas relate to role and social psychological

theories explored in Chapter 7 for two reasons. First, symbolic interaction and related sociological ideas are concerned with social expectations and interpretations which are the meat of role theory, and accepting and interpreting roles are important aspects of the use of symbols in interaction. Second, as we noted in Chapter 7, Goffman's ideas of *role* in which people are seen as presenting themselves in different ways according to the social circumstances of the moment are a significant variant of role theory which stems from symbolic and phenomenological ideas.

Although broadly sociological, such ideas also offer important explanations for intense emotion. Smith (1975), for example, shows how the feelings associated with bereavement may be fully explained not by conventional explanations from psychoanalysis which rely on 'biological, instinctual and internal psychic processes' (p. 79), but by phenomenological explanations. On this basis, grief arises from the unique place allocated to certain relationships (e.g. marriage) within social expectations, and from the reorganisation of our social constructions of our world according to such expectations. When the relationship is lost, a social reconstruction must take place. Moreover, at the personal level, we construct ourselves in such a way that includes the lost person, and that internal reconstruction must also take place.

Understanding social constructions and viewing clients humanistically, so that their own experience and interpretation of events is given importance, may also be essential in working within ethnic groups who do not share the same assumptions about social experience as the dominant culture. For example, de la Rosa (1988) discusses spiritualism in Puerto Rican culture, which tends to conflict with certain aspects of conventional casework, and requires behaving in accordance with clients' expectations and being aware of certain cultural expectations in assessment, and in intervention.

Wilkes (1981) argues from a broadly humanist standpoint, that many 'undervalued groups' of clients whose disability or problem is not capable of immediate 'cure' would benefit from social work which was concerned with exploring meaning within their lives. The social worker's approach would be to share experiences in a liberating way, rather than to make a fetish of method and the achievement of specific therapeutic aims, which are inappropriate with many clients.

Existential social work: Krill

Krill's work, formulated in articles in the 1960s (e.g. Krill, 1969)
reached full expression in his book *Existential Social Work* (1978).
It is an eclectic model, taking insights from Rogers, gestalt
psychology, zen and similar philosophies, but its starting point is
existential philosophy. Existentialism is presented as being about
how we cope with the fact that existence makes us want to live
a life which, nonetheless, has many unsatisfactory aspects. People
often question the value of their lives and their identity. Our need
for security and a fixed identity conflicts with our need to fulfil our
potential and seek personal growth, because doing new things is
risky. People often accept security, but are anxious and guilty
about doing so because they want to fulfil themselves, and they
become *alienated* from their unfulfilled lives.

Social forces support this process through *seduction* and *oppression*. Seductive forces encourage people to seek naive and ulti-
mately unsatisfying stereotypes such as material success, 'macho'
behaviour or excessive femininity. Oppressive forces reinforce
self-doubt by class, sexual and racial prejudice. If these forces can
be overcome, we can begin to explore and accept our own identity.

We then experience a frightening reality, *dread*, which is an
emptiness and overwhelming dissatisfaction with life. Responses
to dread may be:

● accepting and trying to understand it better
● accepting the experience of dread but blaming it on social,
  psychological or economic forces which should be exting-
  uished (as for example a Marxist would – this is an implicit
  criticism of radical views of social work)
● countering it by filling life with activity
● rebelling against it as a mark of the absurdity and chaos of
  life, promoting human solidarity against our absurd existence (hence, for example the theatre of the absurd which has
  connections with existentialist philosophy)
● religious, so that this life is unsatisfactory, but fulfilment will
  be achieved in the next.

Picardie (1980) argues that in many social work cases, clients are
facing 'dreadful' moments in which an ordinary path through life is

suddenly disturbed. The only effective response is for the worker to experience with the client the feelings of despair, then re-establish a sense of security and contact with the world for themselves through exploring the moments of despair that they have shared together. This seems to be a humanistic interpretation of some of the ideas about the stage of active crisis found in crisis intervention theory.

Being (existing) in this world, then, essentially requires us to experience *nothingness*. If we experience nothingness while finding the courage to go on with life, we gain affirmation (a rather similar idea to Laing's idea of confirmation and disconfirmation – see above) both of the power of being and also of the fact that the power and worth of existing or being gives some meaning to our lives even while we are experiencing nothingness. Many clients who are depressed have these experiences. For example, a former school teacher who had been through a period of depression after the death of his wife and father at much the same time had lost his job and become obsessed with keeping souvenirs of his lost ones. He felt there was nothing to go on for. He was encouraged to take part in a group in a day centre, and eventually took on respons-ibilities for teaching literacy skills to others. He never left behind his feelings sufficiently to return to ordinary teaching work, but this voluntary work gave him some worthwhile experiences in his new life which encouraged him to carry on.

The essential paradox that being and nothingness discloses about life removes the division between ourselves and the outside world. Instead, inside and outside of ourselves is a unity. If we achieve this, we have a leap in our conscious understanding ('satori' in zen). Such ideas, claims Krill, underlie the use of paradox in various forms of therapy – it helps us to make that leap. Paradox is an essential part of learning about life, for example in zen stories or in Christian parables.

Effective workers help people find meaning in their experiences, displaying detachment but compassion arising from understanding seduction. We should confront people with the way they use power to oppress others, including attempts at oppression by dictators, bureaucrats, helping professionals and idealists who want to change the world. So, in dealing with an elderly isolated lady living on her memories, I encouraged her to talk about her two failed marriages and her return to her first husband in later life, through simple interest and fascination with her experiences. Other agencies and relatives were anxious because of her forget-fulness, and induced me, rather against my inclinations because of my interest in her as a person, to play safe and admit her to an old people's home. This process led to a breach in what had been an effective relationship with her, and she deteriorated very quickly and died. In this case, I think I failed to act authentically, and accepted the bureaucratic oppression of concern with safety, failing to 'listen' to her happiness and accept the risks which, with hindsight, I think could have been accepted, particularly if I had worked out some mechanisms to check on her. This sort of experience, which I am sure many social workers share, draws attention to the importance of listening in an authentic way and responding according to our perceptions, rather than falling in with an oppressive concern from outside forces.

We gain an identity from this understanding of ourselves and through making sense of the world. There is a constant interplay between the person and the situation (to use psychosocial jargon – see Chapter 3). Maturation and personal development means open-ing people to experiencing and understanding the outside world and integrating it with themselves as a whole. Other forms of therapy which concentrate on helping people deal with the outside world (e.g. ego psychology) increase alienation, because they separate us from the outside world rather than allowing us to integrate with it. Instead, we should promote true maturation through *being activity* in which there is constant interchange between ourselves and the outside world. This is achieved by three processes:

- *process-identity* exists when we are aware of the totality of our life situation, our feelings and experiencing of the world without making judgements or suffering any external limita-tion; this may be achieved by meditation or perhaps drugs
- *creative power* lies in achieving a satisfactory product (the job well done) and the experience of 'quality' of a product and freedom from limitations at the point of achievement (the opposite of the sort of feelings I had when completing my work with the elderly lady described above)
- *love-generating-acceptance* is a painful experience of trying to accept the reality and value of other people or experiences no matter how they confront our own identity

In existential social work we must help clients develop worthwhile relationships with people other than themselves – the *significant-other system* (S-O-S). Being involves choices, actions and communications with the S-O-S and perceptions and conclusions about these interactions. To understand these we must examine:

- rules and roles within the S-O-S
- wider systems (e.g. economic, social oppression) influencing the S-O-S
- clients' belief systems
- how clients handle fear and insecurity
- the interactions between these.

Most emotional problems arise from four sources of alienation:

- when people who are important to us fail to 'confirm' us
- inconsistency or deception over value conflicts
- disillusionment, confusion or loss of personal values
- loss of people who are important to us (e.g. by death).

Krill argues (1978, p. 118) that many writers on existential therapy over-emphasise searching for personal meaning. He suggests that it is more important to see how such meaning is expressed towards others, leading to struggles. This approach reduces intellectualising and self-preoccupation which is typical of insight therapies.

The aim of therapy is to help people attain a satisfying life style. Problems are dealt with by accepting the client's lifestyle and philosophy, exploring and resolving problems within it, avoiding oppression and paternalism. The three *principles of treatment* are:

- an emphasis on experiential change
- being client-centred
- personal engagement by the worker, modelling how to deal with values, feelings and attitudes.

At first the worker seeks to engage clients in exploring themselves and their environment. Early interviews concentrate on exploring clients' sense of being. Diagnostic categories are inappropriate, because they only deal with the worker's insecurity and need to compartmentalise a whole human being. Working should avoid helping the client seek self-knowledge, which is a seduction to accept a naive utopia, or pressing the client to conform to some set standard, which is oppressive. Reason should be used (as in cognitive approaches) to dispute rigid ideas which clients use to maintain themselves in their problems; this gives them greater freedom to explore alternative ways of being.

As treatment progresses, the client can be offered new experiences within the worker-client relationship, by demonstration or practice within the security of the contact between them. New experiences in daily living, given as tasks or homework may also be used.

Treatment goals and activities related are set out in Table 8.1. The treatment process undertaken by the worker comprises:

- *centring* where workers show to clients that they are ready for involvement with the client, and then gain understanding and active contact with those problems
- *vitalisation* which is giving a sense that things are happening and progressing, avoiding endless self-exploration
- *action* as the worker demonstrates openness and the client sees that maintaining security is not always vital to being.

The worker has no model of how clients or society should be, so there is no diagnosis or prognosis, and the aim is to encourage the client to explore options in their life. There may be (ethical) limits about what kinds of exploration will retain their involvement. For example, one adolescent client wanted to discuss with me his income in illicit drug-dealing. I made the point to him, in effect withdrawing from involvement with this aspect of his life, that I could not accept involvement in this; I might be obliged to take official action, and refer him to law enforcement or other helping agencies, but I could not receive this information and do nothing. I tried to help him see that I must reject this behaviour (indeed by my values must try to get him to avoid these activities), while continuing to be interested in and support him in other areas of his life – he had difficulties in his relationship with his father. Since there are no worker-defined objectives or standards, clients terminate the contact when they wish.

Table 8.1 *Existential treatment goals*

Treatment	Aims	Methods
Provocative contact	help unreachable or unwilling clients	active confrontation, reality or rational techniques, behaviour modification
Sustaining relationship	give clients affirmation	offer experience of worker being available and genuinely interested; may lead to personal growth and further attempts to seek change
Specific behaviour change	alter symptoms or behaviour which depend on changing attitudes or reactions to problem	avoiding alcohol despite compulsion, working while depressed, caring for a child while under stress; use support and behaviour change methods
Environmental change	promote realistic action to deal with problems	find creative outlets if anxious, prepare for death if suffering from fatal disease; getting a job, getting more social security
Relationship change	deal with problems in interpersonal relationships	examine and work on S-O-S
Directional change	help client change direction in life	clarify values and aims using transactional analysis, paradox, reality or cognitive models
Insightful analysis	clarify internal mental and emotional conflicts	use insight techniques

Source: Krill (1978).

Commentary

The importance of considering humanist and existential contributions does not lie in their formal impact on social work theory actually in use within most agencies, which is slight. They are important in two ways. First, social work values are essentially humanist. Thus, the idea of treating people as wholes, and as being in interaction with their environment, of respecting their understanding and interpretation of their experience, and seeing clients at the centre of what workers are doing, are all approaches which fit well with individualisation, and the approach with relationship and advocacy which I have argued is central to social work. Humanist therapies thus find a sympathetic fit with social work practice.

The failure to import these potentially sympathetic ideas lies in the framework of social work in agencies which perform social control and bureaucratic functions, as well as in the fact that many of the fundamental philosophies of humanism already exist in social work and do not need explicit importation. Agency function and social control imply that a range of external objectives and targets have to be imposed on social work activities which are inimical to the extremely free approach of humanist therapies, where clients are in control of the exploration and this is facilitated, but not directed, by workers. This was true in the case of my drug-dealing client, for example.

The second area of great importance in present ideas in social work of the material discussed in this chapter has been the influence of symbolic interaction and phenomenological ideas as a basis for understanding human beings which is more flexible, less deterministic and less judgemental than many psychological ideas which are used by social work. The interaction of clients' perceptions and interpretations of the world and the reaction of the world to clients shows how situations arise in which clients' apparently bizarre or bad behaviour is established or amplified by social processes. For the social work function of advocacy, and for assessing need, these ideas can be a useful way of explaining clients' behaviour and problems without blaming clients who are victims of these social processes.

The problem with these ideas and approaches to therapy is, however, their lack of clarity and the difficulty of forming clear targets and agreed explanations about the behaviour. This means that, although these ideas have potential explanatory power in advocacy for clients, they may not be widely accepted among powerful groups in society that workers seek to influence on behalf of clients.

Also, they may be criticised for their vagueness and lack of rigour by positivists, and for the lack of any evidence of effectiveness of the techniques proposed. In answer to this, it is important to note the work on the effectiveness of therapeutic relationships which has originated from Rogers' work, and which demonstrates the importance of empathic valuing and genuine relationships and has made attempts to measure these elements. Though such relationships are not sufficient for therapy to be effective, they are necessary to therapeutic success. So, while they must be present for these techniques to be useful, they have to be part of other activities which actually intervene effectively in clients' behaviour or social circumstances. This material does not tell us, however, what we should do within the relationship once it has been achieved to intervene effectively in the client's situation.

A reasonable judgement seems to be, therefore, that ideas of respect for whole persons are an essential part of effective practice and of the value base of social work. These are fundamentally humanist ideas, and a reading of humanist therapies gives comprehensive access to ways of implementing these basic values comprehensively, and in a sense provides a benchmark for social work, at least with voluntary, self-motivated clients, which helps us to understand the values and tasks of more directed therapies which are more relevant to social and agency functions.

9

Cognitive Models

Connections

Cognitive theories have established a strong position in social work theory during the 1980s primarily through the work of H. Goldstein (1981, 1984a). Part of the reason for this may be increasing interest in cognitive approaches in psychology and counselling, leading to the availability of more work and broader interests in related occupations. There has also been more time for cognitive theory and practice to develop and mature; and social work's movement away from heavy reliance on psychodynamic theory in the 1970s has probably opened up the possibility of using a range of psychological approaches.

Cognitive theory is concerned with cognition – people's thinking. It assumes that behaviour is directed by thoughts, rather than by unconscious drives, conflicts and feelings. Much of the original research and theory of cognitive approaches develops from behaviourist practice. Cognitive theory usefully leads behavioural social work away from a mechanistic view of behaviour and explores the capacity of human minds to modify and control how stimuli affect behaviour. So, social learning theory which emphasises how people learn in social situations by observing and modelling behaviour leads directly towards cognitive theory which concentrates on how behaviour is guided by our perception and analysis of what we see. Writers on cognitive theory with a behavioural emphasis (e.g. Berlin, 1980, 1982) use explanations which rely on rational control of behaviour, but tend to apply interventions which are fundamentally behaviourist.

Important cognitive theories are Beck's (1978) work on anxiety, Ellis' (1962) rational emotive therapy, and Glasser's (1965) reality therapy, which originates from residential work with adolescent girls. These rational cognitive therapies, none of them designed for social work, concentrate on clients' thinking, and all emphasise fairly authoritarian judgements about irrational attitudes which are disputed. Such approaches seem to sit unhappily with the non-judgemental, non-directive style of social work, and cognitive approaches did not make a significant impact on social work until humanistic elements aligned cognitive concepts with more conventional social work approaches.

Including the humanistic element is, then, the crucial aspect of Goldstein's work and the later writings of Werner (1982, 1986). Goldstein's energetic promotion of cognitive-humanist theories in the journals (Goldstein, 1982, 1983, 1984b, 1986) seems to have struck a chord. Cognitive theory lends itself to including humanism because it emphasises how irrational thoughts or disturbances in perception lead us to process our view of the world incorrectly. Consequently we react inappropriately because we have perceived reality wrongly, or processed our perception of reality wrongly. Humanist, phenomenological and symbolic interaction ideas would go further than this (see Chapter 8), claiming that perceptions and their processing legitimately vary and that the only reality is what is perceived and understood. Allied to cognitive ideas, this allows an acceptance of the accuracy of the clients' understanding of the world, so that there is no need to see clients' perceptions as wrong and to attack them. They are seen merely as different. This element of acceptance renders cognitive and behaviourist therapies in ways which seem more natural to the conventions of social work.

Social learning and change: Goldstein

Goldstein (1981) argues that theories of behaviour change need three connecting parts: a moral code or social philosophy, a theory of personality, and techniques which influence behaviour. He starts, therefore, with his underlying philosophy, summarised in four main points:

- people can best be understood as searching for and moving towards their own goals

- people construct their own versions of reality through what they have learned
- people gain certainty in their lives by *adaptation*, a process by which they manage the outside world
- adaptation is influenced by the *perceiving self*, our concept of ourselves and how that affects our perceptions.

To study people's perceptions and learning, we must see their *self* as active and transactional, that is their self actually affects what they do, and is affected by what happens to them. The self has three main activities as it deals with the outside world:

- *adaptation*: reacting to the outside world, while taking account of our self, and therefore our aims and strivings
- *stabilisation*: keeping our system in equilibrium while dealing with new events
- *setting intentions*: seeking change in accordance with internal aims.

Perception is an important aspect of cognitive theory, since how perception takes place conditions thoughts and actions which respond to the perceptions. Goldstein takes a phenomenological view of perception, which is assumed to shape how people think about themselves. Perception is a series of interactions taking place in a social context in response to a stimulus as shown in Figure 9.1. (This diagram is an attempt to represent Goldstein's statement that perception does not occur in a sequence, and it is not similar to his own figure.) The stimulus may be from within or outside us, but as well as being an objective fact it also becomes a subjective representation inside ourselves. How we perceive the stimulus depends on:

- how well it stands out from other surrounding stimuli
- how close and similar its elements are to one another
- how continuous and consistent it is
- whether it is complete or partial.

Thus, if we are watching a child through a video monitor in a child abuse investigation to see how it behaves when with its parents, we may not see a minor movement behind a table – it does not stand

Figure 9.1 *Goldstein's interpretation of perception*

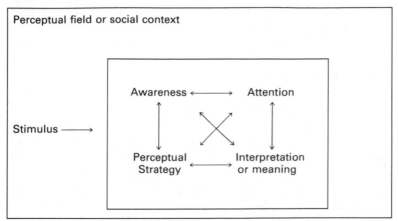

Source: adapted from Goldstein (1981).

out from the surroundings. When the child plays at the other side of a room, it may be so far away, or be doing such a variety of things, that we cannot interpret its feelings because the stimuli are too distant or too diffuse for us to make a judgement. If the child carries on behaving in similar ways for a long period, we may eventually come to notice what its present feelings are. This will be easier if the child completes its game so that we can understand its full import.

The sort of things that make us pay attention are the physical and emotional conditions in which the perception takes place, our own characteristics and habits of attention, and whether we have a mental 'set' towards noticing that kind of event, or alternatively are not disposed to do so. Physical and social contexts will affect how we perceive something, including our cultural assumptions. Many of these ideas are drawn from communication theory and research. Our usual pattern of thinking and the way we normally give meanings to things will also define our perceptions, e.g. whether we are usually creative or very concrete in the way we look at things.

Because our perceptions are inevitably different from those of others, we are always cut off from their worlds, but we can use that estrangement as the basis of a close relationship as we explore each others' understandings of the world. For example, I worked with a man from Pakistan who had recently arrived in Britain to work in a factory. He had become depressed and felt isolated, part of which was related to a feeling that he was cut off from the strange society in which he was living. I started off from a position, wrongly, I now think, in which I took it that he was alienated from our society because of the differences from our own culture. Seeing his reactions simply as alienation denied the individuality of his personal experiences and treated him as merely an example of his culture, and indeed, of a typical social problem. Exploring the struggle to come to England, the pain of cutting himself off from his family, and the meagre relationships which were available at work, I began to get to grips with his world and came to understand the individual reasons for his predicament which belied my general assumptions. Goldstein's view would be that we started off from estranged positions, but in struggling to understand personal, individual experience rather than categories of experience, our estrangement actually helped me to explore and understand his individual world better than I would if the estrangement due to cultural assumptions had not been present.

Perception, according to Goldstein, is crucial to adaptation because it links our thoughts and feelings with the external and social world. This view of perception, he claims, links social and psychological explanations, because it includes both. As in his previous development of systems theory (Goldstein, 1973) he is here trying to combine social and psychological aspects of social work in a whole. Adaptation is not only a personal event but also has social and transactional consequences; adaptation has its effects on the outside world and is affected by it through the self.

The various elements of the self are coalesced by Goldstein into three groups:

- self conception (being)
- perceiving self (knowing)
- intentional self (becoming).

Feeling good about our lives depends on these three aspects of self being in harmony. Conflict between them leads us to search out ways of resolving it which become patterns of dealing with problems. This may be one kind of impulse that, I suggested in Chapter 1, causes clients to seek help from agencies. If these patterns become persistent and powerful, they will affect others through behaviour. When they do so strongly, we are noticed by social institutions and have to respond to their pressures on behaviour, adapting to social requirements. This may force us into compromises with our aims in life, leading to further dissatisfaction, even though it resolves social pressures. Thus social adaptation may limit personal autonomy with a consequent reduction in our capacity for adaptation at a personal level; as we saw, Goldstein's philosophy emphasises the humanist concept of autonomy as an important feature of successful functioning in human beings.

The sort of conflicts between different parts of the self might be:

- between perceiving self and self-concept, where we see others disapprove or dislike us, or where our status or capacity changes as we age, lose jobs or become disabled
- between intentional self and perceiving self, where we seek particular goals and are frustrated by the society we live in or where there are opportunities but we do not have the motivation or belief in ourselves to take them up, perhaps having lost it through past oppression or racism or sexism
- between self-concept and intentional self, when our conception of ourselves is at odds with our motivation, values or beliefs (e.g. putting up with an unsatisfactory marriage when we would prefer something better; drifting along without any goals in life).

How we adapt personally to these sorts of conflicts also has public meaning, because it affects others around us. As they react, we have to deal with their response to us with adaptive mechanisms which are already damaged by the conflicts in our personal adaptation.

Adaptation implies change. If we seek to help someone adapt, we will be helping them to change. Planned change implies change for the better, towards some aim which is preferred to the present state. Since the person and environment are seen as a whole, in Goldstein's view change means improving a client's capacity to solve problems; it is a learning experience. Three main types of learning can be outlined:

- *strategic* learning means acquiring information and skills towards some set objective

- *tactical* learning is concerned with adapting to the pressures of daily living
- *adaptive* learning implies altering the self and its construction of the world as part of a process of dealing with life in a different way.

Learning of all kinds happens when people's movement towards some desired aim is blocked by something in their environment or in themselves.

Goldstein sets out four stages of learning, each of which must be achieved before the next. They are:

- *discrimination learning*, so that clients gain more awareness and/or sensitivity to problems and circumstances in their worlds
- *concept learning*, so that clients learn the symbols and ideas that they conventionally use in processing information
- *principle learning*, concerned with values and self-concept
- *problem-solving*, the overall way in which clients resolve difficulties in their environment.

Each of these are now considered in greater detail.

Discrimination learning raises our consciousness of ourselves and our environment, and improves our capacity to pay attention to things which are or may be important to us. Discrimination takes place before perceptions are turned into ideas. Often, people are unable to judge priorities in their lives and the things it may be important to learn about.

How well we learn discrimination depends on a number of conditions. These include the environment and its effects on our capacity to learn. For example, children from poor families often have less experience in learning than children from well-off backgrounds. They may be less well taught and stimulated, and never learn self-understanding or get out of practice in exploring themselves. Similarly, people from oppressed and depressing environments are less likely to have been able to refine their discriminatory skills. Many settings in which social workers operate blunt discriminatory skills because they make people dependent on others' care rather than independent, e.g. hospitals or residential care. Other conditions which are relevant to capacity to learn discriminatory skills are perceptual. People with poor eyesight or hearing are less able to make important distinctions between things in their environment. Consciousness and attention are also relevant. Workers need to expand clients' consciousness of the detail and range of experiences in their lives, help them to focus on detail of their experiences, and also to generalise from specific events. So, rather than feeling general dissatisfaction with life, a client can be helped to find precisely what it is that is problematic. Then, it may be possible to see how that aspect of their lives is affecting all the other problems that they have.

As a simple example, I was once responsible for a child living in a children's home, and was called by the residential worker, because the child was becoming bored and difficult at school. In conversation with him, I noticed the way in which he looked at me, and because of my own experience of being short-sighted I enquired whether he had ever worn spectacles. It turned out that these had been prescribed some time before, and had been broken; his mother had never encouraged him to wear them and could not afford to have them replaced. His lack of interest in school was partly explained by the pressure of trying to understand lessons without being able to see the blackboard, or to read comfortably. This simple physical lack reduced the capacity to use discriminatory skills, which were already poor because of an unstimulating home environment and the dependence-creating experience of living in the children's home, where he did not receive enough encouragement to develop interests and activities of his own.

Various obstacles to discriminatory learning exist. A disorganised lifestyle makes it hard to see connections and distinctions between things; it may seem that things just happen. Alternatively, a client may make causal connections between things which are uncertain or non-existent. Motivation is important. We have to be open to learning and new experience to get the most from it. People who are preoccupied with themselves cannot lift their eyes to broader issues. On the other hand, some people may spend all their time worrying about outside problems or practicalities, and not focus enough on their own feelings and emotions. This is common, for example, in parents of large families with many practical responsibilities who are unable to give enough time to their own emotional needs.

Evaluation of discriminatory learning involves seeking meanings within clients' behaviour which show how the environment has affected their ways of perceiving things, how they normally go about perceiving their world, and what their motivation is. Appropriate ways of improving discriminatory learning are:

- strengthening consciousness so that clients become more aware of the aspects of their life that they have not explored
- focusing attention and raising consciousness of areas that the clients have not yet explored or wish to avoid
- directing and focusing attention which is diffuse and confused, filtering out irrelevancies in the clients' perceptions
- helping clients to examine the patterns in their own environment and how it affects them
- encouraging sudden leaps in awareness (this idea uses humanist and zen ideas) and helping clients express and appreciate them
- encouraging clients to keep diaries so that they can understand the details of their day, and understand its connections with their thoughts and feelings
- homework and exercises (this idea connects with work of Ellis – see above) to strengthen powers of discrimination in everyday life and encourage clients to practice them.

Concept learning takes place when our minds create ideas about our world from the perceptions and adaptations that we have made. We sort things out into categories and react to the category rather than particular events. So, a client who sees all officials as being like the police would probably include social workers in that category and react accordingly. To do social work would involve changing this categorisation into something less crude, so that such a client would accept help. For example, a homeless man was introduced to me at an emergency shelter because he had problems of mental illness. He was afraid that I would have him admitted compulsorily to hospital, as police officers had occasionally done when they found him wandering; he knew that this was one of my functions. I arranged for him to join a day centre and receive some new clothing, and then spent some time discussing his life and experiences with him. On future occasions he sometimes visited me, and later came when he was experiencing hallucinations and asked to be admitted to hospital. He would still not have considered the police station as a place to go for help, and I think he was still cautious about my compulsory powers, but he had been prepared to recategorise me as being helpful where these were not at issue.

Concept learning may be done:

- *systematically*, as informal education
- *informally*, as we constantly change our understanding of the world through daily experience.

People have various ways of learning; they need to know how to learn particular sorts of information, and workers need to understand clients' ways of learning.

Concepts are not only information, but also carry personal and symbolic meanings for people. So, the fact that a wife is out when her husband returns home may be insignificant to one person, but important to another who gains comfort or power from the expectation that she should always be there. Symbolic meaning comes from experience, thought and consideration, often over a long period of time.

Environment and culture affect how people learn concepts, as with discrimination learning. People have particular cognitive *styles*, which can be identified. Obstacles to effective cognitive learning may be inadequate learning *skills*, arising from poor perceptions and thinking, inadequate *knowledge* to understand what is perceived and an *inflexibility* arising from getting stuck in particular patterns of understanding.

Most concept learning comes from interactions with other people – it is transactional and interpersonal. Everyone is, however, limited by their own personal outlook or *premises* in what they can understand of others. Trying to achieve change in a relationship requires the participants' commitment to involvement, or change cannot be attained because the interpersonal element is not there.

The *content* of change using concept learning is communication and metacommunication (see Chapter 7). Workers should examine the whole range of communication especially language to find out about:

- clients' *cognitions* about themselves and their life
- their *symbolic assumptions* about the world and how they experience it

- cognitive *style*, whether it is concrete or creative
- their *personal responsibility* and how they explain what happens to them
- their *self-concept*
- how they feel about various aspects of their *personal history*.

An important aspect of the change transaction is the expectation clients have of it, which may be uncertain, and which the worker may have of the client. There may be particular confusion about power, and a good deal of resulting ambivalence about the relationship. In one case, for example, I was asked to help a couple consider whether they wished to be reconciled in their marriage rather than seek a legal separation. The wife was hopeful of this, the husband opposed, and I was doubtful about the motives of the lawyer who referred the case, and so I did not really believe that I would be effective. The wife saw me as having the power to convince her husband to return to her; the husband was afraid that I might do so; I was anxious to display the fact that I did not have any power, and that they must in the end make their own decision. As a result, the husband resisted any real involvement in the process, and I failed to use the personal and professional influence that I might have had to induce an engagement in the process of working out a resolution which both could understand and accept, even if it was that divorce was necessary. This illustrates how expectations among workers and clients may doom an otherwise useful relationship, and the problem of power within those expectations.

Assessment should not consist of testing characteristics of the client against systems of knowledge, or set diagnostic categories, but of attempts to understand this client or group of clients in this situation. Workers will always be prejudiced by their own view of the world, and an examination of this prejudice should always be included in any assessment.

Having gained a preliminary understanding of the client's premises and present modes of concept learning, strategies for change can be established. The three major strategies are:

- set up a climate which will improve the clients' learning
- remove obstacles to learning
- help clients change their premises and views of reality.

Some strategies are based in the environment. The first essential is to ensure that clients who do not have the basic resources for living have improved access to them; housing and social security problems should be the first priority where they are an issue. Taking such action does not nourish the whole person however. Clients may be damaged emotionally by their dependency on the services provided. Instead of being patronising helpers, workers should help clients explore parts of their lives and capacities which will allow them to gain some satisfactions and personal growth. Their expectations, currently unsatisfied, should be investigated for some which could be met. Where clients have very disorganised lives, the first priority is to help achieve some level of organisation which will allow the client to begin learning again.

Social services and other agencies often contribute to the disorganisation and oppression which clients experience. Strategies to overcome this are: providing information and advice, particularly about rights; trying to remove the unreasonable emotions that some clients have about dealing with officialdom, so that they are more able to manage their own affairs; advocacy on their behalf; negotiation among agencies to gain some degree of co-ordination and prevent the fragmentation of services to particular clients. All workers have the professional responsibility to seek changes in the system of services which will benefit their clients in general.

Cognitive strategies aim to change clients' views of the world. Clients may not have enough knowledge of themselves or of things outside themselves; they may misinterpret what they know or be poor at reasoning from it. Uncertainty and conflict may limit their capacity to use their knowledge and conceptions.

Conceptual reorientation is the first cognitive strategy. The helper may act as a model for new ways of thinking and understanding, give information and advice, help the client to connect their thinking with the things that they have experienced, and pull out from the client any conceptions which are inhibited by others' expectations (e.g. what parents said was 'good').

The client's involvement in cognitive learning is crucial. The aim is to help clients find evidence in their lives for problems in thinking and understanding their world. *Self-examination* encourages the clients to look closely and analytically at their daily lives to gain new insights. *Explanation* involves giving information not previously available to or used by, the clients. Methods of doing so include interpretation and confrontation where attempts are made to present new or resisted information, reflection and feedback to the client of the feelings being shown, questioning to get the client to think about new concepts, and suggestion and exhortation which apply pressure directly. *Self-demonstration* involves putting the client in situations where problems with perceptions and thinking can be more clearly seen. *Vicarisation* involves helping clients to model themselves on others, either the worker, or people they approve of, or people from books, films and television.

From these approaches, clients can grasp what is getting in the way of fulfilling their aims. What they know, however, does not necessarily affect what they can do – a connection has to be made between their thinking and action. This involves finding and using different ways of thinking. *Convergent* thinking is limiting because it pushes people to put ideas into set and known categories. *Divergent* thinking expands and creates new ideas from initial knowledge or thoughts. It is more dialectical and promotes clients' capacity to apply symbolic and personal meanings to information. Some types of activity require one rather than the other mode of thinking, and good thinking requires the capacity to switch appropriately between the two.

Changing convergent thinking obliges workers to start where the client is (Goldstein, 1983), by accepting their present understanding of reality. Four possible strategies proceed from this:

- *extracting meaning* – clients expand on their ideas and concepts so that inconsistencies and faulty thinking are exposed
- *projecting meaning* – clients show how their thinking works. Role play, or detailed examination of possible situations, enable the worker to show where problems in thinking lead to. It is important to avoid asking for explanations from the client which only leads to self-justification, but, rather, to ask 'what happens when . . ?'
- *dialectic reversal* sets up a situation in which it becomes impossible for clients to continue holding particular views. The worker gets the client to consider alternatives which are equally problematic, and in this way move towards a suitable compromise

- *exchanging frames of reference* – helping the client to see alternative ways of doing things. A teenager who is constantly arguing with parents, for example, can be asked to imagine how a friend without this problem would behave in dealing with the parents. This can give people new ideas, and help them to see the possibility of change – things do not have to be as they are.

One of the difficulties to be faced is the existential crisis of dread of the insecurity which may arise when we change. So, we should get the client's commitment to change. Whatever is done has to achieve the client's purposes, and we may need to alter or expand those purposes as part of achieving change. This involves reaching a new understanding of the problem, of the conflict and discomfort that the client feels, and thinking about the possible consequences for living (which may not all be good), which would be brought about by the changes proposed.

Principle learning is the third form of learning in which we establish general guides to behaviour. These come from the dialectic or interaction between values, adaptation and our personal constructions of the world. Principles allow certainty in relationships between human beings. Values are a particularly important element. Identifying principles of living can be difficult because they cannot be determined by empirical study, and they often form groups associated with parts of human experience so that they cannot easily be separated out and studied on their own. Principles tend to be enduring, but they alter as social change requires it.

Principle learning takes place, therefore, in a social context, and learning can only be enhanced if there is an environment in which the client feels free to take part in dialogue with others in a fairly open way, to isolate, study and test out various principles of living. An oppressive family or community makes it difficult to do this. The way in which the worker manages their own power and authority in relationships with the client affects whether a suitable environment for principle learning can be provided within social work. Openness about the worker's role and activity is essential. Reflection and dialogue with the worker about how clients guide their lives is the main method of approach.

Problem-solving is the fourth type of learning covered by

Table 9.1   *Basic principles of Goldstein's cognitive-humanist model*

Principle	Practice
make social services accessible	many clients are excluded from access, because of the agency's tailing or workers' prejudices
social forces affect problem-solving	clients' attempts to deal with problems are damaged by their environment, and workers must explore ways of helping within that environment
solutions, not problems, are important	we all have problems; how we try to solve them produces most of life's problems; social work is about finding better solutions
start where the client is	worker's should always begin with the client's unique, personal view of the world and symbolic understanding of reality
workers' role is to manage learning and change	clients do the changing, but workers must provide an environment and help to enable clients to change
use the client's own learning style	learning will be quicker and more enduring if the client's own ways of learning are respected
values and action	make clients aware of how principles and values are crucially connected to what they do
risk-taking	clients should be encouraged to use less rational and more creative forms of thinking; also all change will involve clients in facing the insecurity of change
learning is transferable	help clients see how learning can be transferred to other problems of living
motivation	while this is important, the reasons for poor motivation should be explored, rather than rejecting or criticising clients
clarity and openness	these are crucial to providing an environment in which clients can take the risks necessary to make changes
immediacy	particularly with unwilling clients, try to react at once to the most stressful or difficult matter which has caused the referral
use contracts	this helps to make the obligations and roles of all concerned explicit, limits unrealistic and possibly frightening implications, and encourages clients to express their own goals and expectations
advice, guidance and direction	these techniques use the worker's special skills and experience and make available knowledge of the systems within which clients live; help should be offered without

Principle	Practice
	preventing clients from finding their own solutions
locus of practice	use a variety of settings, whichever are most effective for achieving aims
security and stability	ensure that clients receive necessities of living as the basis for future independence, which cannot even be started upon if basic needs are unmet
hope	as part of motivation, it is essential that client and worker have hope, which consists both of realistic expectation and an element of emotion and belief about the future (Korner, 1973)
autonomy	a basic need for everyone which the worker should try to enhance for the client

Source: Goldstein (1981)

Goldstein's book and is at the highest level. Problem-solving is both a process and a way of applying logic to a situation. There are three main phases. The first, *induction*, is where the problem is felt, explored and understood. In the *core*, it is analysed, various alternatives are tested out for its resolution and a strategy for dealing with it identified. In the *ending* phase, the eventual strategy is used and evaluated and taken into the client's repertoire of techniques for dealing with problems in the future. Problem-solving involves all the elements of learning, the environment, the client's self and dialogue with others with whom the client is in contact.

Motivation is a significant part of enabling clients to learn.

Goldstein sets out a number of basic principles of his approach, and these are summarised in Table 9.1.

Commentary

Cognitive theory has only begun to make a significant impact in social work since the early 1980s. Social workers' reaction to the use of the original forms of cognitive therapy within psychology was one of uncertainty that the fairly aggressive methods of disputation were appropriate ethically with clients, congenial to social work's fairly non-directive approach and, particularly, appropriate to social work's clientele. The model runs the risk, if used regularly, of identifying practical problems of poverty and oppression, which is what leads many clients to social work agencies, as irrational reactions, and this would be unfortunate if it failed to acknowlege real problems in the environment. However, more explicit alliances of these methods with a humanist philosophy seems to have overcome some of these problems. Such approaches, which are developments of social learning theory, may have particular benefits for people with mental illnesses, and for training work with parents unable to manage their children's behaviour effectively. There is research support for their effectiveness in such circumstances. The approach introduces into social work a useful educative element as against the therapeutic approach of many social work methods.

Overall, we can see cognitive approaches as offering a useful way of understanding social work in a way which emphasises clients' rational capacity to manage their lives, and enhances that capacity with clear and well-tried techniques. Allied with humanist views of the process and related values which respect and involve clients, cognitive approaches to social work retain many of social work's basic caring values within a framework of effective action. They are, as yet, relatively untried in everyday social work practice.

10

Radical and Marxist Approaches

Connections

Radical views of social work gained in significance in the 1970s. While their influence has waned, some ideas have become embedded in social work thought. An element of social criticism deriving from radical thought is now more essential to social work theory than it was before this period of influence. These approaches also created a theoretical environment in which the development of forms of social work such as empowerment, advocacy and consciousness-raising grew up and became acceptable.

Rojek (1986) distinguishes three Marxist views of social work:

- the *progressive* position – social work is a positive agent of change because it connects more general bourgeois society (i.e. a society in which capitalism has created a system which exploits the working class) with representatives of the working class; social workers are significant in promoting collective action and consciousness raising, so helping to achieve change
- the *reproductive* position – social workers are agents of class control enhancing the oppression by capitalist societies of the working class
- the *contradictory* position – social workers are both agents of capitalist control and undermine (at least potentially) class society; although acting as agents of social control they also increase working-class capacities to function, and offer some of the knowledge and power of the state to clients in the

working class; the existence of this contradiction in their role leads to other contradictions which eventually contribute to the overthrow of capitalist society.

The progressive position is that taken by writers usually described as radical, such as Galper (1980), and books edited by Bailey and Brake (1975a, 1980). One account of the reproductive position is that of Skenridge and Lennie (1971). The contradictory position is represented by the work of Corrigan and Leonard (1978), a Marxist perspective considered later in this Chapter as the best example of this approach.

Radical social work arises from criticism of 'traditional' (psychodynamic) social work, of other theories relying on psychological explanations of social problems, and of functionalist theories which tend to take for granted the present social order. McIntyre (1982) usefully summarises the radical critique of traditional social work:

- explanations in traditional social work reduce complex social problems to individual psychological ones; it tends to 'blame the victim', making clients responsible for problems which have social origins; it deflects attention from social circumstances
- it 'privatises' people with social problems, cutting them off from others who would share that experience and possibly deal jointly with it, and
- it strengthens and follows the oppressive social order of capitalism.

In spite of this critique, there are links between many radical theories and traditional social work. Webb (1981) identifies four main ones:

- both accept that society contributes to generating personal problems, but traditional social work accounts of the process by which this happens and interventions within it are inadequate, as we saw in the case of psychosocial and systems theory
- in both, the relationship between people and society is

transactional, reflexive or interactive, so that we can affect our social circumstances as they affect us

- both seek client autonomy, but traditional social work criticises radical social work for ignoring it in pursuit of general social objectives which may conflict with individual needs and autonomy, while radicalism criticises traditional social work for ignoring the social constraints to conform
- both value insight so that clients can understand their circumstances in order to act on them, but the purposes and means of action are different, and each would deny the value of each other's forms of action.

Allied to the radical critique of social work methods, there is criticism of social work's system of service. Because agencies are part of the social system which supports capitalism, they have inherent failings in helping the working class. Ryant (1969) summarises these as follows:

- agencies have limited and *fragmented* roles making it difficult to deal with the clients' problems as a whole and the range of social problems which need addressing
- agency *financing* restricts the resources available, and exerts control against solutions which are contrary to the interests of the financiers; public and corporate roles of agencies tend to lead to collective views within them which are aligned with conventional views in society
- hierarchical and bureaucratic *organisation* in agencies tends to reinforce caution and acceptance of rules and conventions
- *representation* on management committees and public bodies responsible for agencies' policy tends to be made up of people who represent or accept the existing system, rather than clients or representatives of oppressed or disadvantaged communities
- *professionalisation* of social work leads to social workers being rewarded by society with status, income and other advantages of the profession, thus promoting their acceptance of the status quo and rejection of critical analyses of the problems that they are dealing with.

From these brief summaries of radical views on social work, it is possible to identify a number of issues which are the central concern:

- *social control* and the extent to which social work exercises it through the state on behalf of ruling classes
- *professionalisation* and the extent to which it is promoted by social work education to the disadvantage of the interests of oppressed communities and individuals clients
- is radical *practice* possible?

There would probably be wide agreement that social work has a social control function, in that one of its tasks is to promote conformity with what Pearson (1975, p. 129) calls '... the binding obligations of civil society.' However, if we accept that such functions are always legitimate we fail to question whether that control is always exercised for the benefit of clients, or of the social groups to which clients belong. Satyamurti (1979) argues that care and control are mixed together as part of public policy in British social work agencies, and their functions are hard to separate. This is probably true for many of those countries in which social work is primarily managed by state agencies. Goroff (1974) suggests that the activities of many agencies in the USA reflect coercive social control. Radicals argue that this is often on behalf of the state, representing the dominant interests of capitalist society.

Radical social work has been concerned by the way in which professionalisation of social work disadvantages clients' interests, and leads social workers to become part of the state and social interests which oppress clients, and seek their profession's development even where this is contrary to clients' interests. The work of Illich *et al.* (1977), proposing that professions are often established to act in their own interests rather than (as they would themselves suggest) those of the people they serve, has generated a great deal of interest. The role of social work education is an example of this process. Radicals argue that it trains students for 'traditional' social work, reinforcing social control, individual explanations of clients' problems, and conventional rather than radical interpretations of society (Cannan, 1972). According to Statham (1978, p. 92), radicals should study traditional forms of theory and practice to see where it is oppressive.

Radical practice is presented by Bailey and Brake (1975b, 1980) as '. . . essentially understanding the position of the oppressed in the context of the social and economic structure they live in.' (Bailey and Brake, 1975b, p. 9) Casework is not rejected, only that which supports 'ruling-class hegemony'. Hegemony, here, means the use of ideology by the ruling class to maintain control of the working class.

One form of radical work is through collective action. Workers should ally themselves to working-class institutions, especially trade unions, and participate in political action, and community activity particularly within working-class organisations. Activity outside practice is relevant to practice, particularly since social work as an occupation and a set of agencies cannot expect to have substantial influences on social change (Statham, 1978, pp. 90–94). Decentralising and democratising teamwork is also essential, since it alerts workers to the community in which they operate, improves involvement in community issues, and promotes collective action.

The second major area of radical work, according to Bailey and Brake (1980), is individual work with clients. Workers should help people understand how oppression has alienated them from society, and raise their self-esteem. Personal and material needs should be distinguished; most working-class problems derive from material needs. In explaining clients' problems we should avoid individualising and blaming clients for social problems. In confrontation and negotiation, alliance and collective action with working-class organisations is more powerful than using social workers' influence alone.

One important result of this approach was an emphasis on clients' material needs. We should not see these as signs of personal and emotional problems. The growth of welfare rights and advocacy work on behalf of clients is therefore an important result of radical theory. The development of advocacy as a form of social work practice and theory is considered in the next Chapter.

Radical social work also, significantly, argues that social work emphasises traditional conceptions of the family, which led to the oppression of women, and this is considered further below. Women were often clients of social work when many of the problems should have involved and may have been caused by men. Such approaches became allied with the developing women's movement of the 1960s and 1970s. A distinctively feminist form of social work practice grew up (Statham, 1978; Wilson, 1980; Valentich, 1986; Hanmer and Statham, 1988; Dominelli and McCleod, 1989) which is dealt with later in this Chapter.

A particularly important radical perspective, based on the work of Freire (1972; see also Brigham, 1977), grew up in Latin America during the 1960s and 1970s, arising from a perception that Western social work was inadequate because it did not recognise that in poor countries the struggle merely to exist is the major priority. Rather than a form of social action stemming from reform which maintains society in a steady state, liberation from the struggle to subsist requires revolutionary change (Lusk, 1981). This philosophy led to a 'reconceptualisation' of social work in Latin America. Costa (1987) reviews a range of writing on these developments, emphasising the social worker as a wage earner in alliance with the working class, and political practice as part of social work. Among the techniques used is to seek the democratisation of social institutions so that clients may have influence within them, to create space and services especially appropriate for working-class people (e.g. welfare and civil rights), to become engaged with social movements, and to use professional associations and trade unions to seek change. Costa quotes Faleiros' four strategic alternatives:

- *conservative* – professionalising social work without any political engagement
- *denial* – becoming involved in popular political work without also being committed to changing social institutions for the benefit of clients
- *counter-institutional* – seeking deprofessionalisation, removing professional control and asking clients to make decisions (e.g. anti-psychiatry, which rejects medical and social help for mental illness in favour of self-help)
- *transformation* – seeking the transformation of social institutions through support of clients, professional activity and political action.

By implication, work in one sphere without accepting responsibility for other types of activity is likely to be ineffective.

Freire is concerned with the education of people whose communities are oppressed by poverty and powerlessness. Such people are 'objects' who are acted upon, rather than having the freedom to act that people who are 'subjects' have. However, there is a 'fear of freedom', which must be disposed of. This is done by education through involvement in critical 'dialogue' in which pure activism (trying to act without reflection and analysis) and pure verbalism (constantly talking about what to do without action) are merged together in praxis which involves acting on analyses of social situations, and influencing the analysis by the experience and effects of the action.

One of the important aspects of this is conscientisation which requires the consciousness of oppressed people to be raised. They become aware by this process of their oppression, rather than accepting it as inevitable, and through participation in dialogue and praxis, can take action to lose their fear of freedom and some of their powerlessness. Conscientisation has been connected to ideas of animation and agology which have their influence on the continent of Europe (Resnick, 1976). These are concerned with promoting collective activity, particularly arts and leisure, as an expression of community experience and as a medium of education. Agology is a service in which the worker guides and enables intentional planning of social and personal change. The same radical roots have given rise also to the idea of consciousness-raising as part of the woman's movement, and it has many of the same objectives in freeing women's perceptions, encouraging understanding of their oppressed state and the taking of collaborative action.

A Marxist perspective on social work: Corrigan and Leonard

The starting point of Corrigan and Leonard's book (1978) is that an explanation is needed of why welfare states are attacked for generating dependence and high costs while social structures still create oppression. Corrigan and Leonard argue that the Marxist method of enquiry, *historical materialism*, helps our understanding of these issues. This is an approach to history which studies how materials which are the necessities of life are produced. People are in a *dialectic* relationship with their social world; this means that while it influences and perhaps oppresses them, they may also influence it. Individuals create history, as well as being made by it.

The role of theory is important. The idea of *praxis* means that theories must be implemented in practice, and that practice reflects on and alters the theory. Theory must come partly from ideas outside daily practice, otherwise it would only be a simple reflection of that practice, but it must not be totally outside recognisable practice. Marxism sets out to study both *modes of production* and the *social relations* that they entail through historical materialism. The basic concepts of Marxist theory relevant to social work are set out in the following account, drawing on Corrigan and Leonard.

Production is about the way in which goods are produced in a society, setting the kind of social relationships that exist within it by establishing relationships between people and their natural surroundings and requiring them to work together.

In capitalist societies, labour becomes separated from the means of production, because more complex tools and manufacturing processes are out of the individual worker's financial reach. Labour thus comes to rely on capital accumulated by someone other than the worker to supply the means of production. The capitalist who owns the capital (i.e. the tools, machines, factories and money to buy materials in large quantities) needs to employ large numbers of workers relatively free of other social relations. In return, the capitalist pays a wage, which compensates the worker for part of the value of the labour provided, and retains the remainder of the value of that labour (the surplus value) in the form of profit, having sold the goods produced. Capitalists gain power over labour, tempered by institutions such as trade unions which protect the worker against the employer.

The arrangements necessary for capital production create typical social relations. People live in towns because this is the only way to get a job. Cheap and exploitative forms of housing (e.g. back to back houses and tenements in the 19th century and crowded flats in the 20th century) are devised. Working people suffer from fundamental insecurities because, whatever protections they may have built up, their jobs and livelihood depend on capital which they cannot control. These social relationships must be constantly renewed, otherwise capitalist production would fail. Therefore, capitalist societies must reproduce both capital and labour.

Families provide effective means of reproducing labour, through having and raising children, and reproduction involves socialising children into values which will enable them to accept working in production. The family is one environment in which individual experience can be related to wider social contradictions. Women's oppression arises because of the importance of their role as socialisers of children, in acting as consumers in the economic market, in being the stable centre of a family and in being reserve labour for use if there is not enough male labour, for example where there is war, illness or population decline.

Marx argued that the growth of capitalism broke up close social relationships and damaged, through the demands of production, family relationships in the working class. However, part of the ideological hegemony of the ruling class is the creation of an idealised concept of close family life. The experience of production and life outside the domestic role allows women to challenge the dominance of them by men in a patriarchal society.

There are, of course, many different kinds of family. We have become aware of this particularly because of the variety brought into industrialised societies by different cultural and ethnic groups. These different types of family derive from the different modes of production in the societies from which these cultures come. As they become part of capitalist societies, their traditional family relationships are forced to change or are at least put under conflict.

These social relations are dialectical, so that while industrial work is dehumanising, it also provides experience of human co-operation which enables people to learn its value, and while family life often oppresses women, it gives experience of personal control of an important area of life which is essentially humanising. These are examples of the contradictions which exist everywhere in capitalist life. By analysing and understanding such contradictions, social workers can see where to intervene in people's lives to make them more human. Encouraging involvement in co-operative activities, both for social workers and clients, can be supportive and personally valuable in the face of oppression. Stimulating women's consciousness of their potential and the co-operative and developmental aspects of family living can be valuable in combatting isolation and alienation in society.

Class explains social change in Marxist theory. Change is always taking place; social relations are never static. Classes are social groups with shared interests, which are created by the social relations arising from the mode of production. Critics would dispute whether interests are in fact shared within such large social groupings. In capitalist societies, Marxism says, the interests of the classes grow apart, and there are struggles between them for power. The main class division in society is between those who own the means of production and those who sell their labour, respectively, capitalists (or bourgeoisie) and working classes.

Social workers and similar occupational groups are part of the working class, because they sell their labour, but their role is to act on behalf of the apparatus of the state which seeks to reproduce the social relations of capitalism by the education and adjustment of people in society. Their position is, therefore, another contradiction. The power of capitalist institutions over them through their working role emphasises the importance of collective support among social workers and alliance with working-class organisations if they are to use the contradictions of their position to create social change.

Most people in society are forced to organise themselves to fight the interests of the other class, and this recognition of the importance of the struggle and the conflict of interests between the classes is a form of class consciousness. However, most people's experience of this struggle is as subordinates, so that they always feel without power and influence, and simply operate on the basis of protecting their interests rather than actively seeking change. The fact that only class struggle brings about significant social change means that to make progress in influencing society, social workers or anyone else seeking major social change need to ally themselves with working-class organisations, rather than attempting minor change through their own roles. We should demystify welfare issues and link them in working-class organisations with their more central activities. Thus, information-giving and welfare rights advice helps working-class organisations understand the effect of the state as part of oppression by capitalist societies of working-class people.

The *state*, by which social workers are employed, is the means by which society is established in the interests of capitalism and by which the working class or proletariat is maintained and reproduced. The state is autonomous from the ruling class since it represents the present results of class struggle and therefore the balance between the interests of the classes. Political and economic power do not always go together, therefore. Ruling class hegemony is, however, maintained in the long term.

Capitalism needs an 'efficient environment' for success, so that workers are well educated and healthy, and both capital and labour are reproduced. Welfare activities within the state also act as part of the presentation of the ideology of the ruling class. The system is evidently not wholly oppressive, and workers accept this, becoming apathetic about the possibilities of social change or achieving improvements in their lot. Thus the social worker acts both in the interests of the ruling class, and also represents achievements of the welfare state for the benefit of the working class.

Workers maintain an ideological resistance to the hegemony of the ruling class in the state. They do not give up opposing attitudes, but play the system to get benefits, and accept requirements made of them to achieve services and benefits from the welfare state. Ideological resistance of this kind is supported by actual resistance, through campaigns for welfare benefits and resistance to unwanted legislative change.

Social workers cannot be neutral between the state and the working class. Nobody is ever neutral in social relations, because they always have a role in the class struggle; neutrality implies accepting the status quo which always represents the interests of the ruling class. Similarly, positivist science in its acceptance of conservatively defined evidence and expertise tends to promote the interests of the ruling class because it assumes that the fundamental purpose of society (production) is not disputed, only the ways of achieving it efficiently are uncertain and need to be tested or sought.

Since the welfare state is part of the ideological apparatus of the state rather than being directly repressive, there is room for social workers to manoeuvre to the benefit of their clients. Therefore, how social workers tackle their role affects how their social functions may be defined. Their role is contradictory and the extent of the contradiction created depends on the function that they undertake.

Alienation from the means of production, because they are owned by the ruling class, leads to working-class people becoming fundamentally dissatisfied with their lives. Capitalist society encourages individualism because people must be mobile and in competition with each other. Capitalist ideology associates such alienation with the loneliness of isolation arising from individualism and assumes that this is part of the human condition. This would be the assumption of humanist and existential thought, for example. The cult of the individual also invades the state in the form of a philosophy of concern for the individual and for individualisation, which, we noted in Chapter 1, is a characteristic of social work.

Traditionally, Marxism has rejected the idea of personality and individual psychology being relevant to social understanding, but Leonard (1984) expands on his view of a Marxist psychology which is relevant for social work. He argues that this must start from acknowledgement that our psychology and personality comes from the social relations which are formed by the modes of production and reproduction. We experience contradictions which arise out of these modes in the form of ideology deriving from the demands made by the social order upon us. Thus, needs to consume products come from social pressures to consume which are there because the mode of production requires both consumption and an attitude that consumption is important. Synthesis between Marxist and conventional psychologies is not possible because their philosophical bases are irreconcilable. Instead, according to Leonard, we are constructed by our experiences of the economy and its consequences in the way we offer labour. Economic experiences also construct our organisation, domestic labour and the role of women, the level of income we receive (which affects our health, motivation and mental strength), the balance of effort which we may put into more satisfying mental activities rather than concrete activities aimed at subsistence and the need to consume. The family provides the physical site for our lives. Also the ideology of the family is required by the capitalist social order – including 'gender and age hierarchies' (i.e. whether men or women, older or younger family members are dominant). Socialisation in the family contributes to capitalist assumption about economic life and to wider social attitudes. The state by defining normal and deviant behaviour, reinforces ideology and divisions created and socialised by the economy and the family, sets up and enforces levels of achievement, stigma, income, discrimination, and promotes ideology generally beneficial to the ruling hegemony.

These determinants form a personality by social and personal control over the balance between concrete and abstract activity (so that some people, for example, are expected to be practical, unthinking types and attempts are not made to educate them otherwise), by the acceptance in our minds of the views that have been constructed by the ideology of the ruling hegemony, by identification with dominant ways of seeing how we should be, and by repression of anything which opposes dominant views of appropriate behaviour.

People have various means of resisting these forces, including stimulating consciousness of alternative and contradictory perceptions of the world, developing neurosis and similar behaviours which are evidence of unconscious resistance, developing personal capacities (which may be personally satisfying even if it does not contribute to the labour market), and participation in collective action. These ideas for a Marxist psychology are an important answer to the criticism that, in its emphasis on social forces, Marxism fails to consider personal and individual aspects of our lives. They also emphasise the family as the origin of, and as a place for dealing with, many social and personal issues.

Marxist approaches for everyday practice are as follows:

- working *collectively* with colleagues relating activity, particularly in a community setting, with working-class collective action in community groups and trade unions
- building up *co-operative* and *consciousness-raising* elements of family life, to make it a setting for good personal experiences creating a contradiction with the alienation and isolation of capitalist society
- helping the family cope with the consequences of being a unit of consumption for the market, and the pressures created by the way the employment market encourages the separation of roles in the family
- helping families seek a changing social pattern, rather than aiming at a fixed 'ideal' family
- helping families deal collectively with the problems of their oppression by capitalist society, rather than concentrating on individual problems, or on children's behaviour or women's roles (because they are not being socialised or being good mothers or housekeepers according to capitalist assumptions)

- understanding the meaning of the family members' work lives for arrangements within their family
- understanding conflicts in the family by looking at expected social relations; for instance disputes between generations (e.g. parents and children) arise within the context of preparing children for the labour market and to accept bourgeois ideological views of appropriate behaviour, which they often resist
- helping clients understand and reveal wider social conflicts and contradictions through family relationships, especially by looking, with elderly people, at the history of working-class experience in the community being served, and gaining their own view of the experiences that have led to their present position. The isolation of elderly people and their abandonment reflects their uselessness as units of labour for production and the need for families to concentrate on work, by being mobile (so leaving the area where the elderly parent lives) or out during the day and unable to help and support them. This is one of the consequences of capitalist production for the organisation of family life.

Lee and Pithers (1980) claim that radical social work has had little impact on residential work. They propose that residential care could be a significant alternative model for living in a collective community environment, which provides a counter-balance to family socialisation. Residential care practice could combat, in their view, some of the deleterious effects of socialisation into dominant ideologies.

Commentary

Radical social work has been a controversial development, and the debate has stimulated a variety of criticisms of it:

- it tends to neglect the immediate personal needs of clients, in favour of promoting their consciousness or some form of collective action. This is unethical, uncaring or impractical because it is not what the social services are set up to do, and it provides only a partial explanation for the behaviour and events which are met by social workers. Leonard's Marxist individual psychology tries to counter this by connecting broad general explanations from the social theory with understanding of individual responses

- radical theory is weak in dealing with emotional problems because its concentration on material and social issues and promotion of services like welfare rights advice ignores clients' humanity and emotional and personal problems in favour of a prescription which comes from the theory rather than a response to the problems which at least some clients present. So, it risks failing in the opposite way to traditional social work

- it does not prescribe what to do, but merely offers an approach to understanding the situation in which clients and social workers operate. It relies on insight which is criticised in relation to psychodynamic theories (although we saw when considering behavioural theories that it can speed people's responses to problems), but it does not say that insight brings immediate results since class struggle must follow class consciousness. Failure to offer prescriptions is true of other social work theories (e.g. systems theories); it is likely that having a theory which offers an overall perspective on the situation is useful and radical theory can be accepted as one such

- its accumulation of information critical of the treatment of many different groups identifies many problems (which can be demotivating for social workers), but fails to provide a coherent statement of what this means and a co-ordinated view of appropriate action (Rojek *et al.*, 1988)

- it has a limited view of power and equates it with control, allying social workers excessively with oppression, and not fully identifying the complexity of power relations among people at the personal level, where, as existentialists would argue, even victimised clients have a good deal of power (Rojek *et al.*, 1988).

- although it claims to seek social change, it is impossible to ally all the interests of the groups involved, which often conflict, and in practice it seems to move towards achieving only more from existing services for those said to be oppressed (Rojek *et al.*, 1988)

- it is an ideology, rather than a theory: that is, it does not offer an explanation which can be tested empirically. Marxists would answer that their method of investigation through historical analysis and debate is a legitimate form of study. They argue that positivist science maintains the ruling hegemony by accepting and promoting the present social order, and so is an inappropriate form of investigation for a radical theory; and that all theory represents ideological positions, often in support of the ruling class
- like many ideologies, radical theories define objections in their own terms and explain them away (objections are often taken to be representations of ruling ideologies). The same is said of other theories (e.g. in psychodynamic theory, objections or inability to accept the theory is sometimes claimed to arise from unconscious fears or conflicts in the objector)
- some radical theories emphasise inadequate and oppressive environments and services as a better basis for explanation of clients problems than individual psychology, but, at its worst, this can substitute blame for local environments and their occupants in general for blame of an individual victim as an explanation (Galper, 1975; Webb, 1981). This might lead social workers' support for clients to be seen in opposition to the needs and interests of others in the same environment, since the needs and wishes of the poorest cannot always be aligned with those of all the working class – Clarke (1976) gives an example of this in a conflict involving social workers over facilities on a public housing scheme.

To make an overall assessment of these criticisms, most of the practice prescriptions of radical social work concern collective action rather than individual help, or helping people to radical understandings of their personal circumstances, from which position their options are acceptance or long-term resistance. It is hard to see how this is widely helpful. Workers might have difficulties in official agencies which represent the ruling ideology in trying to promote radical approaches, and are likely either to be excluded or to become frustrated in their inability to take action. It is important not to go too far with this criticism. Many agencies and clients in fact welcome radical and community-oriented approaches, and the fact of opposition does not mean that a perspective should be ignored. It may offer a useful view to contribute to work, using other theories, or to organise social workers' ideas, while not conflicting unreasonably with their function in the agency. In this regard, it is important to read carefully the more sophisticated analyses of the contradictory position, rather than assuming that all radical social work will necessarily require a conflictual approach to practice.

One of the advantages of the radical perspective which negates these general criticisms is that it highlights certain aspects of life, including the importance of power, ideological hegemony, class and status, professionalisation, gender and oppression. Marxism makes these ideas available to social work in understandable form, and has led to a substantial development of practice in relation to these ideas. Its emphasis on power in particular draws into social work theory perspectives which have direct relevance to sexism and racism in ways which few other theories adequately achieve. For this reason, an account of feminist and non-sexist approaches to social work is offered in the next section.

Feminist and non-sexist social work

Feminist social work and therapy is help, usually given by women to other women, aimed at exploring and removing the effects of oppression arising from sexism in society and thus enabling clients greater freedom and control over their lives and capacity for personal development and growth. In the longer term, the aim is to remove oppression due to sexism. More broadly, non-sexist work attempts to avoid social work processes being used in ways which oppress or discriminate against women or which confirm attitudes of male dominance in society. There is some difference of opinion about whether men are able to do feminist work; Valentich (1986) says that some writers accept that male involvement is possible.

Feminist and non-sexist social work have their roots in the women's movement of the 1960s and 1970s. Among concerns about oppression of women were doubts about the value of help for women, particularly in psychiatry, and about the psychological theories underlying the theory and practice of helping. We saw in Chapter 3 that there was criticism of the bias of psychodynamic theory in this respect. Feminists seek to understand the lives and experience of women from their own perspectives and values which are different from men's, and thus avoid being looked at from the point of view of men (androcentrism) (A. Hudson, 1985). In social work, it is argued that goal- and task-oriented practice, and positivist demands for scientific practice, are male-defined priorities, using a male language and way of thinking (B. Collins, 1986). Gilligan's work (1982) has been influential. She shows that women and men have different modes of reasoning about moral questions (Rhodes, 1985), and L. Davis (1985) argues that female 'voices' have been suppressed in favour of a male positivist perspective. Alternative ways of defining social work, and particularly of ensuring that agencies are not managed so as to exclude women and their perspectives, are required. Since feminists are concerned with achieving a state of equality between men and women (and, therefore, with attacking, not men, but the present state of patriarchy in which men are on most social assumptions in a dominant position), their practice should reflect an egalitarian approach (Dominelli and McCleod, 1989).

Work on gender issues is important in settings where sexuality and its control become relevant. In residential care, for example, attempts are sometimes made to create asexual or sexually unusual environments (Harris and Lipman, 1984) in order to avoid the complexities of managing sexuality in an abnormal environment; all places where people are living together for substantial periods are likely to raise gender and sexual issues.

Hanmer and Statham (1988) present an approach to social work which is not explicitly Marxist, and seeks to be woman-centred and non-sexist rather than feminist. Dominelli and McCleod (1989) cover similar ground from a Marxist position. Gender, in Hanmer and Statham's account, is the basis of important life experiences for women. They are often defined by their gender (e.g. as mothers, wives), while men are defined by their status (e.g. job titles). Yet, women's gender often becomes invisible because they are socially expected to accept certain roles (e.g. carer, elderly) which are often expected of women rather than men, but that expectation is unstated. So, public policy assumes that informal carers will be the main helpers of people with difficulties, but informal carers are nearly always women.

Women have many things in common, e.g. managing both home and job, living with and caring for men, and being mothers and caring for dependents. Important differences between them which lead to diverse experiences and expectations are: different employment patterns and status, ethnic differences, different experiences of being powerful or feeling powerless. Thus, a white woman in a professional job with experience of being seen as competent and powerful on occasions, will have a different view of life and have different expectations made of her than a black woman in a manual job who has felt powerless to affect her life. Dominelli and McCleod (1989) make the point that gender cannot be separated from other forms of oppression, and in particular class and ethnic differences, although women often have a special experience of such differences. Nonetheless, Hanmer and Statham argue that women are treated as dependent on and inferior to men, and share the experience of the expectations that arise from this. Social workers should start from recognising the common experiences of women, and should always move on to examining the diversities between one particular woman and others. Then, gender is an important theme in defining women in three main ways: women are always expected to be *carers*, to be *subordinate to men*, and for effective work their *personal identity* is crucial to overcoming many problems that they face.

Assessment of women clients should always contain knowledge of life patterns and policies that affect women, and assumptions which often affect how they are assessed. Relevant life patterns include demographic factors, such as the fact that there are increasing numbers of one-parent families, reductions in the number of children in households, increase in divorce and remarriage, and more working mothers. We should not always make assumptions about normal or acceptable behaviour in women without taking these developments into account. Women are often poorer than men, and experience more strongly the effects of poor family income, poor housing and transport. The importance of women's work both to family income and to self-respect is often underestimated by social workers.

Especially important in assessing women clients is their role as carers. Most women have and care for children, and often other dependents at different stages of their lives. Our assessment of their capacity to do so often reflects cultural assumptions, which may be questioned. Different ethnic groups, for example, may expect different kinds of approach to child care. We may also have expectations that might be questioned, such as expecting that clients will always be able to have stable monogamous relationships with a man, or will be able to care without relief for several young children in a more material and home environment. Because women are assumed to be able and willing to care, their contribution may be taken for granted and they are often given less help than men in similar circumstances. Workers should avoid making resource allocations on such assumptions.

It should not be assumed that women will usually be dependent upon, care for and be subordinate to men. Their status and relationships will be defined by marriage, or the legal consequences of divorce, or the fact that they are unmarried. Their caring role requires skill and commitment, but is often undervalued compared with men's social status defined by their job. Work can usefully focus on promoting women's identity, self-image and self-esteem. Women can be encouraged to see their achievements, to demand support and resources for the important work that they do.

To recognise and share the experiences of women clients in this position, women social workers must recognise power imbalances and unequal treatment that they receive as employees in agencies which are dominated by men and male attitudes. Women are often excluded from promotion and have difficulties in using their perspective in management, which is often defined in male language and expectations. There are a variety of shared and collaborative approaches to dealing with this recommended by Hanmer and Statham (1988).

In working with clients, they propose a variety of strategies for women-centred work, and these are summarised in Table 10.1.

Table 10.1 *Principles of woman-centred work*

Principle	Practice of social worker
preparation	clarify aims, accept writing and recording as helpful in meeting aims rather than feeling disabled by demands for this, check facts and research about women, develop skills and knowledge to be able to challenge from a strong position, take risks to ask for appropriate help, support and resources, define services and policies which are unhelpful to women, keep information on resources for women clients

Principle	Practice of social worker
devise principles for women-centred practice	like and value women, use experience of women as a resource, believe and accept women, share with and learn from clients in non-hierarchical ways, use all women groups, ensure space of women to get away from caring and dependence on men, avoid using conventional assumptions which treat women's ordinary behaviour as bad (e.g. sexuality), encourage women to feel in control of their lives and behaviour, use a wide range of social
make methods relevant to gender	work theories and methods give importance and time to women alone, adapt theories so that they affirm rather than criticise women, avoid stereotyping and sexualising women's behaviour, avoid sexist language, accept oppression and unhappiness, accept disagreement with feminist views, avoid jargon about oppression, aim for success in limited tasks, use groups to stress shared experience and support, use separate groups because men tend to dominate groups which include both sexes
link clients to agencies specialising in women's needs	generalist agencies may not provide enough help of the right kind
increase resources for women	encourage expresssion of needs and formalise and gain support for new resources, encourage equal opportunity policies and structures
involve women in decision-making and policy-making of the agency	set up representative arrangements
create a code for feminist practice	establish women's groups and training

Source: Hanmer and Statham (1988).

McCleod's (1979) work with prostitutes is an example of feminist social work showing the reality of poverty and the need to maintain their families which leads prostitutes to gain the high material rewards from this work, contrary to the more conventional assumption that they become committed to prostitution through contact with deviant subcultures and personal inadequacies. Donnelly (1986) gives one of a number of accounts of groupwork with women clients, raising the sense of shared experience and understanding of women on a deprived housing estate. Both are aimed in various ways at consciousness raising, which Longres and McCleod (1980) relate to the conscientisation of Freire (1972), discussed above, and is thus explicitly radical. Not all feminist therapy and social work is radical, however. Their analysis is that consciousness raising aims to encourage reflection, so as to understand dehumanising social structures, and action to change such social conditions. It involves dialogue between equals, concern for ideology and how dominant ideologies in society may create misfortune and social problems, mutual and shared exploration and respect for each other's views, and making connections between private troubles and public issues and individual and class interests. Consciousness raising is best done in groups for mutual support and broader exploration. It may be harder to find the time and commitment in individual work, and harder to empathise where the relationship between an individual client and worker is usually unequal. There needs to be a commitment to action to change situations which are identified in groups, otherwise complaining about the 'system' simply leads to complaining acceptance of it. Donnelly's work (1986) brought together a group of women from a run-down public housing estate in England, with the aim of helping them realise that they shared many problems and experiences, and that they could understand and take control of their lives.

Commentary

Feminist and non-sexist work has raised great interest since the early 1980s and has become important to many women. It also offers lessons to male social workers in understanding and approaching their women clients, leading to new and less judgemental approaches to women's sexuality and lives. It has close relationships to empowerment strategies, which are the subject of the next Chapter.

One of the problems of creating feminist therapies (which also applies to the empowerment concepts deriving from work with ethnic minorities used in the next Chapter) is that it may detract from the need to permeate all social work with a concern with non-racist and non-sexist work and ideas. Much of the relevant social work literature goes out of its way to emphasise that patriarchy and gender oppression oppress men as well as women, but the creation of a separate category of activity seems in some cases to raise conflict with men and male-dominated institutions. There is not yet a well-developed theory for working in this way with men in difficulties, whose priorities are likely to be elsewhere. Similarly, it could also be claimed that giving too great a priority to this work with many women clients may take resources and effort away from a more practical attention to their poverty and social problems.

Theoretically, there is difficulty in balancing attention to gender oppression with attention to oppression due to class and ethnic minorities, as well as a variety of other stigmas; this has led to a tendency to separate these concerns, which have so far proved hard to integrate. Non-sexist and feminist social work also raises the difficulty that it is based on insight techniques, which some-times, as with other social work theories, do not specify clearly how to intervene once problems are revealed; it tends to be assumed that insight into oppression will naturally lead to action from the client and that the insights are relevant to the clients' priorities in seeking help.

11

Empowerment and Advocacy

Connections

In the previous Chapter, we saw that radical and Marxist theories attempt to offer a perspective on social work which concentrates on social change, but, at least in their more sophisticated formulations, these theories recognise that most workers are concerned with relatively small communities or with individuals, families and small groups rather than political action. So, efforts are made to give guidance for practice which acknowledges and does not conflict with wider social objectives and which might contribute to social change by promoting positive aspects of human experience which would help towards such change. One application of such ideas in non-sexist and feminist social work demonstrated how they could be taken up.

Radical social work has achieved considerable influence in social work, particularly in Europe, and has succeeded in ensuring that social workers are aware of the social-control functions of their work, and potential conflicts between their caring and enabling roles and their official and controlling functions. There is also greater consciousness of the tendency of much social work theory to accept and assume that social workers should reinforce the current social order. Many clients' oppression by and alienation from powerful groups in society is better recognised, as is the close relationship of social workers and their agencies with those groups.

Concern for the needs of clearly-identifiable groups in society (particularly ethnic minorities and groups suffering from various forms of social stigma due to disability) who are oppressed in this way has led to the development of models of practice designed to meet their needs. These tend to concentrate explicitly on the advocacy role of social work.

The most important concept is that of *empowerment*. A full and comprehensive analysis of practice according to this perspective is contained in Solomon's (1976) book, which is outlined below as an example of this approach. Furlong (1987) sees empowerment as an important goal in casework because it avoids a crude polarisation of social action and individualised perspectives, placing work with individuals and families in a context of concern for social objectives. Russel-Erlich and Rivera (1986) argue that promoting empowerment in oppressed communities is an essential response to trends in political and economic life which add to oppression.

Rojek (1986) argues that, although closely related to radical and Marxist perspectives, advocacy and empowerment strategies have fundamentally different objectives. They are rationalist in nature, assuming that it is possible to change the environment in clients' favour. Radical approaches are materialist and claim that the social system needs broad change before true empowerment is possible. Radical and Marxist social workers would seek empowerment in order to create contradictions in society which would lead to eventual change, rather than, as the rationalist would, expect to change society directly.

Advocacy

Advocacy is another important strand of social work practice which seeks to promote clients' own control and involvement in their lives, communities and services. It is a formal application of that feature of social work identified in Chapter 1. Early in its development, advocacy was seen as a service to clients; *case advocacy* was provided by professionals to enhance clients' access to provision designed to benefit them; *cause advocacy* sought to promote social change for the benefit of social groups from which clients came.

More recently, a process of increasing the capacity of people with mental illness and mental handicaps to manage their own lives has led to a movement to provide them with assistance to achieve their civil rights within institutions and to leave institutions where they may have been held by compulsion. This movement, growing up in the USA, has moved to the UK and has been particularly important in promoting the independence of people with disabilities.

Related to advocacy is the idea of *normalisation*, which seeks to offer people in institutions an environment which gives them valued social roles and a lifestyle as close to those valued by people outside institutions. This has proved to be an influential development in the residential care field and in work with people with learning disabilities (Towell, 1988; Sinclair, 1988).

Many of these developments are brought together together in the work of Rose and Black (1985) which describes a project promoting independent living for mentally-ill people in the community. Their approach is based explicitly on the work of Freire (see Chapter 10) in that they seek to empower people to become subjects rather than objects in their lives, by involving them in the process of advocacy. *Critical debate* with clients enters their present subjective reality and explores objective reality with them, so that they can see various situations where their subjective reality limits their control of the environment. Clients are engaged in a *transformation* from dependence to interdependence with collective networks of social support. Total autonomy is not desirable (or attainable for many people): we are all interdependent with others to some extent.

The work is broadly educational, following Freire's perspective. All social exchanges have a political content in that they either accept or deny the present social order. By *dialogue* in a situation of trust, with people who behave authentically (in humanist terms), clients engage in a *praxis*, acting and experiencing the reality that results from their actions which then affects later actions. (Praxis is reflexive in this way.) Workers try to get inside and understand clients' reality. They are oppressed by the institutionalisation, poverty and material deprivation which they have taken into their own view of the world caused by their history in mental hospitals. Self-expression is encouraged, helping them gain vitality and acceptance of their own capacity and worth. *Validation* is the main treatment process, aimed at reconnecting clients to their capacity for self-expression. This is done through trying to understand the reality of their own life history, and rejecting internalised judgements that they are incompetent. Clients become 'producer-participants' in their lives rather than passively consuming services.

The process of the work is set out in Table 11.1. From this account, it will be seen that although the approach is avowedly radical, it has many connections with humanist and existential ideas, and emphasises values of self-knowledge and self-control which also accept that clients can have rational cognitive control of their lives.

Table 11.1 *Advocacy and empowerment processes*

Phase	Process	Activity
beginning	limit-setting	identify specific areas of praxis
	problem-posing	elaborate problems as client explores their perceptions, so that client can see how the world has created that problem; explore differences between worker's and client's view of problems; enhance trust through authenticity
	identifying options for action	use worker's knowledge to help client understand how world may be affected; identify how client may be an actor rather than an object in relation to particular problems; avoid leadership domination – shared responsibility for decisions
advocacy/ empowerment practice	'verstehen'	understanding client's perspective, especially their self-concept; demonstrate trust, non-domination; offer opportunities for new language, understanding and reference points
	thematisation	establish *generative themes* in clients' lives (central ideas about the distortions and oppression in their lives); look for *alienation* arising from poverty, exploitation and powerlessness, or *submergence* from legitimation of oppression and mystification of reality
	problemisation	evaluate clients' elaborated description of their world critically; see where world can be changed rather than seen as unchangeable

Table 11.1 (*contd.*)

Phase	Process	Activity
	anomie	help clients understand that it is understandable to fear the loss of certainty of previous life of dependence; support rational planning for the future rather than fear reactions
	analysis of consequences of action	strategic planning; assess possible realistic actions; help clients understand power differences and conflicts of interest that will make some actions impossible
	choice	choose targets for action; join in process of struggling with decision about whether to act or not
	action	reflect and analyse actions and their outcomes so that praxis is continuous
	evaluation	assess what has been achieved after completion of action; assess what process felt like; begin critical reflection to improve future action
	'verstehen'	assess how clients and workers have been changed by the action, and the process begins all over again, in a new cycle of activity

Source: Rose and Black (1985).

Black empowerment: Barbara Solomon

Solomon's book (1976) applies to all oppressed communities, but she is particularly concerned with black ethnic minorities. We all need personal and financial resources to accept valued identities and roles. *Powerlessness* in individuals or social groups is defined by Solomon as 'the inability to manage emotions, skills, knowledge and/or material resources in a way that effective performance of valued social roles will lead to personal gratification' (p. 16).

In some communities, people have been negatively valued so much and for so long that their powerlessness is extensive and crippling. *Negative valuations* occur in practices, organisations and events which discriminate against minority groups and also in language which attaches derogatory words to such groups.

Empowerment aims to use specific strategies to reduce, eliminate, combat and reverse negative valuations by powerful groups in society affecting certain individuals and social groups. It may be particularly useful to apply it in family work since mutual support may strengthen the development of capacity among family members, and help to interpret the worker's intervention jointly within the family's culture (Weaver, 1982; Pinderhughes, 1983).

Social workers have difficulties with empowerment strategies because their agencies are part of a social system which routinely devalues certain minority groups. Making equal responses to all people who come to an agency may reduce discrimination. Since negative valuations are so widespread, agencies may unthinkingly implement them, so that potential clients are discouraged from using the agency and so do not receive the equal treatment available. Also, agencies may reflect negative valuations in their own organisation, for example by not employing any black people in senior positions or by deciding not to have an office in an area with a predominantly ethnic minority population in order to protect staff from potential violence. In relation to ethnic minorities, this endemic and widespread negative valuation is called *institutionalised racism*. Negative valuations of minorities (not only ethnic minorites) may be so institutionalised that the problem may not be perceived. In many cases, therefore, such groups suffer from *power absence* rather than *power failure* (meaning that they have tried to use power and failed).

An empowerment strategy requires commitment to *both* maintenance and improvement of effective equal services and *also* to confrontation of pervasive negative valuations.

Most people, according to Solomon, move through *three levels of development*. They have:

- positive experiences in early family life which give them confidence and competence in social interactions, and this
- reinforces their ability to manage social relationships and use social institutions (e.g. schools) to gain further competence, with which
- they can accept and perform well in valued social roles.

Indirect power blocks can affect each level. Negative early experiences (e.g. stigma due to race, disability or poverty) reduce confidence in social interaction which in turn reduces the gain to be made at the second level and therefore obstructs the growth of capacity to perform valued social roles at the third level. *Direct power blocks* similarly affect each level. Poor services, for example, might mean bad health, retarded early growth; discrimination in education may restrict access to learning and equally may prevent people taking on valued social roles.

Solomon argues that because social work has concentrated on changing individuals rather than social institutions it is weak at dealing with power blocks.

The *aims* of empowerment are to help clients see:

- themselves as *causal agents* in finding solutions to their problems
- social workers as having knowledge and skills that clients can use
- social workers as peers and partners in solving problems and
- the power structure as complex and partly open to influence.

The *model of practice* is:

- to overcome responses among clients that arise from negative valuations so that they see themselves as able to have some impact on their problem
- to locate and remove blocks and find and reinforce supports to effective problem-solving.

Social workers must always be aware of powerlessness. For example, advocacy for a social security allowance might be seen as using the worker's skills or as taking away clients' freedom to act for themselves. These possibilities and their implications for individuals should be assessed. Workers should also beware of seeing clients as the cause of their problems simply because they are trying to see clients as causal agents in solving their problems. For example, I worked with a woman who was accused of neglecting her child because she was not developing properly. As part of this, I was trying to help her to see ways in which she could play with the child regularly as part of her day. This is to treat her as a causal agent who can actively do something about her problem, rather than sending the child to a nursery where someone else would take over from her. While doing this, I found myself becoming frustrated and blaming her for her inability to organise her day to make time for the child, and for her lack of creativity in playing with the child, who became bored. This was, wrongly, to see her as the cause of these problems. It was more appropriate to acknowledge that the poverty of her surroundings and the constant struggle to make ends meet took up much of her time and energy, and the lack of experience of mothering in her own childhood limited her capacity. It was more effective to involve an older woman assistant who could offer her more personal time, and help her also to plan her domestic responsibilities to make space for the child.

The *characteristics of a non-racist practitioner* may be extended to apply to work with many oppressed groups:

- the ability to see alternative explanations for any behaviour, and especially those alternatives which we might most want to reject as false
- the ability to use many cues to choose the alternative explanation which is most relevant to the client
- the ability to feel warmth, genuine concern and empathy regardless of race or other characteristics
- the ability to confront clients when true feelings of warmth have been misinterpreted or distorted.

Solomon's approach to engaging black-client systems in work can also usefully be applied to a wide range of oppressed groups. The underlying assumption is that most blacks coming to social agencies have been sent by others and will not be convinced that workers have anything to offer. Rapport must be established across the racial divide, in spite of a pervasive distrust of whites and of established agencies. We can see these feelings in many other clients of social work agencies. Workers should show familiarity with the communication patterns, life styles and life experience of the client and must present themselves 'authentically' in the humanist sense. It is often important to make clear the helping role of the worker in contrast to experiences that clients may have had of other agencies.

Assessing *motivation, capacity and opportunity* is crucial, since access to services is often obstructed by failings in the way this is done. Our criteria for motivation may be inappropriate, because the worker values things which the client's culture does not value. Knowing appropriate cultural expectations and patterns gives clues about what will motivate clients. Capacity may be more accurately assessed in an environment which is more secure for the client than an office or formal setting. Opportunity needs weighing carefully, since the client may be blamed for not taking up opportunities which in reality have not been available, because of various blocks, as in the case of the mother being unable to play with her child. Contracts should always place the client as the main causal agent.

The *worker's roles* which work best in empowerment are:

- resources consultant – linking clients to resources in ways which improve their self-esteem and problem-solving abilities
- sensitiser – assisting clients to gain self-knowledge
- teacher/trainer – teaching processes and skills which will enable the client to complete specific tasks.

For example, I worked with an elderly man from an Asian community who was becoming disabled, and was isolated because several friends had returned to Malaysia. Rather than arrange attendance at a day centre, which I thought might be unsympathetic, I suggested that we both investigate various possibilites for social contact through organisations that we knew. We sat down to identify some that we each knew, and he came with me as I approached one organisation that I had not been in touch with before. It proved uncongenial for him. Having had this experience, however, he followed up some of the other contacts for himself; while he did not become involved with these groups for various reasons, he seemed happier to go out more and made one or two contacts in the community. I think this came from the social skills and confidence acquired and having learned how to make new approaches.

An important strategy is to help the client to provide services in their family, neighbourhood or community. A more equal relationship between client and worker often results, since both are offering something, and mutuality and complementarity of relationships in the community also improves. For example, helping a woman to improve her child-care skills may improve her self-esteem, give her skills to feed back into the community, improve relationships in the family, and help to prevent the child having poor experiences at the first stage of development.

Learned helplessness theory

Barber (1986) proposes that learned helplessness theory may be a useful perspective for social work. These ideas are closely related to, and offer some research support for, ideas of empowerment. Seligman's (1975) theory is based on experiments with animals and humans which shows that if people have important experiences which show that what they do has no effect on what happens to them, they form the expectation that their actions will generally not produce any useful results. Their capacity to learn useful behaviour in other situations becomes impaired. People may lose motivation, become anxious and depressed and poor at thinking and learning. This evidence clearly supports some of Solomon's (1976) ideas about powerlessness. People who are powerless throughout their lives would carry a sizeable burden of learned helplessness. The response should be, according to Barber (1986), *environmental enrichment* by giving such people experience of situations in which they are in control and achieve successful results.

Commentary

Advocacy and empowerment strategies have proved attractive in recent years as a development and implementation of radical social work, and one of social work's fundamental features. Concern about dealing with oppression and prejudice, particularly against black people, has strengthened interest. Advocacy has evolved strongly as part of the movement to discharge many people from long-stay institutions in which they would previously have been cared for.

These approaches are idealistic, but it is a practical idealism, which can be implemented. Some forms of therapy can, if used incautiously, make people dependent on the expertise of the worker. Therefore, it may be argued that advocacy and empowerment represent an ideology of treatment which is radically different, or at least is experienced differently by client and, perhaps, worker.

The philosophy of self-control, personal responsibility and self-actualisation through empowerment has relationships with cognitive and particularly humanist approaches, although humanist therapies tend not to emphasise so clearly (although it is present in Rogers' later work, and Goldstein's) the importance of power differentials, class, and oppression, as aspects of society which obstruct self-actualisation and need actively to be overcome. Critical review of empowerment and advocacy theories has not developed yet, but potential criticisms may be identified. Like insight therapies, empowerment concentrates on developing clients' capacities and does not seek direct change in oppressive social structures, except by the effects of individual cases through advocacy. It thus tends to place the responsibility for social change upon clients, who may be strengthened, but still face formidable social obstacles. The practice prescriptions do not address powerless people whose own capacities are inadequate to the assumption of full power over their lives; there is a danger that workers will act as though all clients can achieve a high degree of empowerment. There is no doubt that many very damaged, oppressed and institutionalised clients can achieve significantly greater degrees of self-control and power through such techniques, but this should not exclude therapeutic work for their benefit as well. Another difficulty, where social workers are dealing with individuals, is that it is not clear that empowerment of individuals generalises to their wider community or networks, so that the empowered individual may be taking up power and resources from others in their oppressed environment, to their disadvantage, rather than taking it from wider society. In a social and political environment where resources are limited, empowerment may be setting one oppressed or deprived group against another, rather than uniting them.

12

Assessing Social Work Theories

How can we assess the role of social work theory in social work and the place of the various theories in practice? In the first Chapter, I argued that theory, like social work itself, was socially constructed by the participants and the context in which they met to carry out the activity of social work. It follows from this view that theory is not solely an intellectual development, but responds to the social forces creating social work at this moment, many of which come from practice. We need to look at the social circumstances in which social work theory is used in practice to see how current trends and developments in theory reflect present social assumptions.

This Chapter is concerned with how social workers may assess and integrate theories into their practice in modern circumstances. The first point is that different theories may be used for different purposes. Research into their effectiveness can help to assess their validity, but it does not give us all the answers about usefulness, because many theories are about ideas and interpretation rather than prescription for actions. The uses of different theories conflict, and also build up trends in the development of theories in which there are clear parallels with the social and political roles of social work in society.

Different uses of theory

A number of the theories examined set out to be comprehensive in their applicability, others less so. The nature of their comprehensiveness also varies. So, one way of deciding on the value of theories is to fit them into a series of categories which define the circumstances in which they claim to be useful:

- *comprehensive* theories offer a system of thought to cover all the practice that social workers might want to undertake in casework, residential work and groupwork; they might also claim an applicability to community work, but as a central theory of practice, I have argued that psychological approaches are not within the tradition of community work theory. Examples of theories which claim to be comprehensive are psychodynamic, behavioural, systems and ecological and cognitive ideas
- *comprehensive inclusive* theories would also accept the inclusion of many other perspectives and methods drawn from other theories. Examples are systems and ecological approaches

One of the reasons why these theories are so broadly applicable is that they are relatively mature systems of thought, usually because they are built on very well-established sets of ideas in psychology or sociology, and they have had time within social work to be subjected to development and debate, and to acquire evidence of broad application. On this count, there is some doubt about cognitive theory, which is well-established in psychology and counselling, but a relative upstart; and in social work it is very much a theory of the 1980s, whose implications have not yet been worked through.

Three categories remain:

- *specific* theories at the other end of the spectrum offer ideas and techniques which would benefit social workers in their work, whichever theory they were using. An example is communication theory. It offers a broad way of looking at the world, but not an overall approach to doing social work
- *perspective* theories offer a way of looking at the world, and particularly personal and social change, which would be beneficial for social workers. Into this category, I would put humanist and existential and radical theories. Attached to them are a number of ideas about practice, some fairly

exclusive, others drawn from more general theories of sociology, psychology and therapy. Some would argue that systems and ecological theories also fall into this group

- *application* theories offer both useful broad ideas, which are widely applicable, and some specific techniques designed to apply to particular target problems or social and personal situations. Crisis, task-centred, empowerment and advocacy, and perhaps also non-sexist or feminist work fall into this group.

In many cases, specific and application theories may be used together with comprehensive, inclusive and perspective theories, to enhance them where their prescriptions for action are inadequate or seem limited. Perspective theories may also offer alternative ideas and systems of thought to help us understand groups of clients or social situations where another theory, which may generally be preferred, is inadequate, undeveloped or rejected by clients. For example, we may generally think that behavioural theories are practically useful and effective, but not where we are dealing with groups in political conflict or which have social ideologies that are opposed to this individual approach. At least to understand their view, and perhaps to intervene in a different way, we might find radical or empowerment theory useful. This does not imply a rejection of behavioural theory, merely that we have reserved it for its most useful place in our work.

As I showed in Chapter 2 when considering eclecticism, we should be cautious in selecting from theories to use together. Different types of theory might be most usefully combined; but we should be careful of trying to combine, say, two comprehensive theories, since their assumptions, which are intended to cover many eventualities and hence probably the one we are considering, will probably be in conflict and thus should not be used together.

Using research to assess theory

Another valid way of selecting appropriate theories for use is the research which shows that they are likely to be effective. Perspective and inclusive theories are not generally supported by research;

they are intended to help us organise our ideas. There is some research evidence about many other theories, but much of it is in dispute. Much research is about problems or social programme evaluation (Brawley and Martinez-Brawley, 1988), rather than attempting to validate theoretical approaches (Jenkins, 1987), so it does not help us to say whether this or that theory is 'true' in any sense. In any case, Sainsbury (1987) makes the point that often research does not produce direct changes in practice, because it would be too much to expect people already committed to particular services to make major changes in direction, even if sufficiently convincing findings could help them to do so. There is also a problem about creating a bridge between people who generate research findings and those who might use them (Brawley and Martinez-Brawley, 1988). What happens is that research tends to affect the professional climate of opinion, and lead to slowly changing and developing progress.

Research perspectives on specific theories have been given briefly in the relevant chapters; the purpose of this section is to consider research validity in a general way to see which theories might be selected that are generally well-supported by research. Since many approaches have been imported into social work from psychology, psychotherapy and medicine, research sometimes exists in these disciplines, although where treatment techniques have been substantially changed within social work, research in original disciplines may not be applicable. Research into psychoanalysis, for example, is not encouraging, but social work uses of psychodynamic theory are distant from its formal application as therapy, and constitute more of a comprehensive perspective which informs social work practice values, than something to which the original research should apply.

Research, generally in recent years of a small-scale nature, exists in social work on specific techniques, and some rather older broad outcome studies also exist. It is not possible to review all these studies, which have led to several other tomes; all that is possible is to offer some overall summary. Rachman and Wilson (1980) in an authoritative review of the clinical psychotherapeutic literature, conclude that there is no quantitative evidence 'to support the view that psychoanalysis is an effective treatment (p. 76)' although a good deal of clinical evidence does exist, and many would argue that quantitative evidence is not appropriate for testing psychotherapeutic activity, because it is essentially subjective and clinical in nature and hard to test rigorously. Rachman and Wilson judge that rigorous testing is feasible, although many of the studies purporting to show success do not meet high standards of statistical and research design, and they consider that 'there is only modest evidence to support the view that psychotherapy produces beneficial effects (p. 77).'

Behaviour therapy, including social skills techniques, are well-researched. According to Rachman and Wilson:

> . . . it is clear that [it] has demonstrated value in the treatment of several clinical disorders. Most of the available evidence indicates the short-term success of behavioural methods. Well controlled studies of the long-term clinical efficacy of behaviour therapy are needed (p. 194) . . .

There are doubts about Rogerian (i.e. humanist) therapies, in their view, partly because the research concentrates on therapist skills, which, as we have seen, are acknowledged, and therefore there is little evidence on what particular techniques work with what particular conditions. There is evidence that several cognitive therapies are effective in fairly limited circumstances.

Turning to the social work research, reviews of it in recent years conclude that the position is more optimistic than after the first wave of evaluative research in the 1950s and 1960s, which showed that in meeting broad programme objectives, the social work techniques of the time were ineffective. Recent studies are smaller in size and deal with much more limited problems, manageable problems with more controlled methods, such as contracts relying on the client's definition of the problem (Sheldon, 1986). Highly specific techniques, such as task-centred work and behavioural approaches, are well-validated but this may not say anything about the general practice of social work, which on the whole uses (and probably must do so) less specific techniques for much more complex sets of problems. Sheldon (1986) also argues that recent studies do not generally cover long-term, as opposed to short-term, gains, and produce a result which may be statistically significant but is '. . . not one which sets the blood coursing through the veins (p. 237)', since the successes documented are on a small scale and in limited areas of practice.

Overall, while research tells us something about the use and validity of some social work approaches, it does not provide help in making a judgement which would enable us to compare the use and validity of particular theories. Larger studies of particular services indicate that case management techniques, in which there are 'packages of care', and community-oriented techniques, which are trying to build networks of support which mesh with individual casework activities, are proving effective (Goldberg, 1987). This suggests that those therapeutic techniques which lead to social systems development, such as social skills training among behavioural methods and systems theories, are likely to develop and prove most useful within social work, as opposed to other forms of helping.

Changing theoretical responses to social contexts

So far, we have not noted many final answers. I argue that social workers prefer theory which responds to the social demands on them, and which they can develop in this way, to any rational and research-based assessment of theory. In Chapter 1, I argued that social work as an activity was formed by the varying balance of importance in different social contexts of the eight main features. Theories selected by workers and how they are used reflect the current balance of these factors. Table 12.1 notes briefly each of the main features, and summarises the approach of each of the groups of theories that we have considered to have those features.

From this table, we can see that a range of the theories are broadly individualistic and concentrate on therapy. Their approach to advocacy is to provide explanations of client behaviour which concentrate on clients' personal characteristics, problems and interactions with the environment. There is generally not a set of techniques within these theories for seeking organisational or social change, or for acting vigorously on behalf of a client. Change in these theories is change of clients and their individual circumstances. Problems are 'privatised' and their social consequences, while accepted, are to be dealt with outside social work (as in psychodynamic work according to Hollis and Woods) or as a separate category of activity (as in ecological systems theory, at least as presented by Germain and Gitterman). The need for social change is acknowledged, and so is the influence of clients' environments on their circumstances and the need to do something about it. The unhelpfulness of agencies is often accepted in these theories, and is seen as an unhappy feature of modern bureaucratic times.

The last group of theories, on the other hand, while not rejecting the importance of individual work, have general explanations for many of the oppressions which clients feel, and place social workers and their agencies firmly in that system of oppressions. Attempts are made to offer models of work which at least do not reinforce those social evils, and conceivably might help to mitigate some of their effects and begin a process in which they would be changed. While not hostile, at least as presented, they are often critical of the structures within which social work is practised. However, as forms of practice, themselves, much of what is to be done with individual clients is borrowed from therapeutic styles of social work, and their concentration on certain established sorts of explanation means that problems must either be fitted into preconceived ideas, or therapeutic models of intervention must be used. So, the radical, feminist and Marxist social worker has ideas and perspectives which help social workers understand how clients are oppressed in society in a way that none of the other theories do. There are actions which can be taken to deal with these; generally, methods of advocacy and empowerment are well-developed. But in dealing with personal problems of clients within these perspectives, the worker will have to use the techniques of therapeutic models of social work, particularly where the problems are not particularly relevant to the forms of oppression that the theories deal with or where at any time little can be done to combat oppression. Here, theories like empowerment offer a way of doing traditional work which meets some of the needs of oppressed people and avoids making the oppression worse.

None of these theories, I would contend, make a wholly satisfactory basis for social work on its own. This is even more apparent when we look at the context of modern practice.

Three areas of modern practice seem important. First there is the *political and economic climate* within which social work is practised. For more than a decade in many countries, the worth and effectiveness of social work and broader welfare services has been questioned. In many non-Western countries its value has been

Table 12.1   *How theories meet the requirements of social work*

Theories	Individualisation	Evidence from psychology and sociology	Relationship
Psycho-dynamic	strong emphasis	strong use of psychoanalytic theory, very little use of sociology and other psychologies, some pragmatic use of other concepts	strong emphasis on relationship
Crisis/ task-centred	strong emphasis	crisis uses ego-psychology, Erikson with some social aspects; task-centred uses any and all useful information	yes, but both use contracts and activities as focus of work
Behavioural	strong emphasis	learning theory, including social learning theory; minimal sociology	important, but emphasis on specific procedures
Systems	yes, but individual is seen as part of wider system	social systems theory, but allows use of many other psychological and sociological ideas	relationships needed, but not only with client
Humanistic	strong emphasis	existential, subjective philosophies; objective knowledge less important	strong emphasis
Role communica-tion	yes, but emphasises social and personal interaction	social psychology	techniques and knowledge more important
Cognitive	yes, but emphasis on learning and adaptation to environment	mainly cognitive and learning theory	yes, but emphasis on client's own work
Marxist, radical	yes, but general ideas about social causation of problems are applied	sociological; psychology underdeveloped	yes to promote for sharing but not for personal change
Empower-ment, advocacy	yes, but social oppression the main feature of explanation	sociological; social psychological explanations of oppression	yes, especially to overcome obstructions

seriously doubted. Economic pressures in many countries seem destined for some time to limit expenditure on social work and related services. Most of these theories have not attempted to test the cost-effectiveness of their models of practice, or the economic and political worth of what they attempt to achieve. Advocacy for clients is seen as a duty based on clients' need, rather than on priorities in the provision of services. Managerial and resource

Organisational context	Defining needs	Maintains social structures	Advocacy
not crucial but may give a focus to work	strong emphasis; diagnosis and medical model; internal needs a strong feature	family is origin of problem and treatment focus; community is less important	explanations of personal origins of problems; no techniques for advocacy
not crucial	strong emphasis on diagnosis or assessment	family and other support needed in crisis work: social issues not questioned	only to resolve specific problems
not crucial	strong emphasis on careful diagnosis and assessment	social issues not questioned; family support used	not an aim; credible action and explanations available
important system for intervention	some emphasis on assessment; need socially defined by system	family and community important systems	may be important function
not crucial	selfactualisation, internal needs important	not important; strongly individualistic	not important; client's own aims main focus
not crucial	not important, behaviour socially defined	not important	not important but credible specific explanations available
not crucial, may contribute to clients' problems	not crucial, clients' role important	strongly individualistic	not an aim, clients' activity a focus
strong emphasis on power, class and organisational aspects of work	important, but many needs are general to social classes	crucial elements of origins and resolution of problems	important as interim strategy, leading to social change
strong emphasis; important to deal with organisational problems	important, especially to combat stereotypes	important as sources of support and sharing; community more important	central aspect of the theory

decisions are to be dealt with as matters external to social work practice (perhaps to be undertaken by managers or politicians) or as the province of alternative models and theories of practice. The development of case management systems, of informal and community care and of networking represents an attempt to deal with political and economic exigencies outside social work theory. Some of the theories (see Chapter 10 on social support systems) respond to these demands with a technology of methods but without a political and economic context. Some of them (e.g. Marxism) offer a perspective and direction for action, but little methodology except political and class action outside social work.

Second, there is the growth in most countries of *welfare bureaucracies* of substantial size and importance. In many Western countries, these are large government agencies, with considerable budgets and political power. Involvement and action in them, and use of their power, may be the answer to some of the problems discussed in the preceding paragraph. But many of the theories, again, have little to say about taking action in bureaucracies for the benefit of clients, and give little importance to the organisational issues involved in doing social work. Those that do, offer ideas that again do not link well with the therapeutic and individualist style of many of the daily interactions of social workers.

The third aspect of modern social work worthy of note is greater awareness of *oppression* of important groups in society through sexism, racism, ageism and other forms of socially established tyrannies. Clients and workers must be aware of divisive and personally and socially damaging policies; of a rising tide of violence and stress for both of them. Social work must respond to these issues in ways which acknowledge their importance, but also retain the personal individualised relationship which the therapeutic theories of social work offer.

In meeting these modern practice issues, social work theories have so far been inadequate. Yet, pragmatically, many social workers manage to combine many of these ideas in their practice. I argue that the reasons for this are:

- trends in theoretical development, because they are responding to modern practice needs, are tending towards theories which integrate many of these ideas
- the process by which social work theory is used (as opposed to the process by which it is created and debated) tends to merge ideas as they naturalise into a general social work paradigm
- a number of important features are shared between many theories which provide crossover points and indicate likely trends for future development.

The final three sections examine each of these points.

Theoretical trends

Since the 1960s, there has been a trend away from the centrality of psychodynamic theory as the conceptual base of social work, which I have shown to come from demands for demonstrated effectiveness, clarity and focus, a stronger social orientation, recognition of the importance of oppression in clients' lives, and rejection of strongly deterministic theories in favour of those which acknowledge the centrality of clients' ability to control their environment. While some of the alternative theories are themselves in opposition to one another, they have tended to develop simultaneously, rather than one after another, and their position seems to be a response to psychodynamic theory as the traditional form of social work, rather than a response to each other. Thus, they are presented as alternatives to or critiques or modifications of traditional forms of social work.

Many of these theories represent similar developments. All except behavioural and humanist approaches give importance to social environment and how clients deal with it. All give importance to enhancing clients' capacity to control the environment through their own thinking, social action, empowerment, or advocacy. All are concerned to clarify in some way the worker's and client's perspective on the world. Humanist, radical, Marxist, empowerment and advocacy approaches seek to do this directly by working on their world views. Behaviourist, task-centred and communication approaches seek a form of practice which is focused, directive and capable of explicit understanding.

The fact that these trends are common arises, I argue, because they reflect the dominant political and economic ideologies of our time. They must do so because one of social work's primary activities, as we saw in Chapter 1, is to humanise clients and represent them to society as acceptable to society and capable of acceptance as citizens. In the time of the ascendency of psychodynamic theory, the approach to social work's advocacy role was to use a medical model to demonstrate the dependence and need of clients for help and support; social work's caring role showed how the offered services helped clients to establish capability and independence. In the transitional period of the 1960s, community work showed how the neighbourhood and the community could be enabled to achieve social change jointly.

Now the dominant ideology expects citizens to become self-sufficient; dependence is less acceptable and people must learn to control their own destinies, to play a part in the community, to find their own ways to deal with oppressions that affect them. Social work strategies must assist in these processes, and so the theories and technologies that enable them to do so achieve dominance within the occupational group.

In this way, social work theory has responded to what clients and people around them expect, as they process clients through the route to clienthood, and to what social workers and the institutions which struggle for influence in their occupational grouping come to expect as a result of that power struggle. In the argument of this book, theory has been socially constructed by the society in which it operates.

But, if these are the trends, what does the construction now look like? Does it reflect only the latest trend? In fact, the dominant mode of social work is remarkably stable and still reflects significant elements of psychodynamic practice. This is because of the way in which theoretical trends have naturalised to the fundamental paradigm of social work theory and practice.

The naturalisation of social work theory

The naturalisation of concepts from social work theories is to a dominant mode of practice which retains many aspects of psychoanalytic theory. This is, first, because psychodynamic theory was the first generally applied social work theory, and was a powerful factor in the development of social work theory from the 1920s to the 1960s. This allowed it to develop applications broadly to most fields of social work. Most training and professional language used it for many years. Second, although other theories react to it by rejecting certain aspects, it is capable of including many ideas from apparently conflicting theories. Third, it is a very attractive and rich theory which, as it developed, emphasised different aspects, which have themselves grown into theories, so that parts of psychodynamic theory have potential alliances with a wide variety of other theories as they develop. Fourth, it forms the basis of many ideas which, outside its formal theoretical structure, are central to social work. The typical style of how social workers deal with people is fundamentally psychodynamic. So, relationship, individualisation, assessment and diagnosis, acceptance and non-directiveness, and the medical model of treatment which are so much part of social work, however presented, essentially derive from, and certainly have links and resonances with, psychodynamic theory. Many powerful professions with which social workers must have good relationships in order to do their jobs find the basic model congenial; doctors of course understand and accept the medical model of study, diagnosis and treatment, and lawyers can understand and accept problem-solving as a method.

The process of naturalisation also occurs because other theories, as they were produced, responded to its dominant position. The starting point of a new theory is very often a response to the inadequacies for the social circumstances of the time in some aspect of the traditional mode of social work practice. This is and always was an interpreted, changed – some would say bastardised – form of psychodynamic theory. So, any debate is around the new theories' differences from, and also therefore by implication its similarities to, conventional, broadly psychodynamic theory. Also, since most social workers are using psychodynamic theory as a conventional framework for their daily use of practice concepts, they are not acting as adherents to psychodynamic theory, but as practical users of a conventional set of ideas which happen to be derived from that theory. So, they see no harm in adapting other ideas for equally practical use without a concern for theoretical inconsistencies, which may not arise in occasional practice episodes.

The only possibility of dislodging psychodynamic theory is to replace it with an alternative paradigm, but I have argued that this has not happened, Why not?

One of the reasons is that some of the possible alternatives offended against some basic value systems in social work. These alternatives are fundamentally humanist in nature. So, theories involving a positivistic technology, such as behavioural approaches, or unrelieved cognitive theories have not proved attractive to social workers. Their role is not only to change people who have particular conditions in a therapeutic way but also to gain a personal contact with and feeling for them, to humanise and advocate for them. Humanist theories have not proved successful as a replacement paradigm partly because they are not ideologically distant from psychodynamic ideas as they have come to be interpreted in social work, and so do not constitute a very different view, but also because they are out of sympathy with the political and economic ideology of the times, which, I have argued, social work must, particularly of the helping occupations, always align with because of its advocacy role. Thus, humanist therapies have become aligned in later formulations with cognitive theory, both to humanise and make acceptable its intrusive and directive methodology, and to form a way of developing attractive humanist therapies in tune with political demands on, and modern social constructions of, social work.

Other theories are presented and accepted as being merely contributory, such as role or communication theory, or intend to be inclusive or organising theories, such as systems or radical theory, or focus on other issues and do not centrally concern themselves with therapeutic method, such as Marxist or empowerment theory. In these cases, the central nature of social work practice remains basically undisturbed.

If this is so, why does naturalisation of parts of other theories take place, instead of their being rejected? The reason for this is that, for social work practice, some aspects of psychodynamic theory are, as we have noted, very unsatisfactory. It is very weak in offering tools to deal with the environment. It offers much attacked and therefore decreasingly credible explanations of behaviour for advocacy purposes, and it offers few practice techniques for advocacy. It offers long-term, rather unfocused treatment methods, much concerned with feeling and emotion, when the political and economic pressures are towards a focused and directive treatment methodology. It fails to offer a perspective which can deal with quite evident failings in social policy and institutions, with oppression and inequity in society which particularly affect the sort of people who are clients of social workers. While it is humanist in style as interpreted in social work, its basic view is determinist (people's problems are caused by events in the past and are not fully within their control) and yet the role of social workers is to change people and their position so that they can be humanised and advocated for as citizens. All of these features of the psychodynamic basic orientation in social work limit its usefulness and inspire criticism which leads to amendment and accretions to the basic style of social work.

But, as we have seen, total change does not take place because of the hold of the basic social work approach, because of the flexibility of psychodynamic theory as it is used within social work in accepting amendment, and because of its breadth, general applicability and attractiveness as a fundamental orientation for social work.

Important shared features of social work theories

In the trends away from formal psychodynamic theory, and the development of it into a common form of social work by naturalisation of elements of other theories, it is possible to see clear directions for social work theory. The purpose of this final section is to note some of them, as showing the way to the future for social work theory.

First, social work treatment techniques are becoming more *focused*, setting clear aims and methods for achieving them. Aside from the borrowing of occasional aspects of behavioural methods, particularly social learning methods, and the achieving of a technology for making the plans through contracting and task-centred work, it is less clear how we will implement changes that we want to make. This may well offer a role for borrowings from educational settings (perhaps in the social pedagogy of continental Europe and the radical ideas of agology, animation and conscientisation) and the methods of communication and understandings from social psychology. The managerialism of the 1980s, and economic difficulties in countries where social work is strongest, have led to proposals for management systems of social service delivery which concentrate on techniques of case management, involvement in community networking as a technique and moves to decentralise services. These developments encourage the use of structured and focused theories, and it is not surprising to see their strength increasing.

Second, social work is moving away from determinist, positivist ideas as the basis for practice (but not for assessment of effectiveness) and we may expect to see a strengthening of ideas from *humanist* psychologies. This is because of social movements about the quality of life and the environment, which encourage us to take a broader view of human needs, treating them as part of a whole person. We may expect to see this as a significant area of exploration.

Third, social work is becoming, consistent with its move away from determinism and towards humanism, much more *interactive* in its approach, so that there is a move away from the catalytic model of pure professionalism towards a much more open model of practice in which workers share with clients in a joint exploration and learning experience. We noted an interactive approach particularly in ecological systems theory, radical and cognitive approaches. With the use of educational rather than treatment methodologies suggested as a trend above, and the influence of systems, cognitive, humanist, radical, Marxist and feminist ideas and a commitment to empowerment and advocacy, we may expect to see a more open and sharing occupational group.

Fourth, social work has an increasing awareness of its place and role as an occupational group within the *powerful institutional* networks in society, and we may expect a growing technology and theory base to achieve influence for clients within it. We can see this already in the development of theory to deal with sexism, racism and other oppressions in which social workers and clients interactively seek to share experiences and actions together. Movements for more client and consumer participation, managerial techniques such as case management, and community social work in the UK are examples of this trend.

Fifth, and related to that, social work is much more concerned with the *social environment*, and achieving influence through and within it. We may expect to see the theoretical development of social support and network theory to permit this.

Sixth, again related to these issues, an explicit focus on *advocacy* is developing as part of many social work theories, and we may expect to see the evolution of theoretical and practical means to implement it effectively.

Finally, although social work is international, it has so far been dominated by Western culture in its theoretical development. Learning about different cultural and ethnic groups in a more interactive style of social work in the West will enable a variety of perspectives to open up which may permit a different and more representative set of models for social work to emerge.

Bibliography

Abrams, Philip (1980) 'Social change, social networks and neighbourhood care', *Social Work Service*, 22 12–23.

Abrams, Sandra (1983) 'Casework: a problem-solving process' in Carol H. Meyer (ed.), *Clinical Social Work in the Eco-Systems Perspective* (New York, Columbia University Press).

Ainsworth, Frank and Leon C. Fulcher (eds) (1981) *Group Care for Children* (London, Tavistock).

Alexander, Leslie B. (1972) 'Social work's Freudian deluge: myth or reality?', *Social Service Review*, 46(4) 517–38.

Allan, Graham (1983) 'Informal networks of care: issues raised by Barclay', *British Journal of Social Work*, 13(4) 417–34.

Arnold, Magda B. and J. A. Gasson (1979) 'Logotherapy's place in psychology' in Joseph B. Fabry, Reuven P. Bulka and William S. Sahakian (eds), *Logotherapy in Action* (London, Jason Aronson).

Asamoah, Yvonne and D. N. A. Nortey (1987) 'Ghana' in John Dixon (ed.), *Social Welfare in Africa* (London, Routledge).

Asamoah, Yvonne and Creigs C. Beverly (1988) 'Collaboration between Western and African schools of social work: problems and possibilities', *International Social Work*, 31(3) 177–94.

Attlee, Clement R. (1920) *The Social Worker* (London, Bell).

Bailey, Roy and Mike Brake (eds) (1975a) *Radical Social Work* (London, Edward Arnold).

—— (1975b) 'Introduction: social work in the welfare state' in Roy Bailey and Mike Brake (eds) *Radical Social Work* (London, Edward Arnold).

—— (1980) 'Contributions to a radical practice in social work' in Mike Brake and Roy Bailey (eds) *Radical Social Work and Practice* (London, Edward Arnold).

Balgopal, Pallasana R. and Thomas Vassil (1983) *Groups in Social Work: an Ecological Perspective* (New York, Macmillan).

Bandura, Albert (1977) *Social Learning Theory* (Englewood Cliffs, NJ, Prentice-Hall).

Barber, James G. (1986) 'The promise and pitfalls of learned helplessness theory for social work practice', *British Journal of Social Work*, 16(5) 557–70.

Barbour, Rosaline S. (1984) 'Social work education: tackling the theory-practice dilemma', *British Journal of Social Work*, 14(6) 557–78.

Barclay Report (1982) *Social Workers: their Role and Tasks* (London, Bedford Square Press).

Barker, Mary and Pauline Hardiker (eds) (1981) *Theories of Practice in Social Work* (London, Academic Press).

Bateson, Gregory, Don Jackson, Jay Haley, and J. Weakland (1956) 'Toward a theory of schizophrenia', *Behavioral Science*, 1 251–264.

Batten, T. R. (with Madge Batten) (1967) *The Non-directive Approach in Group and Community Work* (London, Oxford University Press).

Beck, Aaron T. (1989) *Cognitive Therapy and the Emotional Disorders* (Harmondsworth, Middlesex, Penguin).

Becker, Howard (1963) *Outsiders: Studies in the Sociology of Deviance* (New York, Free Press).

Bellamy, Donald F. and Allan Irving (1989) 'Canada' in John Dixon and Robert P. Scheurell (eds) *Social Welfare in Developed Market Countries* (London, Routledge).

Berger, Peter L. and Thomas Luckmann (1971) *The Social Construction of Reality* (Harmondsworth, Middlesex, Penguin) (original American publication 1966).

Berlin, Sharon (1980) 'A cognitive-learning perspective for social work', *Social Service Review*, 54(4) 537–55.

_____ (1982) 'Cognitive behaviourial interventions for social work practice', *Social Work*, 27(3) 218–26.

Berne, Eric (1961) *Transactional Analysis in Psychotherapy* (New York, Grove Press).

_____ (1964) *Games People Play* (Harmondsworth, Middlesex, Penguin).

Biddle, Bruce J. and Edwin J. Thomas (eds) (1979) *Role Theory: Concepts and Research* (Huntington, New York, Robert S Krieger Publishing).

Biestek, Felix P. (1965) *The Casework Relationship* (London, George Allen and Unwin).

Bion, W. R. (1961) *Experiences in Groups and Other Papers* (London, Tavistock).

Birchwood, Max, Stephen Hallett and Martin Preston (1988) *Schizophrenia: an Integrated Approach to Research and Treatment* (London, Longman).

Birdwhistell, Ray L. (1973) *Kinesics and Context: Essays on Body-motion Communications* (Harmondsworth, Middlesex, Penguin).

Birks, Colin (1987) 'Social welfare provision in France' in Roslyn Ford and Mono Chakrabarti (eds) *Welfare Abroad: an Introduction to Social Welfare in Seven Countries* (Edinburgh, Scottish Academic Press).

Black, Clifford and Richard Enos (1981) 'Using phenomenology in clinical social work: a poetic pilgrimage', *Clinical Social Work Journal*, 9(1) 34–43.

Blumer, Herbert (1969) *Symbolic Interactionism: Perspective and Method* (Englewood Cliffs, New Jersey, Prentice-Hall).

Bocock, Robert (1988) 'Psychoanalysis and social theory' in Geoffrey

Pearson, Judith Treseder and Margaret Yelloly (eds) *Social Work and the Legacy of Freud: Psychoanalysis and its Uses* (London, Macmillan).

Booth, Charles (1892–1903) *Life and Labour of the People of London* (vols 1–7) (London, Macmillan).

Borensweig, Herman (1980) 'Jungian theory and social work practice', *Journal of Sociology and Social Welfare*, 7(4) 571–85.

Bowlby, John (1951) *Maternal Care and Mental Health* (Geneva, World Health Organisation).

_____ (1969) *Attachment and Loss, vol I: Attachment* (London, Hogarth Press).

_____ (1973) *Attachment and Loss, vol II: Separation* (London, Hogarth Press).

_____ (1980) *Attachment and Loss, vol III: Loss* (London, Hogarth Press).

Bradshaw, Jonathan (1972) 'The taxonomy of social need' in G. McLachlan (ed.) *Problems and Progress in Medical Care* (Oxford, Oxford University Press).

Brake, Mike and Roy Bailey (eds) (1980) *Radical Social Work and Practice* (London, Edward Arnold).

Brandon, David (1976) *Zen in the Art of Helping* (London, Routledge and Kegan Paul).

Brawley, Edward Allan and Emilia E. Martinez-Brawley (1988) 'Social programme evaluation in the USA: trends and issues', *British Journal of Social Work*, 18(4) 391–414.

Breakwell, Glynis M. and Colin Rowett (1982) *Social Work: the Social Psychological Approach* (Wokingham, Berks, Van Nostrand Reinhold).

Brennan, William C. (1973) 'The practitioner as theoretician', *Journal of Education for Social Work*, 9(1) 5–12.

Brigham, Thomas M. (1977) 'Liberation in social work education: applications from Paulo Freire', *Journal of Education for Social Work*, 13(3) 5–11.

Brown, Phil (1985) *The Transfer of Care: Psychiatric Deinstitutionalisation and its Aftermath* (New York, Routledge).

Brown, Robert, Stanley Bute and Peter Ford (1986) *Social Workers at Risk: the Prevention and Management of Violence* (London, Macmillan).

Browne, Elizabeth (1978) 'Social work activities' in DHSS *Social Service teams: the Practitioner's View* (London, HMSO).

Bryant, Coralie (1985) 'Rural development: Asian lessons and African perspectives', *Indian Journal of Social Work*, 46(3) 399–409.

Buchanan, Ann and Alec Webster (1982) 'Bedtime without battles: using a behavioural approach to establish bedtime routines: giving parents of nursery and primary age children a focus for their difficulties', *British Journal of Social Work*, 12(2) 197–204.

Bulmer, Martin (1987) *The Social Basis of Community Care* (London, Allen and Unwin).

Bunston, Terry (1985) 'Mapping practice: problem-solving in clinical social work', *Social Casework*, 66(4) 225–36.

Burgess, Robin, Robert Jewitt, James Sandham and Barbara L. Hudson

(1980) 'Working with sex offenders: a social skills training group', *British Journal of Social Work*, 10(2) 133–42.

Burn, Michael (1956) *Mr Lyward's Answer: a Successful Experiment in Education* (London, Hamish Hamilton).

Burrell, Gibson and Gareth Morgan (1979) *Sociological Paradigms and Organisational Analysis* (London, Heinemann).

Butler-Sloss, Lord Justice (Elizabeth) (1988) *Report of the Inquiry into Child Abuse in Cleveland 1987* (Cm 412) (London, HMSO).

Cannan, Crescy (1972) 'Social workers: training and professionalism' in Trevor Pateman (ed.) *Counter Course: a Handbook for Course Criticism* (Harmondsworth, Middlesex, Penguin).

Caplan, Gerald (1965) *Principles of Preventive Psychiatry* (London, Tavistock).

—— (1974) *Support Systems and Community Mental Health: Lectures on Concept Development* (New York, Behavioral Publications).

—— and Marie Killilea (eds) (1976) *Support Systems and Mutual Help: Multidisciplinary Explorations* (New York, Grune and Stratton).

Carew, Robert (1979) 'The place of knowledge in social work activity', *British Journal of Social Work*, 9(3) 349–64.

Carkhuff, Robert R. and Bernard C. Berenson (1977) *Beyond Counseling and Therapy*, (2nd edn) (New York, Holt, Rinehart and Winston).

Carr, Wilfred (1986) 'Theories of theory and practice', *Journal of the Philosophy of Education*, 20(2) 177–86.

Case, Lois P. and Neverlyn B. Lingerfelt (1974) 'Name-calling: the labeling process in the social work interview', *Social Service Review*, 18(2) 75–86.

Cecil, Rosanne, John Offer and Fred St Leger (1987) *Informal Welfare: a Sociological Study of Care in Northern Ireland* (Aldershot, Hants, Gower).

Chaiklin, Harris (1979) 'Symbolic interaction and social practice', *Journal of Sociology and Social Welfare*, 6(1) 3–7.

Chakrabarti, Mono (1987) 'Social welfare provision in India' in Roslyn Ford and Mono Chakrabarti (eds) *Welfare Abroad: an Introduction to Social Welfare in Seven Countries* (Edinburgh, Scottish Academic Press).

Cheers, Brian (1978) 'Things and theories – me, people I help and theories', *Contemporary Social Work Education*, 2(2) 99–107.

Cherniss, Cary (1980) *Staff Burnout: Job Stress in the Human Services* (Beverly Hills, Sage).

Chow, Nelson W. S. (1987) 'Western and Chinese ideas of social welfare', *International Social Work*, 30(1) 31–41.

Cigno, Katy (1985) 'The other Italian experiment: neighbourhood social work in the health and social services', *British Journal of Social Work*, 15(2) 173–86.

Cingolani, Judith (1984) 'Social conflict perspective on work with involuntary clients', *Social Work*, 29(5) 442–6.

Clarke, Michael (1976) 'The limits of radical social work', *British Journal of Social Work*, 6(4) 501–6.

Clough, Roger (1982) *Residential Work* (London, Macmillan).
Coburn, Denise Capps (1986 – 3rd ed.) 'Transactional analysis: a social work treatment model' in Francis J. Turner (ed.) *Social Work Treatment: Interlocking Theoretical Approaches* (New York, Free Press).
Cocozzelli, Carmelo and Robert T. Constable (1985) 'An empirical analysis of the relation between theory and practice in clinical social work', *Journal of Social Service Research*, 9(1) 47–64.
Cohen, Stan (1972) *Folk Devils and Moral Panics* (London, Paladin).
Collier, Andrew (1977) *R. D. Laing: The Philosophy and Politics of Psychotherapy* (Brighton, Sussex, Harvester).
Collins, Anne H. and Diane L. Pancoast (1976) *Natural Helping Networks* (Washington, DC, NASW).
Collins, Barbara G. (1986) 'Defining feminist social work', *Social Work*, 31(3) 214–19.
Corden, John and Michael Preston-Shoot (1987a) *Contracts in Social Work* (Aldershot, Hants, Gower).
—— (1987b) 'Contract or con trick? a reply to Rojek and Collins', *British Journal of Social Work*, 17(5) 535–43.
—— (1988) 'Contract or con trick? a postscript', *British Journal of Social Work*, 18(6) 623–34.
Corrigan, Paul and Peter Leonard (1978) *Social Work Practice Under Capitalism: a Marxist Approach* (London, Macmillan).
Costa, Maria das Dores (1987) 'Current influences on social work in Brazil: practice and education', *International Social Work* 30(2) 115–28.
Curnock, Katherine and Pauline Hardiker (1979) *Towards Practice Theory: Skills and Methods in Social Assessments* (London, Routledge and Kegan Paul).
Danisoglu, Emel (1987) 'Turkey' in John Dixon (ed.) *Social Welfare in the Middle East* (London, Croom Helm).
Davies, Martin (1977) *Support Systems in Social Work* (London, Routledge and Kegan Paul).
—— (1985 – 2nd ed.) *The Essential Social Worker: a Guide to Positive Practice* (Aldershot, Hants, Gower).
Davis, Ann (1981) *The Residential Solution* (London, Tavistock).
—— Steve Newton and Dave Smith (1985) 'Coventry crisis intervention: the consumer's view', *Social Services Research*, 14(1) 7–32.
Davis, Liane V. (1985) 'Female and male voices in social work', *Social Work*, 30(2) 106–13.
—— (1986) 'Role theory' in Francis J. Turner (ed.) *Social Work Treatment: Interlocking Theoretical Approaches* (New York, Free Press).
Davis-Sacks, Mary Lou Srinika Jayaratne and Wayne A. Cheis (1985) 'A comparison of the effects of social support on the incidence of burnout', *Social Work*, 30(3) 240–4.
de Hoyos, Genevieve and Claigh Jensen (1985) 'The systems approach in American social work', *Social Casework*, 66(8) 490–7.
de la Rosa, Mario (1988) 'Puerto Rican spiritualism: a key dimension for effective casework practice with Puerto Ricans', *International Social Work*, 31(4) 273–83.

Devore, Wynetta (1983) 'Ethnic reality: the life model and work with black families', *Social Casework*, 64(9) 525–31.

DHSS (1978) *Social Services Teams: The Practitioner's View* (London, HMSO).

DHSS (1988) *Report of the Inquiry into Child Abuse in Cleveland 1987*, Cm.412 (London, HMSO)

Dimmock, Brian and David Dungworth (1983) 'Creating manoeuvrability for family/systems therapists in social services departments', *Journal of Family Therapy*, 5(1) 53–70.

Dixon, John (ed.) (1987) *Social Welfare in Africa* (London, Croom Helm).

_____ and Robert P. Scheurall (eds) (1989) *Social Welfare in Developed Market Countries* (London, Routledge).

Dominelli, Lena (1988) *Anti-racist Social Work* (London, Macmillan).

_____ and Eileen McLeod (1989) *Feminist Social Work* (London, Macmillan).

Donnelly, A. (1986) *Feminist Social Work with a Women's Group* (Norwich, Norfolk, Social Work Monographs).

Douglas, Tom (1979) *Group Processes in Social Work: a Theoretical Synthesis* (Chichester, Hants, John Wiley).

Dowrick, Christopher (1983) 'Strange meeting: Marxism, psychoanalysis and social work', *British Journal of Social Work*, 13(1) 1–18.

Dryden, Windy (1984) *Individual Therapy in Britain* (London, Harper and Row).

Durkheim, Emile (1938) *The Rules of Sociological Method*, 8th edn, translated (New York, Free Press).

Eisenhuth, Elizabeth (1981) 'The theories of Heinz Kohut and clinical social work practice', *Clinical Social Work Journal*, 9(2) 80–90.

Ellis, Albert (1962) *Reason and Emotion in Psychotherapy* (Secaucus, NJ, Lyle Stuart).

Ellis, June (1977) 'Differing conceptions of a child's needs: some implications for social work with West African children and their parents', *British Journal of Social Work*, 7(2) 155–72.

England, Hugh (1986) *Social Work as Art* (London, Allen and Unwin).

Epstein, Laura (1978) *Helping People: a Task-Centred Approach* (St Louis, Mo., C. V. Mosby).

Erikson, Erik (1965) *Childhood and Society*, 2nd edn. (London, Hogarth Press).

Etzioni, Amitai (1975) *A Comparative Analysis of Complex Organisations: on Power, Involvement and Their Correlates* (New York, Free Press).

Evans, Roger (1976) 'Some implications of an integrated model of social work for theory and practice', *British Journal of Social Work*, 6(2) 177–200.

Fairbairn, W. R. D. (1954) *An Object Relations Theory of Personality* (New York, Basic Books).

Feldman, Ronald A. and John S. Wodarski (1975) *Contemporary Approaches to Group Treatment* (San Francisco, Jossey-Bass).

Ferrera, Maurizio (1989) 'Italy' in John Dixon and Robert Scheurell (eds), *Social Welfare in Developed Market Countries* (London, Routledge).

Fineman, Stephen (1985) *Social Work Stress and Intervention* (Aldershot, Hants, Gower).

Fischer, Joel (1973) 'Is casework effective? a review', *Social Work*, 18(1) 5–20.

____ (1976) *The Effectiveness of Social Casework* (Springfield, Ill., Charles C. Thomas).

____ (1978) *Effective Casework Practice: an Eclectic Approach* (New York, McGraw-Hill).

____ (1981) 'The social work revolution', *Social Work*, 26(3) 199–207.

____ and Harvey L. Gochros (1975) *Planned Behaviour Change: Behaviour Modification in Social Work* (New York, Free Press).

Forder, Anthony (1976) 'Social work and systems theory', *British Journal of Social Work*, 6(1) 24–41.

Fraiberg, Selma (1978) 'Psychoanalysis and social work: a re-examination of the issues', *Smith College Studies in Social Work*, 48(2) 87–106.

Franklin, Marjorie E. (1968) 'The meaning of planned environment therapy' in Arthur T. Barron (ed.) *Studies in Environment Therapy*, vol 1 (Worth, Sussex, Planned Environment Therapy Trust).

Freedberg, Sharon (1986) 'Religion, profession and politics: Bertha Capen Reynolds' challenge to social work', *Smith College Studies in Social Work*, 56(2) 95–110.

Freire, Paulo (1972) *Pedagogy of the Oppressed* (Harmondsworth, Middlesex, Penguin).

Freud, Sigmund (1974 edn) *Introductory Lectures on Psychoanalysis* (Harmondsworth, Middx. Penguin).

Fulcher, Leon C. and Frank Ainsworth (eds) (1985) *Group Care Practice with Children* (London, Tavistock).

Furlong, Mark (1987) 'A rationale for the use of empowerment as a goal in casework', *Australian Social Work*, 40(3) 25–30.

Galper, Jeffrey (1975) *The Politics of Social Service* (Englewood Cliffs, NJ, Prentice-Hall).

____ (1980) *Social Work Practice: a Radical Approach* (Englewood Cliffs, NJ, Prentice-Hall).

Gambrill, Eileen (1981) 'The use of behavioural procedures in cases of child abuse and neglect', *International Journal of Behavioural Social Work and Abstracts*, 1(1) 3–26.

Gangrade, K. D. (1970) 'Western social work and the Indian world', *International Social Work*, 13(3) 4–12.

Garbarino, James (1983) 'Social support networks: Rx for the helping professions' in James K. Whittaker and James Garbarino (eds), *Social Support Networks: Informal Helping in the Human Services* (New York, Aldine).

Germain, Carel (1970) 'Casework and science: a historical encounter' in Robert W. Roberts and Robert H. Nee (eds) *Theories of Social Casework* (Chicago, University of Chicago Press).

_____ (1976) 'Time: an ecological variable in social work practice', *Social Casework*, 57(7) 419–26.

_____ (1978) 'General-systems theory and ego psychology: an ecological perspective', *Social Service Review*, 59(4) 534–50.

_____ (ed.) (1979a) *Social Work Practice: People and Environments – an Ecological Perspective* (New York, Columbia University Press).

_____ (1979b) 'Introduction: ecology and social work' in Carel B. Germain (ed.) *Social Work Practice: People and Environments – an Ecological Approach* (New York, Columbia University Press).

_____ (1981) 'The ecological approach to people-environment transactions', *Social Casework*, 62(6) 323–31.

_____ and Alex Gitterman (1980) *The Life Model of Social Work Practice* (New York, Columbia University Press).

_____ and Ann Hartman (1980) 'People and ideas in the history of social work practice', *Social Casework*, 61(6) 323–31.

Ghosh, H. (1984) 'Social work contribution to population programme management', *Indian Journal of Social Work*, 44(4) 409–18.

Gibson, Faith, Anne McGrath and Norma Reid (1989) 'Occupational stress in social work', *British Journal of Social Work*, 19(1) 1–16.

Gilligan, Carol (1982) *In a Different Voice: Psychological Theory and Women's Development* (Cambridge, Mass., Harvard University Press).

Gingerich, Wallace J., Mark Kleczewski and Stuart A. Kirk (1982) 'Name-calling in social work', *Social Service Review*, 56(3) 366–74.

Gitterman, Alex (1983) 'Uses of resistance: a transactional view', *Social Work*, 28(2) 127–31.

Glasser, William (1965) *Reality Therapy: a New Approach to Psychiatry* (New York, Harper and Row).

Goffman, Erving (1968a) *Stigma: Notes on the Management of Spoiled Identity* (Harmondsworth, Middlesex, Penguin).

_____ (1968b) *The Presentation of Self in Everyday Life* (Harmondsworth Middlesex, Penguin).

_____ (1972a) *Relations in Public: Microstudies of the Public Order* (Harmondsworth, Middlesex, Penguin).

_____ (1972b) *Interaction Ritual: Essays on Face-to-Face Behaviour* (Harmondsworth, Middlesex, Penguin).

_____ (1972c) *Encounters: Two Studies in the Sociology of Interaction* (Harmondsworth, Middlesex, Penguin).

Golan, Naomi (1978) *Treatment in Crisis Situations* (New York, Free Press).

_____ (1986) 'Crisis theory' in Francis J. Turner (ed.), *Social Work Treatment: Interlocking Theoretical Approaches* (New York, Free Press).

Goldberg, E. Matilda (1987) 'The effectiveness of social care: a selective exploration', *British Journal of Social Work*, 17(6) 595–614.

_____ Jane Gibbons and Ian Sinclair (1985) *Problems, Tasks and Outcomes* (London, Allen and Unwin).

Goldstein, Eda G. (1984) *Ego Psychology and Social Work Practice* (New York, Free Press).

Goldstein, Howard (1973) *Social Work Practice: A Unitary Approach* (Columbia, South Carolina, University of South Carolina Press).

___ (1981) *Social Learning and Change: a Cognitive approach to Human Services* (Columbia, South Carolina, University of South Carolina Press).

___ (1982) 'Cognitive approaches to direct practice', *Social Service Review*, 56(4) 539–55.

___ (1983) 'Starting where the client is', *Social Casework*, 64(5) 267–75.

___ (ed.) (1984a) *Creative Change: a Cognitive-Humanistic Approach to Social Work Practice* (New York, Tavistock).

___ (1984b) 'Cognitive theory and social work practice revisited', *Social Service Review*, 58(3) 462–65.

___ (1986) 'A cognitive-humanistic approach to the hard-to-reach client', *Social Casework*, 67(1) 27–36.

Gordon, William E. (1983) 'Social work revolution or evolution?' *Social Work*, 28(3) 181–5.

Goroff, Norman N. (1974) 'Social welfare as coercive social control', *Journal of Sociology and Social Welfare*, 2(1) 19–26.

Granger, Jean M. and Doreen L. Portner (1985) 'Ethnic- and gender-sensitive social work practice', *Journal of Social Work Education*, 21(1) 38–47.

Greif, Geoffrey L. (1986) 'The ecosystems perspective "meets the press"', *Social Work*, 31(3) 225–6.

___ and Arthur A. Lynch (1983) 'The eco-systems perspective' in Carol H. Meyer (ed.), *Clinical Social Work in the Eco-Systems Perspective* (New York, Columbia University Press).

Gulbenkian Foundation Study Group (1968) *Community Work and Social Change* (London, Longman).

Guntrip, Harry (1968) *Schizoid Phenomena, Object Relations and the Self* (London, Hogarth Press).

Hadley, Roger and Stephen Hatch (1981) *Social Welfare and the Failure of the State: Centralised Social Services and Participatory Alternatives* (London, Allen and Unwin).

Hadley, Roger and Morag McGrath (1984) *When Social Services are Local: the Normanton Experience* (London, Allen and Unwin).

Hall, Edward T. (1966) *The Hidden Dimension* (Garden City, New York, Doubleday).

Hamalainen, Juha (1989) 'Social pedagogy as a meta-theory of social work education', *International Social Work*, 32(2) 117–28.

Hamilton, Gordon (1951 – 2nd ed.) *Theory and Practice of Social Casework* (New York, Columbia University Press).

___ (1957) 'A theory of personality: Freud's contribution to social work' in Howard J. Parad (ed.), *Ego Psychology and Dynamic Casework* (New York, Family Service Association of America).

Hanmer, Jalna and Daphne Statham (1988) *Women and Social Work: Towards a Women-Centred Practice* (London, Macmillan).

Hanson, Meredith (1983) 'Behavioural approaches to social work practice' in Carol H. Meyer (ed.), *Clinical Social Work in the Eco-Systems Perspective* (New York, Columbia University Press).

Hardiker, Pauline (1981) 'Heart or head – the function and role of knowledge in social work', *Issues in Social Work Education*, 1(2) 85–111.

Harris, Howard and Alan Lipman (1984) 'Gender and the pursuit of respectability: dilemmas of daily life in a home for adolescents', *British Journal of Social Work*, 14(3) 265–76.

Harris, Thomas A. (1973) *I'm OK – You're OK* (London, Pan).

Hartman, Ann (1971) 'But what is social casework?', *Social Casework*, 52(7) 411–19.

―――― (1986) 'The life and work of Bertha Reynolds: implications for education and practice today', *Smith College Studies in Social Work*, 56(2) 79–94.

Hearn, Gordon (1958) *Theory-building in Social Work* (Toronto, University of Toronto Press).

―――― (ed.) (1969) *The General Systems Approach: Contributions toward an Holistic Conception of Social Work* (New York, Council on Social Work Education).

Hearn, Jeff (1982) 'The problem(s) of theory and practice in social work and social work education', *Issues in Social Work Education*, 2(2) 95–118.

Heineman, Martha Brunswick (1981) 'The obsolete scientific imperative in social work research', *Social Service Review*, 55(3) 371–97.

Heisler, Helmuth (1970) 'Social welfare and African development' *Applied Social Studies* 2(2) 81–9.

Herbert, Martin (1987 – 2nd ed.) *Behavioural Treatment of Children with Problems: a Practice Manual* (London, Academic Press).

Hofstein, Saul (1964) 'The nature of process: its implications for social work', *Journal of the Social Work Process*, 14 13–53.

Hollis, Florence and Mary E. Woods (1981) *Casework: a psychosocial therapy* (New York: Random House).

Hopkins, Jeff (1986) *Caseworker* (Birmingham, Pepar Publications).

Howard, Jane (1971) 'Indian society, Indian social work: identifying Indian principles and methods for social work practice', *International Social Work*, 14(4) 16–31.

Howard, Tina U. and Frank C. Johnson (1985) 'An ecological approach to practice with single-parent families', *Social Casework*, 66(8) 482–9.

Howe, David (1987) *An Introduction to Social Work Theory* (Aldershot, Hants, Wildwood House).

Howe, Michael W. and John R. Schuerman (1974) 'Trends in the social work literature: 1957–72', *Social Service Review*, 48(2) 279–85.

Hudson, Annie (1985) 'Feminism and social work: resistance or dialogue?', *British Journal of Social Work*, 15(6) 635–55.

Hudson, Barbara L. (1978) 'Behavioural social work with schizophrenic patients in the community', *British Journal of Social Work*, 8(2) 159–70.

―――― (1982) *Social Work with Psychiatric Patients* (London, Macmillan).

―――― and Geraldine Macdonald (1986) *Behavioural Social Work: an Introduction* (London, Macmillan).

Hugman, Richard (1987) 'The private and the public in personal models of social work: a response to O'Connor and Dalgleish', *British Journal of Social Work*, 17(1) 71–6.

Hutten, Joan M. (1977) *Short-term Contracts in Social Work* (London, Routledge and Kegan Paul).

Ilango, P. (1988) 'Existing models of social work education for community development', *Indian Journal of Social Work*, 49(1) 21–5.

Illich, Ivan, Irving K. Zola, John McKnight, Jonathan Caplan and Harley Shaiken (1977) *Disabling Professions* (London, Marion Boyars).

Irvine, Elizabeth E. (1956) 'Transference and reality in the case-work relationship', *British Journal of Psychiatric Social Work*, 3(4) 1–10.

Jackson, Henry J. and Neville J. King (1982) 'The conceptual basis of behavioural programming: a review with implications for social work', *Contemporary Social Work Education*, 5(3) 227–38.

Jansen, Elly (ed.) (1980) *The Therapeutic Community outside the Hospital* (London, Croom Helm).

Jayaratne, Srinika (1978) 'A study of clinical eclecticism', *Social Service Review*, 52(4) 621–31.

―――, Tony Tripodi and Wayne Cheis (1983) 'Perceptions of emotional support, stress and strain by male and female social workers', *Social Work Research and Abstracts*, 19(Summer) 29–37.

Jehu, Derek (1967) *Learning Theory and Social Work* (London, Routledge and Kegan Paul).

―――(ed.) (1972) *Behaviour Modification in Social Work* (Chichester, John Wiley).

Jenkins, Shirley (1980) 'The ethnic agency defined', *Social Service Review*, 54(2) 249–61.

―――(1987) 'The limited domain of effectiveness research', *British Journal of Social Work*, 17(6) 587–94.

Jones, Chris (1979) 'Social work education, 1900–1977' in Noel Parry, Michael Rustin and Carole Satyamurti (eds), *Social Work, Welfare and the State* (London, Edward Arnold).

Jones, Howard (1979) *The Residential Community* (London, Routledge and Kegan Paul).

Jordan, Bill (1978) 'A comment on "Theory and practice in social work"', *British Journal of Social Work*, 8(1) 23–5.

―――(1987) 'Counselling, advocacy and negotiation', *British Journal of Social Work*, 17(2) 135–46.

―――(1989) Review of David Howe: 'An Introduction to Social Work Theory', *Journal of Social Policy*, 18(3) 462–3.

Joynathsing, Mohipnarain (1987) 'Mauritius' in John Dixon (ed.), *Social Welfare in Africa* (London, Croom Helm).

Karger, H. Jacob (1983) 'Science, research, and social work: who controls the profession?', *Social Work*, 28(2) 200–5.

Kassim Ejaz, Farida (1989) 'The nature of casework practice in India: a study of social workers' perceptions in Bombay', *International Social Work*, 32(1) 25–38.

Katz, Alfred H. (1983) 'Deficiencies in the status quo', *Social Work*, 28(1) 71.

Keefe, Thomas (1986) 'Meditation and social work treatment' in Francis J. Turner (ed.) *Social Work Treatment: Interlocking Theoretical Approaches*, 3rd edn (New York, Free Press).

Kemshall, Hazel (1986) *Defining Clients' Needs in Social Work* (Norwich, Norfolk, Social Work Monographs).

Kennard, David (1983) *An Introduction to Therapeutic Communities* (London, Routledge and Kegan Paul).

Kettner, Peter M. (1975) 'A framework for comparing practice models', *Social Service Review*, 49(4) 629–42.

Kohut, Heinz (1978) *The Search for the Self: Selected Writings of Heinz Kohut: 1950–1978* (2 vols) (New York, International Universities Press).

Kolevson, Michael S. and Jacqueline Maykranz (1982) 'Theoretical orientation and clinical practice: uniformity versus eclecticism?', *Social Service Review*, 58(1) 120–9.

Korner, I. N. (1973) 'Crisis reduction and the psychological consultant' in Gerald A. Spector and William L. Claiborn (eds), *Crisis Intervention* (New York, Behavioral Publications).

Krill, Donald F. (1969) 'Existential psychotherapy and the problem of anomie', *Social Work*, 14(2) 33–49.

—— (1978) *Existential Social Work* (New York, Free Press).

Kuhn, Thomas S. (1970) *The Structure of Scientific Revolutions* (Chicago, University of Chicago Press).

Kurtz, P. David and Eldon K. Marshall (1982) 'Evolution of interpersonal skills training' in E. K. Marshall, P. D. Kurtz *et al.*, *Interpersonal Helping Skills* (San Francisco, Jossey-Bass).

Lacan, Jacques (1979) *The Four Fundamental Concepts of Psychoanalysis* (Harmondsworth, Middlesex, Penguin).

Laing, Ronald D. (1965) *The Divided Self: an Existential Study in Sanity and Madness* (Harmondsworth, Middlesex, Penguin).

—— (1971) *Self and Others*, 2nd edn (Harmondsworth, Middlesex, Penguin).

Lane, Helen J. (1984) 'Self-differentiation in symbolic interactionism and psychoanalysis', *Social Work*, 29(3) 270–4.

Lee, Phil and David Pithers (1980) 'Radical residential child care: Trojan horse or non-runner?' in Mike Brake and Roy Bailey (eds), *Radical Social Work and Practice* (London, Edward Arnold).

Lees, Ray (1971) 'Social work 1925–50: the case for a reappraisal', *British Journal of Social Work*, 1(4) 371–80.

Leighninger, Robert D. (1978) 'Systems theory', *Journal of Sociology and Social Welfare*, 5 446–66.

Lemert, Edwin (1972) *Human Deviance, Social Problems and Social Control*, 2nd edn (Englewood Cliffs, NJ, Prentice-Hall).

Lennox, Daphne (1982) *Residential Group Therapy with Children* (London, Tavistock).

Leonard, Peter (1975a) 'Towards a paradigm for radical practice' in Roy

Bailey and Mike Brake (eds), *Radical Social Work* (London, Edward Arnold).

—— (1975b) 'Explanation and education in social work', *British Journal of Social Work*, 5(3) 325–33.

—— (1984) *Personality and Ideology: Towards a Materialist Understanding of the Individual* (London, Macmillan).

Levy, Charles S. (1981) 'Labeling: the social worker's responsibility', *Social Casework*, 62(6) 332–42.

Lewin, Kurt (1951) *Field Theory in Social Science* (New York, Harper).

Liberman, R. P., L. W. Wing, W. J. Derisi and M. McCann (1975) *Personal Effectiveness: Guiding People to Assert Themselves and Improve Their Social Skills* (Champaign, Ill., Research Press).

Lindemann, Erich (1944) 'Symptomatology and management of acute grief' in Howard J. Parad (ed.) (1965), *Crisis Intervention: Selected Readings* (New York, Family Service Association of America).

Loewenberg, Frank M. (1984) 'Professional ideology, middle range theories and knowledge building for social work practice', *British Journal of Social Work*, 14(4) 309–22.

Longres, John F. and Eileen McCleod (1980) 'Consciousness raising and social work practice', *Social Casework*, 61(5) 267–76.

Lowenstein, Sophie (1985) 'Freud's metapsychology revisited', *Social Casework*, 66(3) 139–51.

Lukton, Rosemary Creed (1982) 'Myths and realities of crisis intervention', *Social Casework*, 63(5) 276–85.

Lum, Doman (1982) 'Toward a framework for social work practice with minorities', *Social Work* 27(3) 244–9.

Lusk, Mark W. (1981) 'Philosophical changes in Latin American social work', *International Social Work*, 24(2) 14–21.

MacLean, Mary (1986) 'The neurolinguistic programming model' in Francis J. Turner (ed.), *Social Work Treatment: Interlocking Theoretical Approaches* (New York, Free Press).

Maluccio, Anthony N. (ed.) (1981) *Promoting Competence in Clients* (New York, Free Press).

Mancoske, Ronald (1981) 'Sociological perspectives on the ecological model', *Journal of Sociology and Social Welfare*, 8(4) 710–32.

Maslow, Abraham (1970) *Motivation and Personality*, 2nd edn (New York, Harper and Row).

McAuley, Roger and Patricia McAuley (1980) 'The effectiveness of behaviour modification with families', *British Journal of Social Work*, 10(1) 43–54.

McCleod, Eileen (1979) 'Working with prostitutes: probation officers' aims and strategies', *British Journal of Social Work*, 9(4) 453–70.

McIntyre, Deborah (1982) 'On the possibility of "radical" casework: a "radical" dissent', *Contemporary Social Work Education*, 5(3) 191–208.

McNamara, James J. (1976) 'Social work designs a humanistic program to enhance patient care', *Social Work in Health Care*, 1(2) 145–54.

Mead, George Herbert (1934) *Mind, Self and Society* (Chicago, University of Chicago Press).

Meyer, Carol H. (ed.) (1983) *Clinical Social Work in the Eco-Systems Perspective* (New York, Columbia University Press).

Midgley, James (1981) *Professional Imperialism: Social Work in the Third World*, (London, Heinemann).

Mitchell, Juliet (1975) *Psychoanalysis and Feminism* (Harmondsworth, Middlesex, Penguin).

Moore, Edith E. (1976) 'Eclecticism and social work practice', *Social Worker*, 44(1) 23–8.

Mor-Barak, Michal E. (1988) 'Support systems intervention in crisis situations: theory, strategies and a case discussion', *International Social Work*, 31(4) 285–304.

Morgan, Roger T. and Gordon C. Young (1972) 'The conditioning treatment of childhood enuresis', *British Journal of Social Work*, 2(4) 503–10.

Muller, C. Wolfgang (1989) 'Germany, West' in John Dixon and Robert Scheurell (eds), *Social Welfare in Developed Market Countries* (London, Routledge).

Munson, Carlton E. and Pallassana Balgopal (1978) 'The worker/client relationship: relevant role theory', *Journal of Sociology and Social Welfare*, 5(3) 404–17.

Muzumdar, Amma Menon (1964) *Social Welfare in India: Mahatma Gandhi's Contributions* (London, Asia Publishing House).

Nagpaul, Hans (1972) 'The diffusion of American social work education to India: problems and issues', *International Social Work*, 15(1) 3–17.

Nanavatty, Meher C. (1981) 'Rural development and social work', *Indian Journal of Social Work*, 42(3) 265–72.

Neill, A. S. (1964) *Summerhill* (London, Victor Gollancz).

Nelson, Judith C. (1986) 'Communication theory and social work treatment' in Francis J Turner (ed.) *Social Work Treatment: Interlocking Theoretical Approaches* (New York, Free Press).

—— (1980) *Communication Theory and Social Work Practice* (Chicago: University of Chicago Press).

Nuttall, Kathryn (1985) *The Place of Family Therapy in Social Work* (Norwich, Norfolk, Social Work Monographs).

O'Connor, Ian and Len Dalgleish (1986) 'Cautionary tales about beginning practitioners: the fate of personal models of social work in beginning practice', *British Journal of Social Work*, 16(4) 431–47.

O'Hagan, Kieran (1986) *Crisis Intervention in Social Services* (London, Macmillan).

Olsen, M. Rolf (ed.) (1978) *The Unitary Model: its Implications for Social Work Theory and Practice* (Birmingham, BASW Publications).

Olsson, Sven E. (1989) 'Sweden' in John Dixon and Robert P. Scheurell (eds) *Social Welfare in Developed Market Countries* (London, Routledge).

Onokerkoraye, Andrew G. (1984) *Social Services in Nigeria: an introduction* (London, Kegan Paul International).

Papell, Catherine P. and Beulah Rothman (1966) 'Social group work models: possession and heritage', *Journal of Education for Social Work*, 2(2) 66–73.

Parad, Howard J. (1958) *Ego Psychology and Dynamic Casework* (New York, Family Service Association of America).

——— (ed.) (1965a) *Crisis Intervention: Selected Readings* (New York, Family Service Association of America).

——— (1965b) 'Introduction' in Howard J. Parad (ed.) *Crisis Intervention: Selected Readings* (New York, Family Service Association of America).

——— and Roger Miller (1963) *Ego-oriented Casework: Problems and Perspectives* (New York, Family Service Association of America).

Parkes, Colin Murray (1972) *Bereavement: Studies of Grief in Adult Life* (Harmondsworth, Middlesex, Penguin).

Patterson, C. H. (1986) *Theories of Counseling and Psychotherapy*, 4th edn. (New York, Harper and Row).

Payne, Malcolm (1986) *Social Care in the Community* (London, Macmillan).

——— (1989) 'Open records and shared work' in Steven Shardlow (ed.), *The Values of Change in Social Work* (London, Routledge).

Pearson, Geoffrey (1975) *The Deviant Imagination: Psychiatry, Social Work and Social Change* (London, Macmillan).

——— Judith Treseder and Margaret Yelloly (eds) (1988) *Social Work and the Legacy of Freud* (London, Macmillan).

Perlman, Helen Harris (1957a) *Social Casework: A Problem-Solving Process* (Chicago: University of Chicago Press).

——— (1957b) 'Freud's contribution to social welfare', *Social Service Review*, 31 (2) pp. 192–202.

——— (1968) *Persona: Social Role and Personality* (Chicago, University of Chicago Press).

——— (1970) 'The problem-solving model in social casework' in Robert W. Roberts and Robert H. Nee (eds) *Theories of Social Casework* (Chicago, University of Chicago Press).

——— (1979) *Relationship: the Heart of Helping People* (Chicago, University of Chicago Press).

——— (1986) 'The Problem-solving model' in Francis J. Turner (ed.) *Social Work Treatment: Interlocking Theoretical Approaches*, 3rd edn. (New York, Free Press).

Perls, Frederick, Ralph F. Hefferline and Paul Goodman (1973) *Gestalt Therapy: Excitement and Growth in the Human Personality* (Harmondsworth, Middlesex, Penguin) (original American ed., 1951).

Phillips, Helen U. (1957) *Essentials of Social Group Work Skill* (New York, Association Press).

Philp, Mark (1979) 'Notes on the form of knowledge in social work', *Sociological Review*, 27(1) 83–111.

Philpot, Terry (ed.) (1986) *Social Work: a Christian Perspective* (Tring, Herts, Lion Publishing).

Picardie, Michael (1980) 'Dreadful moments: existential thoughts on doing social work', *British Journal of Social Work*, 10(4) 483–90.

Pincus, Allen, and Anne Minahan (1973) *Social Work Practice: Model and Method* (Itasca, Ill., Peacock).

Pincus, Lily (1976) *Death and the Family* (London, Faber and Faber).
Pinderhughes, Elaine B. (1983) 'Empowerment for our clients and ourselves', *Social Casework*, 64(6) 331–8.
Pithouse, Andrew (1987) *Social Work: the Social Organisation of an Invisible Trade* (Aldershot, Hants, Gower).
Pitman, Elizabeth (1982a) 'Transactional analysis: an introduction to its theory and practice', *British Journal of Social Work*, 12(1) 47–64.
―――― (1982b) *Transactional Analysis for Social Workers* (London, Routledge and Kegan Paul).
Pizzat, Frank J. (1973) *Behaviour Modification in Residential Treatment for Children: Model of a Program* (New York, Behavioral Publications).
Polsky, Howard (1968) *Cottage Six: the Social System of Delinquent Boys in Residential Treatment* (Chapel Hill, N. Carolina, University of North Carolina Press).
Rachman, S. J. and G. T. Wilson (1980) *The Effects of Psychological Therapy*, 2nd edn (Oxford, Pergamon Press).
Ramon, Shulamit and Maria Grazia Giannichedda (eds) (1988) *Psychiatry in Transition: the British and Italian Experiences* (London, Pluto Press).
Rapoport, Lydia (1970) 'Crisis intervention as a mode of brief treatment' in Robert W. Roberts and Robert H. Nee (eds), *Theories of Social Casework* (Chicago, University of Chicago Press).
Redl, Fritz (1959) 'Strategy and techniques of the life space interview', *American Journal of Orthopsychiatry*, 29 1–18.
Rees, Stewart and Anne Wallace (1982) *Verdicts on Social Work* (London, Edward Arnold).
Reid, William J. (1978) *The Task-Centred System* (New York, Columbia University Press).
―――― (1985) *Family Problem-Solving* (New York, Columbia University Press).
―――― and Ann W. Shyne (1969) *Brief and Extended Casework* (New York, Columbia University Press).
―――― and Laura Epstein (1972) *Task-Centred Casework* (New York, Columbia University Press).
―――― and Laura Epstein (eds) (1972) *Task-Centred Practice* (New York, Columbia University Press).
Rein, Martin and Sheldon H. White (1981) 'Knowledge for practice', *Social Serivce Review*, 55(1) 1–41.
Resnick, Rosa Perla (1976) 'Conscientization: an indigenous approach to international social work', *International Social Work*, 19(1) 21–9.
Rhodes, Margaret L. (1985) 'Gilligan's theory of moral development as applied to social work', *Social Work*, 30(2) 101–105.
Richmond, Mary (1917) *Social Diagnosis* (New York, Free Press).
Righton, Peter (1975) 'Planned environment therapy: a reappraisal', *Association of Workers with Maladjusted Children Journal*, Spring 1975; reprinted in Peter Righton (ed.) *Studies in Environment Therapy*, vol. 3 (Toddington, Glos, Planned Environment Therapy Trust).
Roazen, Paul (1979) *Freud and his Followers* (Harmondsworth, Middlesex, Peregrine).

Roberts, Robert W. and Robert H. Nee (eds) (1970) *Theories of Social Casework* (Chicago, University of Chicago Press).

Roberts, Robert W. and Helen Northen (eds) (1976) *Theories of Social Work with Groups* (New York, Columbia University Press).

Rogers, Carl R. (1951) *Client-Centred Therapy: its Current Practice, Implications and Theory* (London, Constable).

____ (1961) *On Becoming a Person: a Therapist's View of Psychotherapy* (London, Constable).

____ (1977) *Carl Rogers on Personal Power* (London, Constable).

____ and Mary Strauss (1967) *Person to Person: the Problem of Being Human* (London, Souvenir Press).

Rojek, Chris (1986) 'The "Subject" in Social Work', *British Journal of Social Work* 16(1) 65–79.

Rojek, Chris and Stewart Collins (1988) 'Contract or con trick revisited: comments on the reply by Corden and Preston-Shoot', *British Journal of Social Work*, 18(6) 611–22.

____, Geraldine Peacock and Stewart Collins (1989) *Social Work and Received Ideas* (London, Routledge).

____ and Stewart Collins (1987) 'Contract or con trick?' *British Journal of Social Work*, 17(2) 199–211.

Rose, Sheldon (1981) 'Cognitive behavioural modification in groups', *International Journal of Behavioural Social Work and Abstracts*, 1(1) 27–38.

Rose, Stephen M. and Bruce L. Black (1985) *Advocacy and Empowerment: Mental Health Care in the Community* (Boston, Routledge and Kegan Paul).

Ross, Murray G. (1958) *Case Histories in Community Organisation* (New York, Harper).

Rothman, Jack (1968) 'Three models of community organization practice' in *Social Work Practice, 1968* (New York, Columbia University Press).

Rowe, William (1986) 'Client-centred therapy' in Francis J. Turner (ed.), *Social Work Treatment: Interlocking Theoretical Approaches* 3rd edn (New York, Free Press).

Ruckdeschel, Roy A. and Buford E. Farris (1982) 'Science: critical faith or dogmatic ritual?', *Social Casework*, 63(5) 272–5.

Ruddock, Ralph (1969) *Roles and Relationships* (London, Routledge and Kegan Paul).

Russel-Erlich, John L. and Felix G. Rivera (1986) 'Community empowerment as a non-problem', *Journal of Sociology and Social Welfare*, 13(3) 451–65.

Rustin, Michael (1979) 'Social work and the family' in Noel Parry, Michael Rustin and Carole Satyamurti (eds), *Social Work, Welfare and the State* (London, Edward Arnold).

Rutter, Michael (1981) *Maternal Deprivation Reassessed* (Harmondsworth, Middlesex, Penguin).

Ryan, Peter (1979) 'Residential care for the mentally disabled' in J. K. Wing and Rolf Olsen (eds) *Community Care for the Mentally Disabled* (Oxford, Oxford University Press).

Ryant, Joseph C. (1969) 'The revolutionary potential of social work', *Social Worker*, 37(3) 151–6.

Ryder, Eleanor L. (1976) 'A functional approach' in Robert W. Roberts and Helen Northen (eds) (1976) *Theories of Social Work with Groups* (New York, Columbia University Press).

Sainsbury, Eric (1987) 'Client studies: their contributions and limitations in influencing social work practice', *British Journal of Social Work*, 17(6) 635–44.

Salzberger-Wittenberg, Isca (1970) *Psycho-analytic Insights and Relationships: a Kleinian Approach* (London, Routledge and Kegan Paul).

Sanda, A. O. (1987) 'Nigeria' in John Dixon (ed.), *Social Welfare in Africa* (London, Croom Helm).

Satir, Virginia (1964) *Conjoint Family Therapy* (Palo Alto, Science and Behavior Books).

——— (1972) *Peoplemaking* (Palo Alto, Science and Behavior Books).

Satyamurti, Carole (1979) 'Care and control in local authority social work' in Noel Parry, Michael Rustin and Carole Satyamurti (eds), *Social Work, Welfare and the State* (London, Edward Arnold).

Sayers, Janet (1986) *Sexual Contradictions: Psychology, Psychoanalysis and Feminism* (London, Tavistock).

——— (1988) 'Feminism, social work and psychoanalysis' in Geoffrey Pearson, Judith Treseder and Margaret Yelloly (eds) *Social Work and the Legacy of Freud: Psychoanalysis and its uses* (London, Macmillan).

Scheflen, Albert E. (1972) *Body Language and Social Order* (Englewood Cliffs, NJ, Prentice-Hall).

——— and Norman Ashcraft (1976) *Human Territories: How we Behave in Space-Time* (Englewood Cliffs, NJ, Prentice-Hall).

Schenk, Quentin F. and Emmy Lou (1987) 'Ethiopia' in John Dixon (ed.), *Social Welfare in Africa* (London, Croom Helm).

Schriver, Joe M. (1987) 'Harry Lurie's critique: person and environment in early casework practice', *Social Service Review*, 61(3) 514–32.

Schwartz, Arthur and Israel Goldiamond (1975) *Social Casework: a Behavioural Approach* (New York, Columbia University Press).

Sedgwick, Peter (1972) 'R. D. Laing: self, symptom and society' in Robert Boyers and Robert Orrill (eds), *Laing and Anti-psychiatry* (Harmondsworth, Middlesex, Penguin).

Seebohm Report (1968) *Report of the Committee on Local Authority and Allied Personal Social Services*, Cmnd 3703 (London, HMSO).

Seligman, M. E. P. (1975) *Helplessness: on Depression, Development and Death* (San Francisco, Freeman).

Sheldon, Brian (1978) 'Theory and practice in social work: a re-examination of a tenuous relationship', *British Journal of Social Work*, 8(1) 1–22.

——— (1982a) 'A measure of success', *Social Work Today* 13(21) 8–11.

——— (1982b) *Behaviour Modification* (London, Tavistock).

——— (1984) 'Evaluation with one eye closed: the empiricist agenda in social work research – a reply to Peter Raynor', *British Journal of Social Work*, 14(6) 635–7.

_____ (1986) 'Social work effectiveness experiments: review and implications', *British Journal of Social Work*, 16(2) 223–42.

Sibeon, Roger (1982) 'Theory-practice symbolisations: a critical review of the Hardiker/Davies debate', *Issues in Social Work Education*, 2(2) 119–47.

Siegel, Deborah H. (1984) 'Defining empirically-based practice', *Social Work*, 29(4) 325–31.

Sifneos, Peter E. (1967) 'Two kinds of psychotherapy of short duration', *American Journal of Psychiatry* 123(3) 1069–1073.

_____ (1972) *Short-term Psychotherapy and Emotional Crisis* (Cambridge, Mass, Harvard University Press).

Sinclair, Elma (1988) 'The formal evidence' in National Institute for Social Work, *Residential Care: a positive choice* (London, HMSO).

Siporin, Max (1975) *Introduction to Social Work Practice* (New York, Macmillan).

_____ (1980) 'Ecological systems theory in social work', *Journal of Sociology and Social Welfare*, 7(4) 507–532.

Skenridge, P. and I. Lennie (1971) 'Social work: the wolf in sheep's clothing', *Arena*, 5(1).

Small, Neil (1987) 'Putting violence to social workers into context', *Critical Social Policy*, 19 40–5.

Smalley, Ruth E. (1967) *Theory for Social Work Practice* (New York, Columbia University Press).

_____ (1970) 'The functional approach to casework practice' in Robert W. Roberts and Robert H. Nee (eds), *Theories of Social Casework* (Chicago, University of Chicago Press).

Smid, Gerhard and Robert van Krieken (1984) 'Notes on theory and practice in social work: a comparative view', *British Journal of Social Work*, 14(1) 11–22.

Smith, Carole R. (1975) 'Bereavement: the contribution of phenomenological and existential analysis to a greater understanding of the problem', *British Journal of Social Work*, 5(1) 75–94.

_____ (1982) *Social Work with the Dying and Bereaved* (London, Macmillan).

Smith, David (1987) 'The limits of positivism in social work research', *British Journal of Social Work*, 17(4) 401–16.

Smith, Gilbert (1980) *Social Need: Policy, Practice and Research* (London, Routledge and Kegan Paul).

Solomon, Barbara Bryant (1976) *Black Empowerment: Social Work in Oppressed Communities* (New York, Columbia University Press).

Specht, Harry (1986) 'Social support, social networks, social exchange and social work practice', *Social Service Review*, 60(2) 218–240.

_____ and Riva Specht (1986a) 'Social work assessment: the route to clienthood – part 1', *Social Casework*, 67(9) 525–32.

_____ (1986b) 'Social work assessment: the route to clienthood – part II', *Social Casework*, 67(10) 587–93.

_____ and Anne Vickery (eds) (1977) *Integrating Social Work Methods* (London, Allen and Unwin).

Starak, Yaro (1988) 'Hong Kong: a model of "social happiness" for the new China', *International Social Work*, 31(3) 211–7.

Statham, Daphne (1978) *Radicals in Social Work* (London, Routledge and Kegan Paul).

Stenson, Kevin and Nick Gould (1986) 'A comment on "A framework for theory in social work" by Whittington and Holland', *Issues in Social Work Education*, 6(1) 41–45.

Strean, Herbert S. (1971a) 'Introduction' in Herbert S. Strean (ed.), *Social Casework: Theories in Action* (Metuchen, NJ, Scarecrow Press).

—— (1971b) 'The application of the role theory to social casework' in Herbert S. Strean (ed.), *Social Casework: Theories in Action* (Metuchen, NJ, Scarecrow Press).

—— (1971c) *Social Casework: theories in action* (Metuchen, NJ, Scarecrow Press).

—— (1979) *Psychoanalytic Theory and Social Work Practice* (New York, Free Press).

Sucato, Vincent (1978) 'The problem-solving process in short-term and long-term service', *Social Service Review*, 52(2) 244–64.

Sullivan, Michael (1987) *Sociology and Social Welfare* (London, Allen and Unwin).

Taylor, Samuel H. and Robert W. Roberts (eds) (1985), *Theory and Practice of Community Social Work* (New York, Columbia University Press).

Thomas, Edwin J. (1968) 'Selected sociobehavioural techniques and principles: an approach to interpersonal helping', *Social Work*, 13(1) 12–26.

—— (1971) 'The behaviour modification model and social casework' in Herbert S. Strean, *Social Casework: Theories in Action* (Metuchen, NJ, Scarecrow Press).

Timms, Elizabeth (1983) 'On the relevance of informal social networks to social work intervention', *British Journal of Social Work*, 13(4) 405–16.

Timms, Noel (1964) *Psychiatric Social Work in Great Britain (1939–62)* (London, Routledge and Kegan Paul).

Titmuss, Richard M. (1963) *Essays on 'The Welfare State'*, 2nd edn (London, Allen and Unwin).

—— (1968) *Commitment to Welfare* (London, Allen and Unwin).

Towell, David (ed.) (1988) *An Ordinary Life in Practice* (London: King Edward's Hospital Fund).

Truax, Charles B. and Robert R. Carkhuff (1967) *Toward Effective Counseling and Psychotherapy: Training and Practice* (Chicago, Aldine).

Tully, J. Bryan (1976) 'Personal construct theory and psychological changes related to social work training', *British Journal of Social Work*, 6(4) 480–99.

Turner, Francis J. (ed.) (1986) *Differential Diagnosis and Treatment in Social Work*, 3rd edn (New York, Free Press).

Uttley, Stephen (1989) 'New Zealand' in John Dixon and Robert Scheurall (eds), *Social Welfare in Developed Market Countries* (London, Routledge).

Valentich, Mary (1986) 'Feminism and social work practice' in Francis J. Turner (ed.), *Social Work Treatment: Interlocking Theoretical Perspectives* (New York, Free Press).

Vickery, Anne (1974) 'A systems approach to social work intervention: its uses for work with individuals and families', *British Journal of Social Work* 4(4) 389–404.

von Bertalanffy, Ludwig (1971) *General System Theory: Foundations, Development, Application* (London, Allen Lane).

Wadia, A. R. (1961) 'Ethical and spiritual values in the practice of social work' in A. R. Wadia (ed.) *History and Philosophy of Social Work in India* (Bombay, Allied Publishers Private).

Wagner, Gillian (1979) *Barnardo* (London, Weidenfeld and Nicolson).

Walker, Alan (ed.) (1982) *Community Care: the Family, the State and Social Policy* (Oxford, Basil Blackwell and Martin Robertson).

Wallen, JoAnne (1982) 'Listening to the unconscious in case material: Robert Langs' theory applied', *Smith College Studies in Social Work*, 52(3) 203–33.

Walrond-Skinner, Sue (1976) *Family Therapy: the Treatment of Natural Systems* (London, Routledge and Kegan Paul).

Walton, Ronald G. (ed.) (1986) 'Integrating formal and informal care – the utilization of social support networks', *British Journal of Social Work* 16 (Supplement).

Walton, Ronald G. and Medhat M. Abo el Nasr (1988) 'Indigenization and authentization in terms of social work in Egypt', *International Social Work*, 31(2) 135–44.

Ward, Liz (1980) 'The social work task in residential care' in Ronald Walton and Doreen Elliott (eds) *Residential Care: a Reader in Contemporary Theory and Practice* (Oxford, Pergamon).

Watson, David (1980) *Caring for Strangers* (London, Routledge and Kegan Paul).

Weaver, Donna R. (1982) 'Empowering treatment skills for helping black families', *Social Casework*, 63(2) 100–5.

Webb, David (1981) 'Themes and continuities in radical and traditional social work', *British Journal of Social Work*, 11(2) 143–58.

Weick, Ann (1981) 'Reframing the person-in-environment perspective' *Social Work* 26(2) 140–43.

—— (1983) 'Issues in overturning a medical model of social work practice', *Social Work*, 28(6) 467–71.

—— (1986) 'The philosophical context of a health model of social work', *Social Casework*, 67(9) 551–9.

Werner, Harold D. (1982) *Cognitive Therapy: a Humanistic Approach* (New York, Free Press).

—— (1986) 'Cognitive theory' in Francis J. Turner (ed.) *Social Work Treatment: Interlocking Theoretical Approaches*, 3rd edn (New York, Free Press).

Whang, In-Young (1988) 'Social services programmes for the poor in a newly industrialising country: experience in South Korea' in Dennis A. Rondinelli and G. Shalikin Cheema (eds), *Urban Services in*

Developing Countries: Public and Private Roles in Urban Development (London, Macmillan).

Whiteley, J. Stuart (1979) 'The psychiatric hospital as a therapeutic setting' in Peter Righton (ed.), *Studies in Environment Therapy*, vol. 3 (Toddington, Glos, Planned Environment Therapy Trust).

Whittaker, James K. (1974) *Social Treatment: an approach to interpersonal helping* (Chicago, Aldine).

—— and James Garbarino (eds) (1983) *Social Support Networks: Informal Helping in the Human Services* (New York, Aldine).

Whittington, Colin and Ray Holland (1985) 'A framework for theory in social work', *Issues in Social Work Education*, 5(1) 25–50.

Wikler, Meir (1986) 'Pathways to treatment: how orthodox Jews enter therapy', *Social Casework*, 67(2) 113–8.

Wilkes, Ruth (1981) *Social Work with Undervalued Groups* (London Tavistock).

Wills, David (1964) *Homer Lane: a Biography* (London, Allen and Unwin).

Wills, David (1973) 'Planned environment therapy – what is it' in Hugh Klare and David Wills (eds), *Studies in Environment Therapy*, vol. 2 (London, Planned Environment Therapy Trust).

Wilson, Elizabeth (1980) 'Feminism and social work' in Mike Brake and Roy Bailey (eds) *Radical Social Work and Practice* (London, Edward Arnold).

Wood, Katherine M. (1971) 'The contribution of psychoanalysis and ego psychology to social work' in Herbert S. Strean (ed.) *Social Casework: Theories in Action* (Metuchen, NJ: Scarecrow Press).

Woodroofe, Kathleen (1962) *From Charity to Social Work* (London: Routledge and Kegan Paul).

Yelaja, Shankar A. (1970) 'Toward a conceptualization of the social work profession in India', *Applied Social Studies* 2(1) 21–6.

Yelloly, Margaret A. (1980) *Social Work Theory and Psychoanalysis* (Wokingham, Berks, Van Nostrand Reinhold).

York, Alan S. (1984) 'Towards a conceptual model of community social work', *British Journal of Social Work*, 14(3) 241–55.

Young, A.F. and E.T. Ashton (1956) *British Social Work in the Nineteenth Century* (London, Routledge and Kegan Paul).

Name Index

Subject Index